IMAGES
of America

OUTER BANKS

IMAGES
of America

OUTER BANKS

John Hairr

ARCADIA
PUBLISHING

ISBN 978-0-7385-0169-7

Published by Arcadia Publishing
Charleston, South Carolina

Printed in the United States of America

Library of Congress Catalog Card Number: 9962492

For all general information contact Arcadia Publishing at:
Telephone 843-853-2070
Fax 843-853-0044
E-mail sales@arcadiapublishing.com
For customer service and orders:
Toll-Free 1-888-313-2665

Visit us on the Internet at www.arcadiapublishing.com

Contents

INTRODUCTION

This book is but a glimpse into the fascinating history of North Carolina's Outer Banks. Inside are old photographs and postcards of such diverse topics as lighthouses, lifesaving stations, boats, ferries, whalers, and fishermen. There are also a number of old maps and charts to help guide the way.

In addition, the reader will find a good number of photos of people in this book, for it is the people who make places interesting. There are famous people, such as Wilbur and Orville Wright, Captain Otway Burns, and Paul Green, and there are also a lot of local folks, such as Captain John Allen Midgett, William Daly, or Monroe Gilgo. In addition, there are numerous images of tourists doing what tourists do.

Some may ask, "Just what are these Outer Banks?" They are a series of narrow, sandy barrier islands along the coast of North Carolina that stretch south from Virginia to Cape Lookout, and then turn west. How far west is debatable. Most descriptions include the Shackleford Banks and, traditionally, the Bogue Banks.

This work takes readers on a visual journey through time along the Outer Banks. It is the author's hope that the book will be entertaining and stimulate an interest in this unique region of the Old North State.

One

Wash Woods to Bodie Island

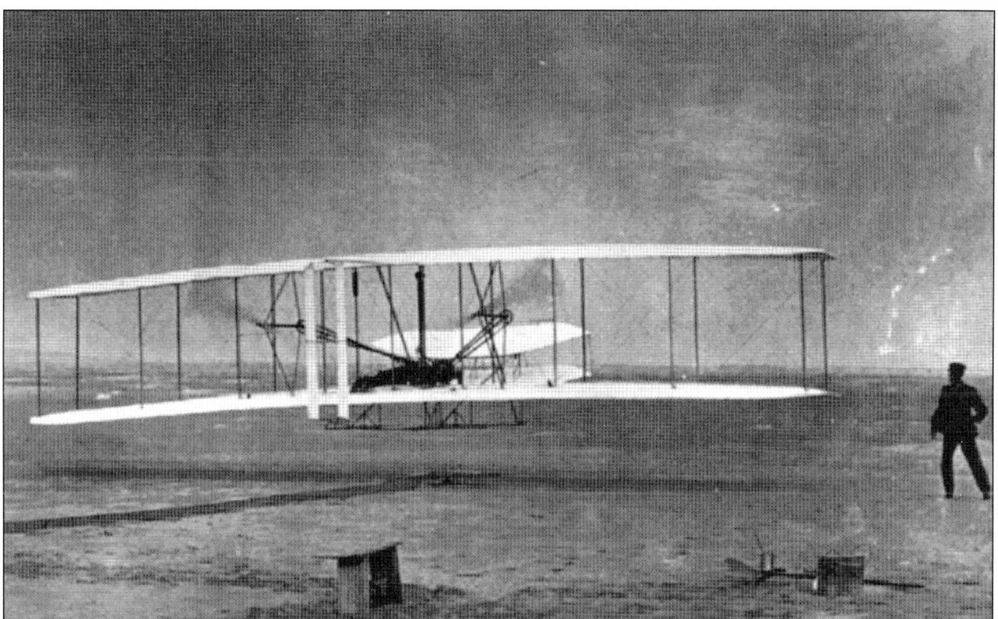

John Daniels captured this well-known image of Orville Wright making his historic flight at Kill Devil Hills on December 17, 1903. (Courtesy Library of Congress.)

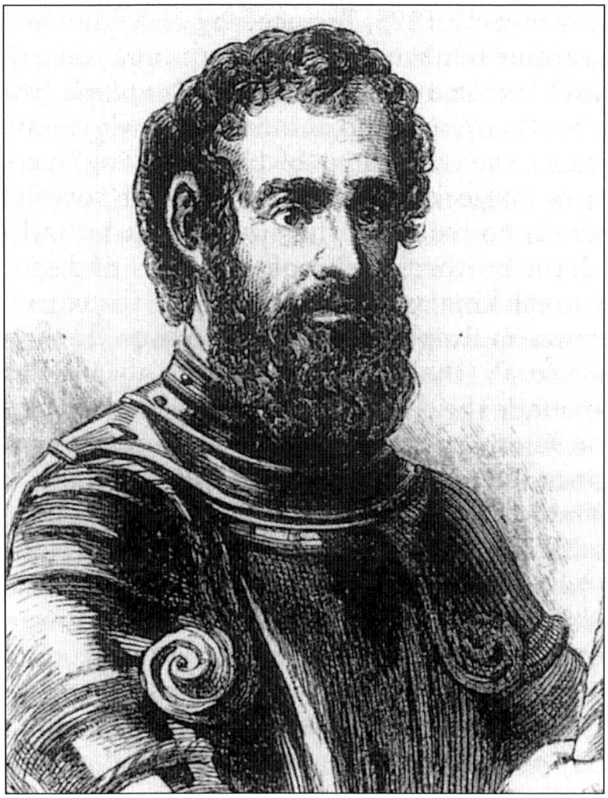

Florentine explorer Giovanni Verrazzano is credited with being the first European to explore the North Carolina coast. His ship, *La Dauphine*, cruised along the Outer Banks in the spring of 1524. Verrazzano mistakenly believed that Pamlico Sound was the Pacific Ocean. Thus, for several years, the Outer Banks were depicted on maps as a narrow isthmus separating the Atlantic and Pacific Oceans.

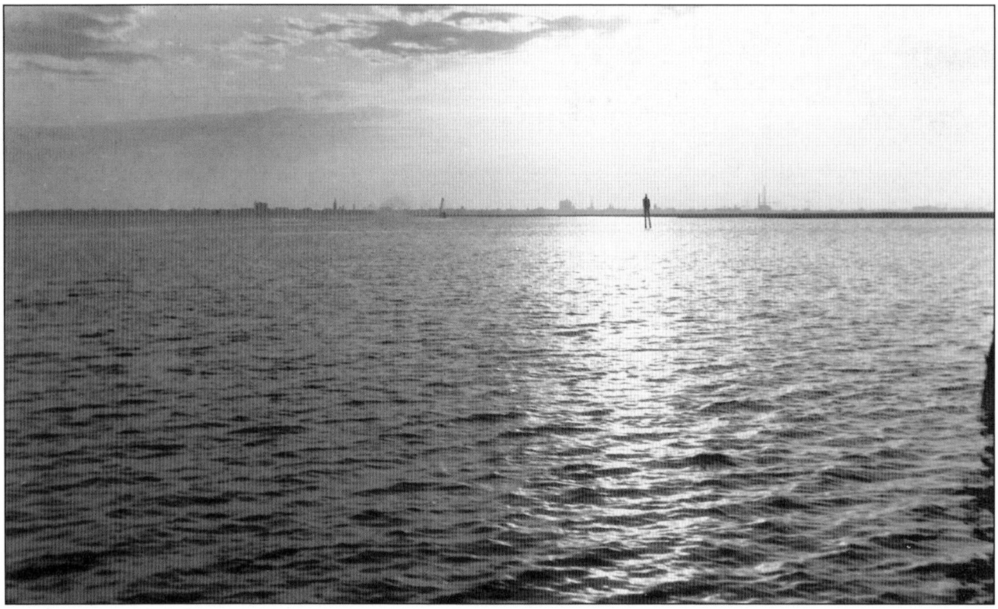

H.H. Brimley captured this tranquil scene on Pamlico Sound in 1927. (Courtesy North Carolina Division of Archives and History.)

This frontispiece comes from Sir Walter Raleigh's book, *History of the World*. Raleigh was behind the efforts to establish the first English colony in North America.

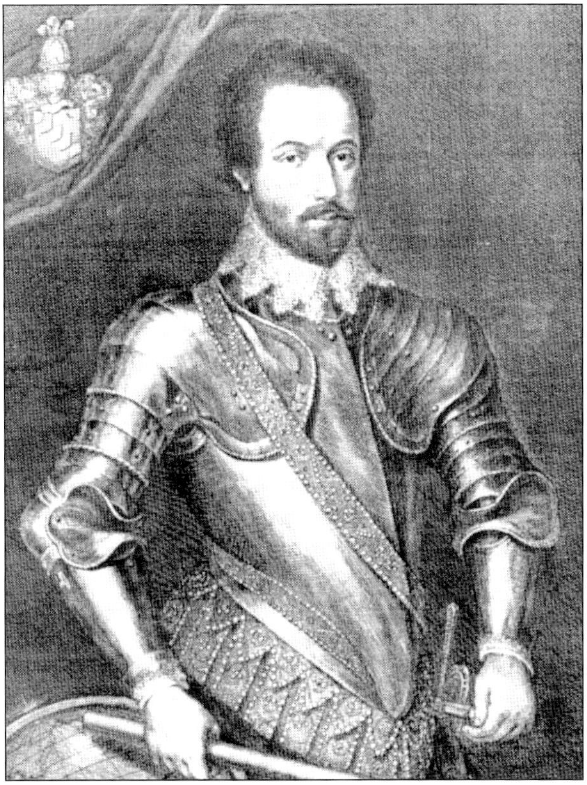

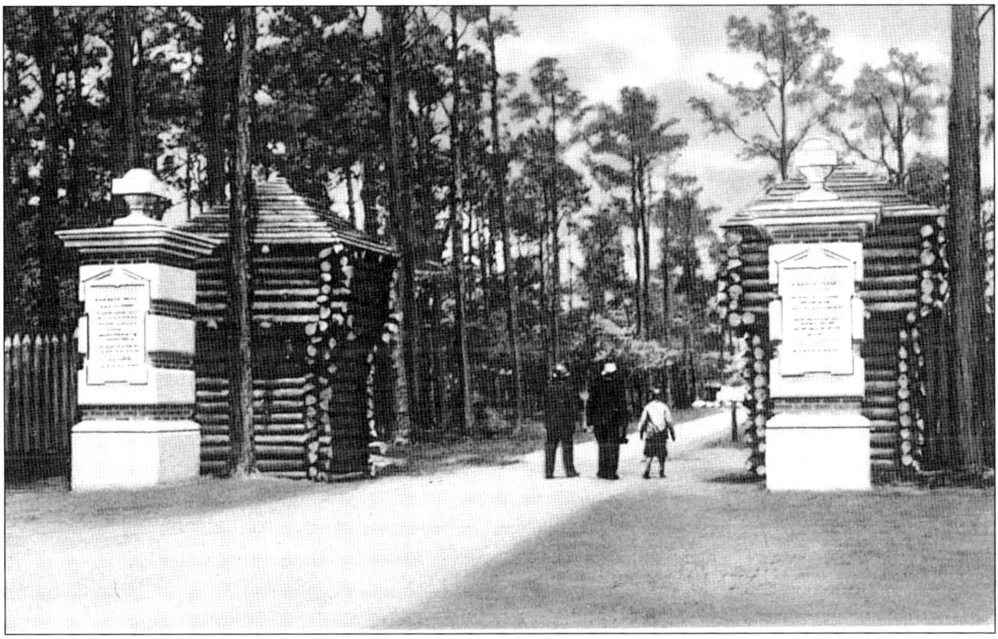

This postcard shows the entrance to the Fort Raleigh National Historic Site on Roanoke Island.

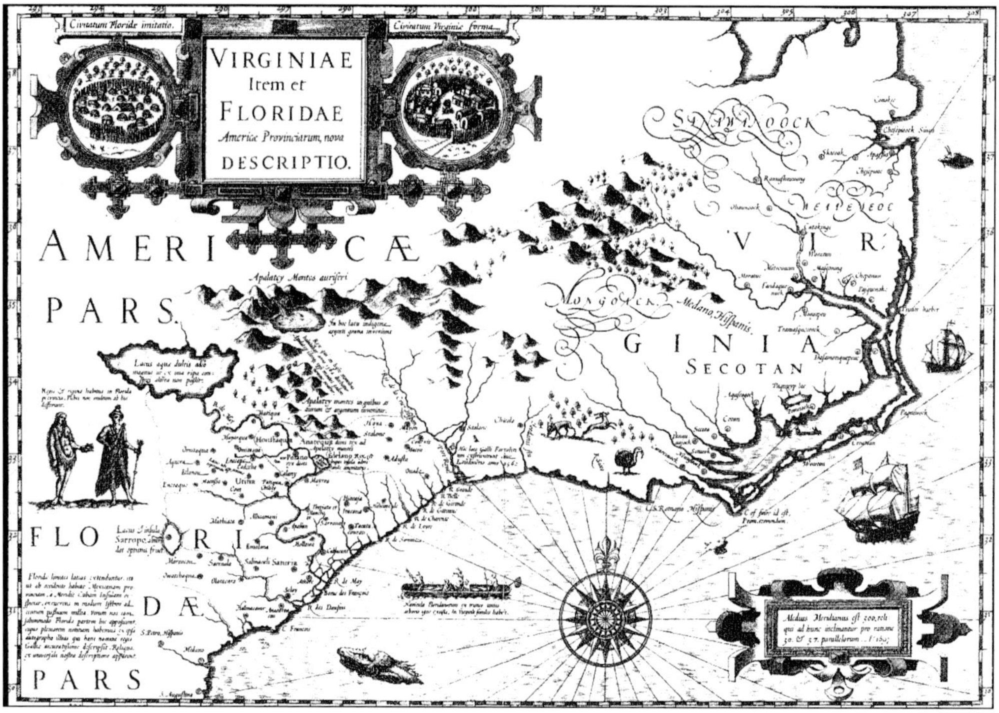

John White prepared this map of Virginia in 1590, based on his explorations of the Outer Banks region.

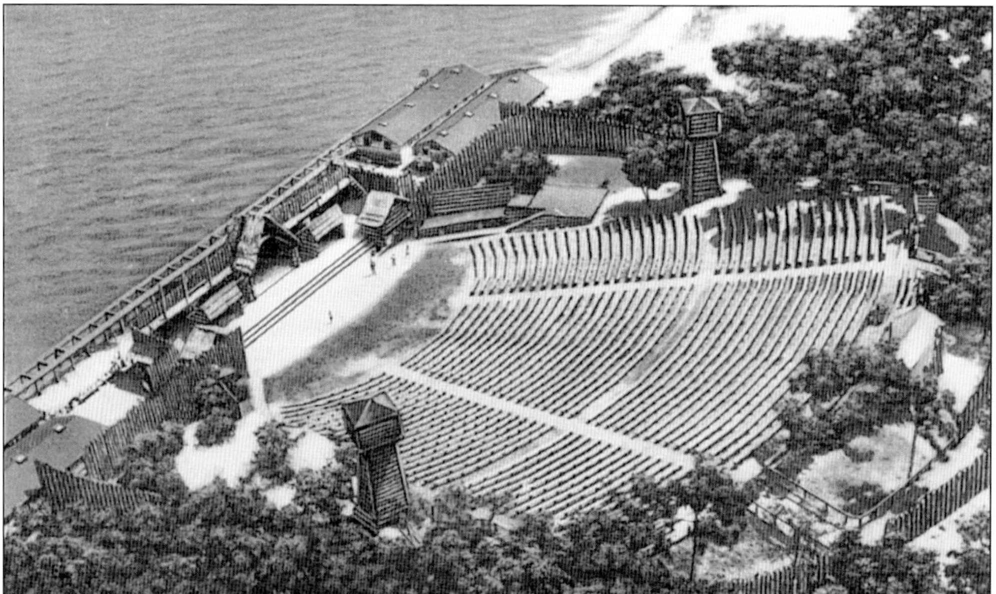

This old postcard shows the Waterside Theatre on Roanoke Island. This is the home of Paul Green's most famous outdoor drama, *The Lost Colony*.

The marker shown on this old postcard was erected in 1896 to commemorate the Lost Colonists and Virginia Dare. Born August 18, 1587, Dare was the first English child born in America.

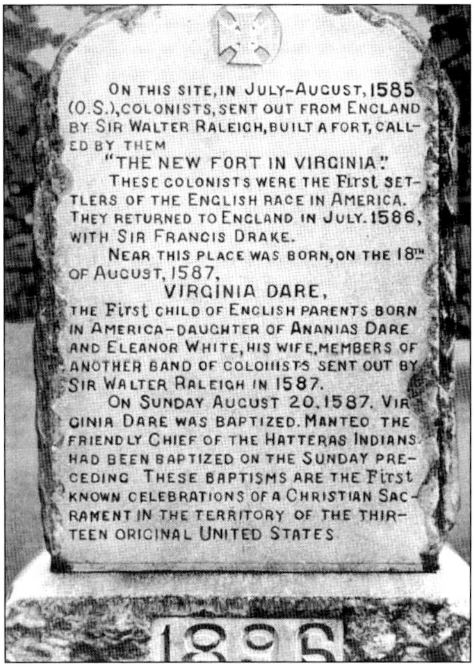

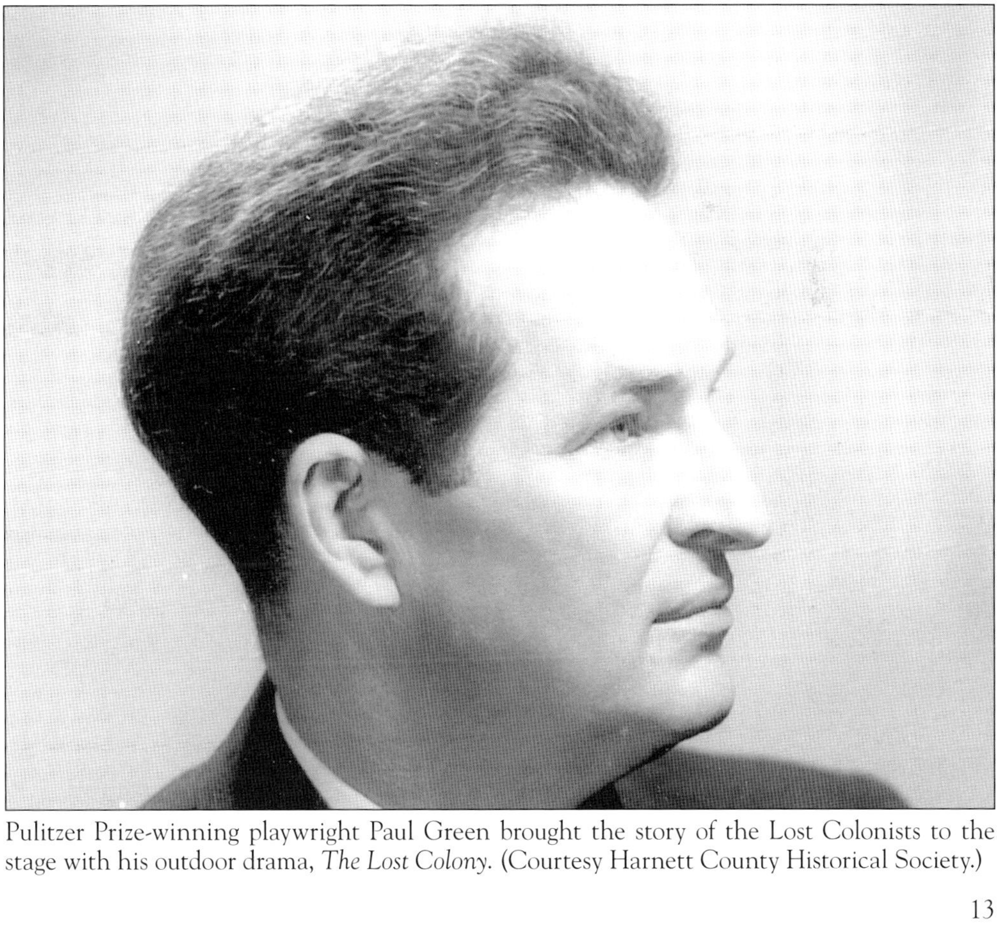

Pulitzer Prize-winning playwright Paul Green brought the story of the Lost Colonists to the stage with his outdoor drama, *The Lost Colony*. (Courtesy Harnett County Historical Society.)

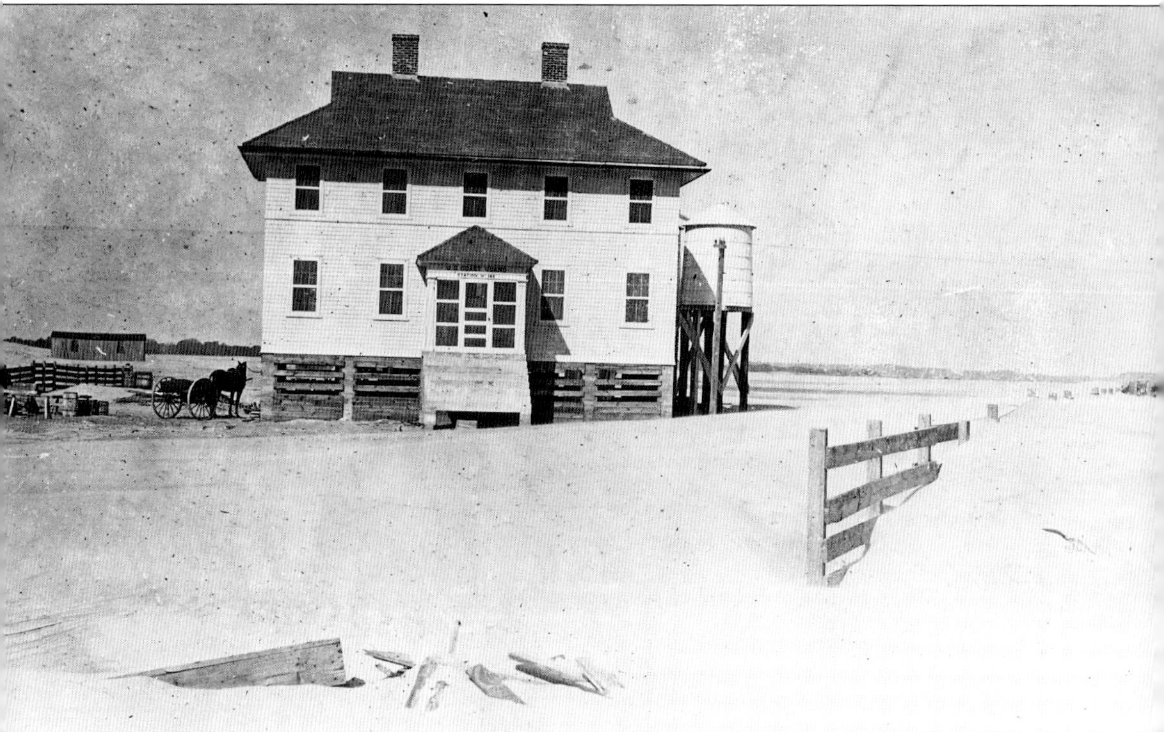

The Wash Woods Life Saving Station was known as Deals Island when it first came into operation in 1878. The U.S. Weather Bureau operated a station here from 1878 to 1888. (U.S. Coast Guard.)

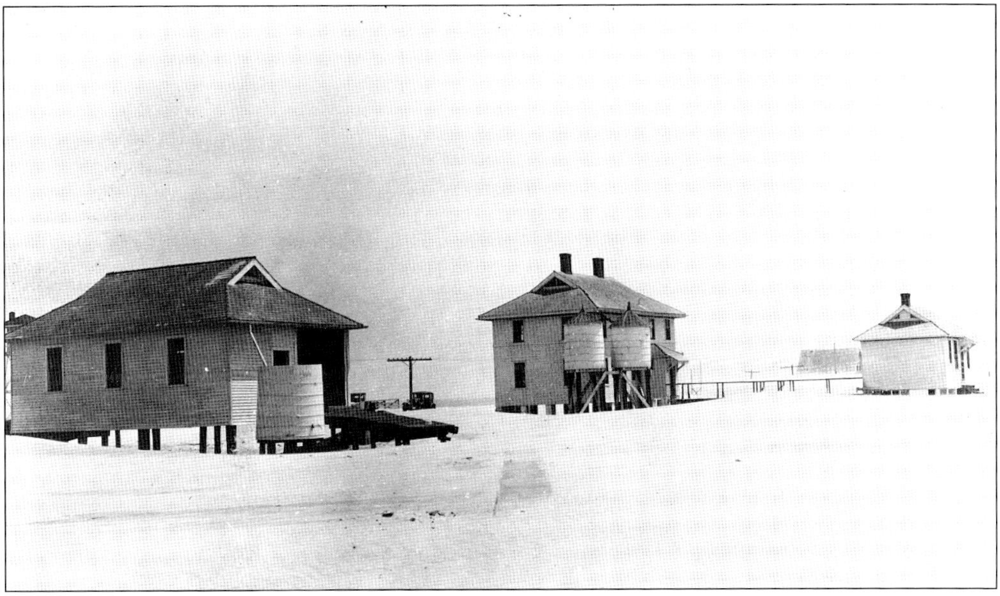

The first keeper of the Wash Woods Station was Calvin Cason, who served from December 9, 1878, to December 27, 1881. (U.S. Coast Guard.)

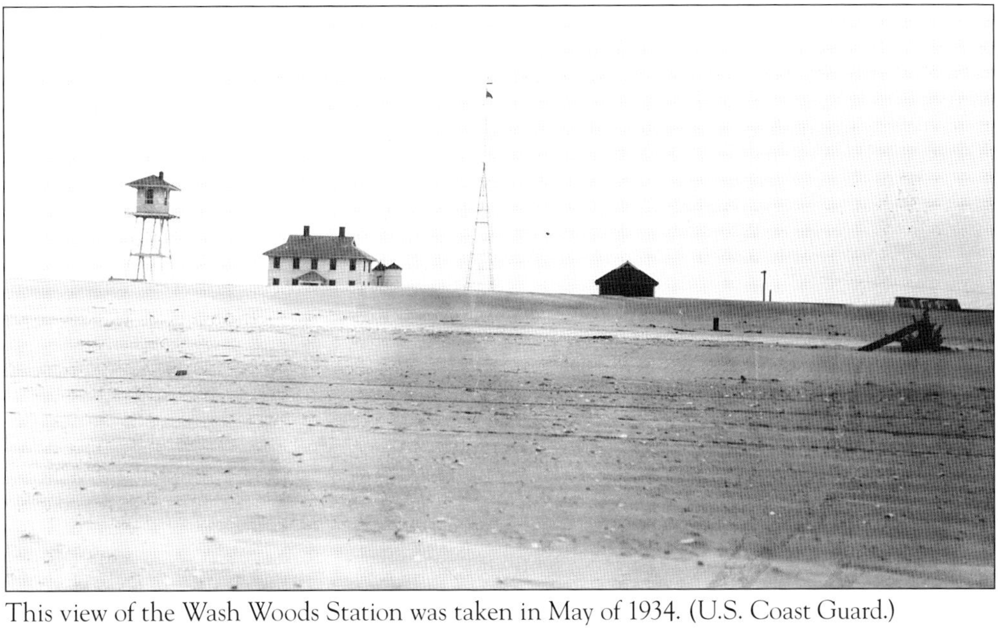

This view of the Wash Woods Station was taken in May of 1934. (U.S. Coast Guard.)

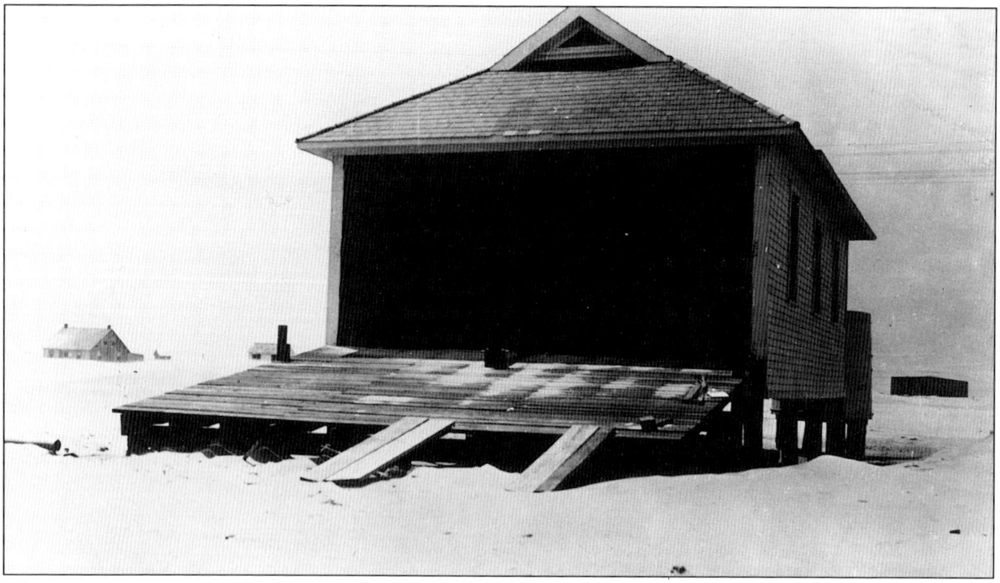

The May 1934 view of the Wash Woods Station was photographed from the east. (U.S. Coast Guard.)

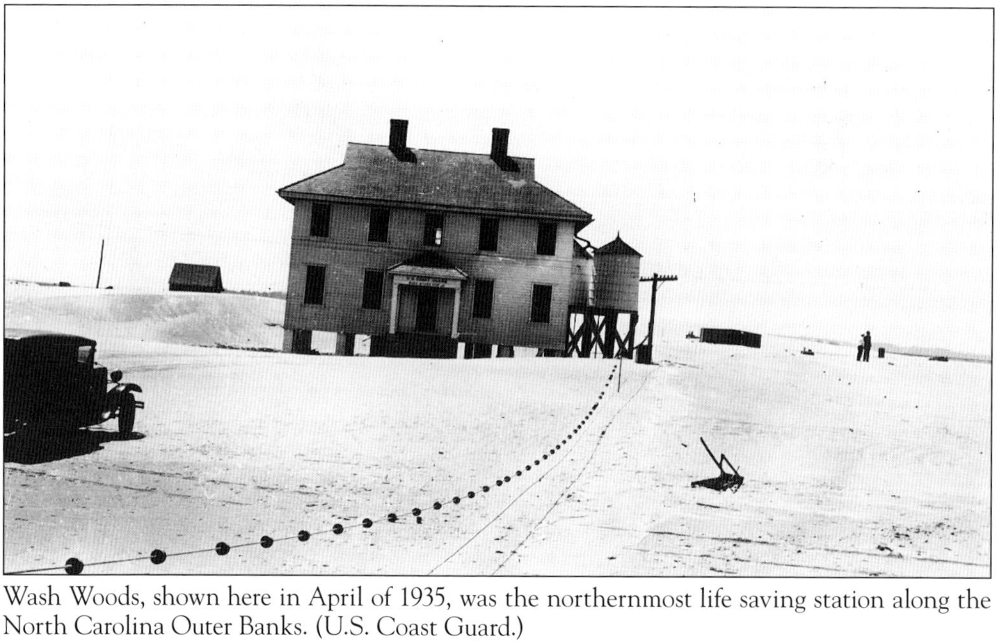

Wash Woods, shown here in April of 1935, was the northernmost life saving station along the North Carolina Outer Banks. (U.S. Coast Guard.)

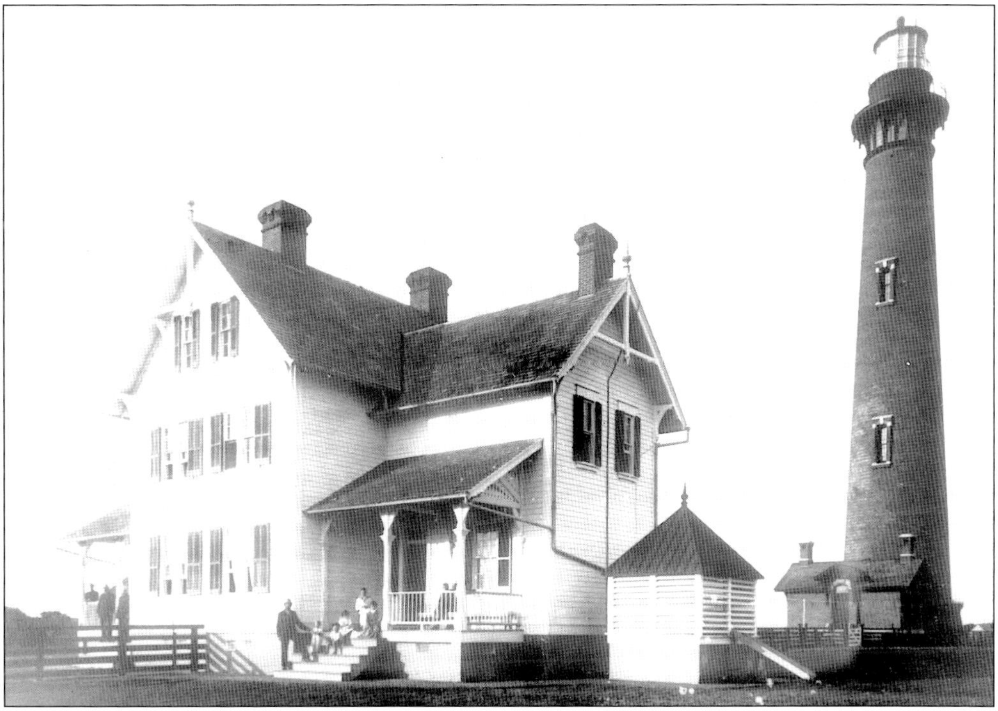

The Currituck Lighthouse, photographed here *c.* 1880, is located near Corolla. The lighthouse was completed in 1875 and was the last of the major lighthouses constructed on the Outer Banks. (Courtesy North Carolina Division of Archives and History.)

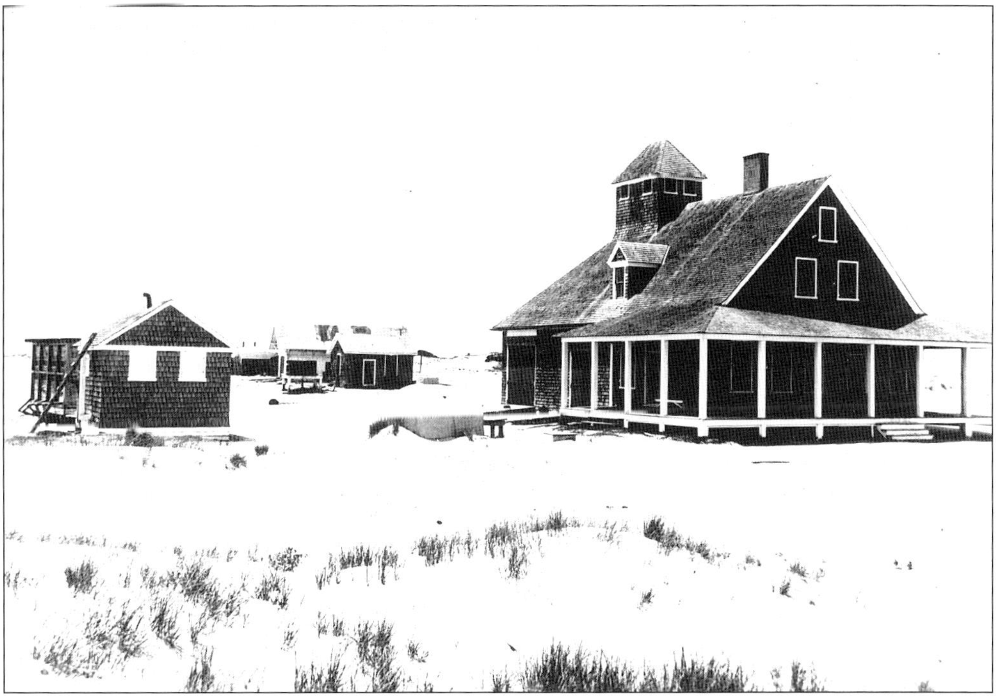

This view of the Currituck Beach Lifeboat Station was taken in 1927. (U.S. Coast Guard.)

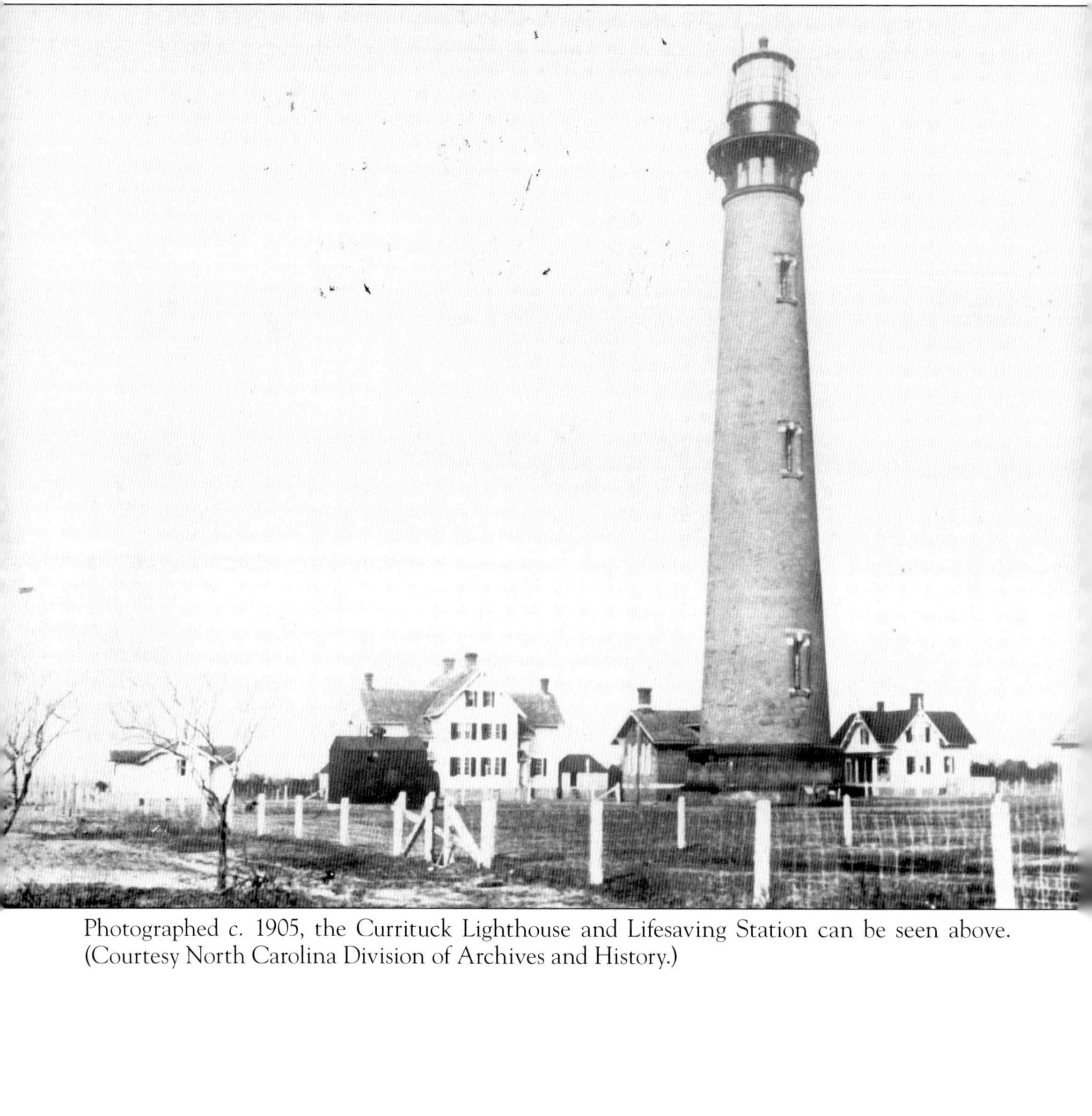

Photographed c. 1905, the Currituck Lighthouse and Lifesaving Station can be seen above. (Courtesy North Carolina Division of Archives and History.)

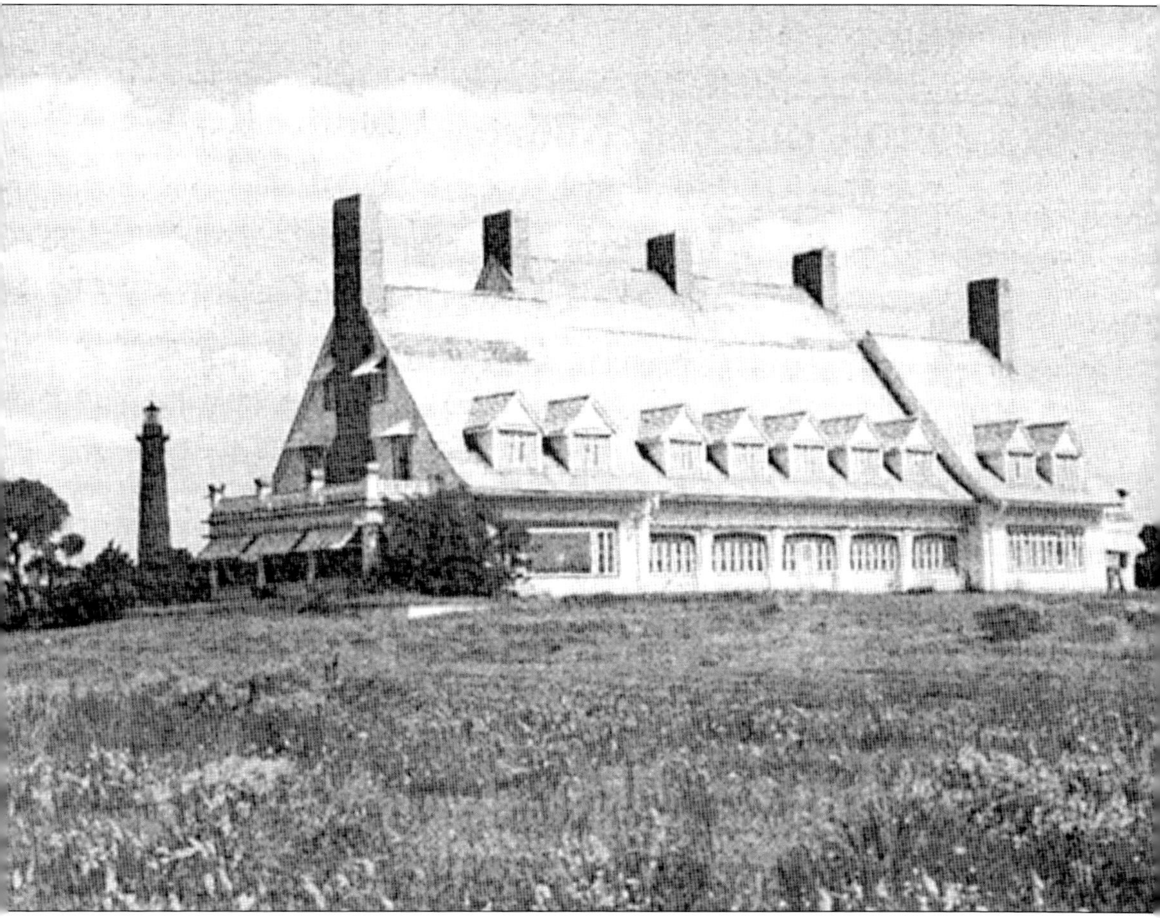

The famous Whalehead Club can be seen with the Currituck Lighthouse in the background. (Federal Writer's Project.)

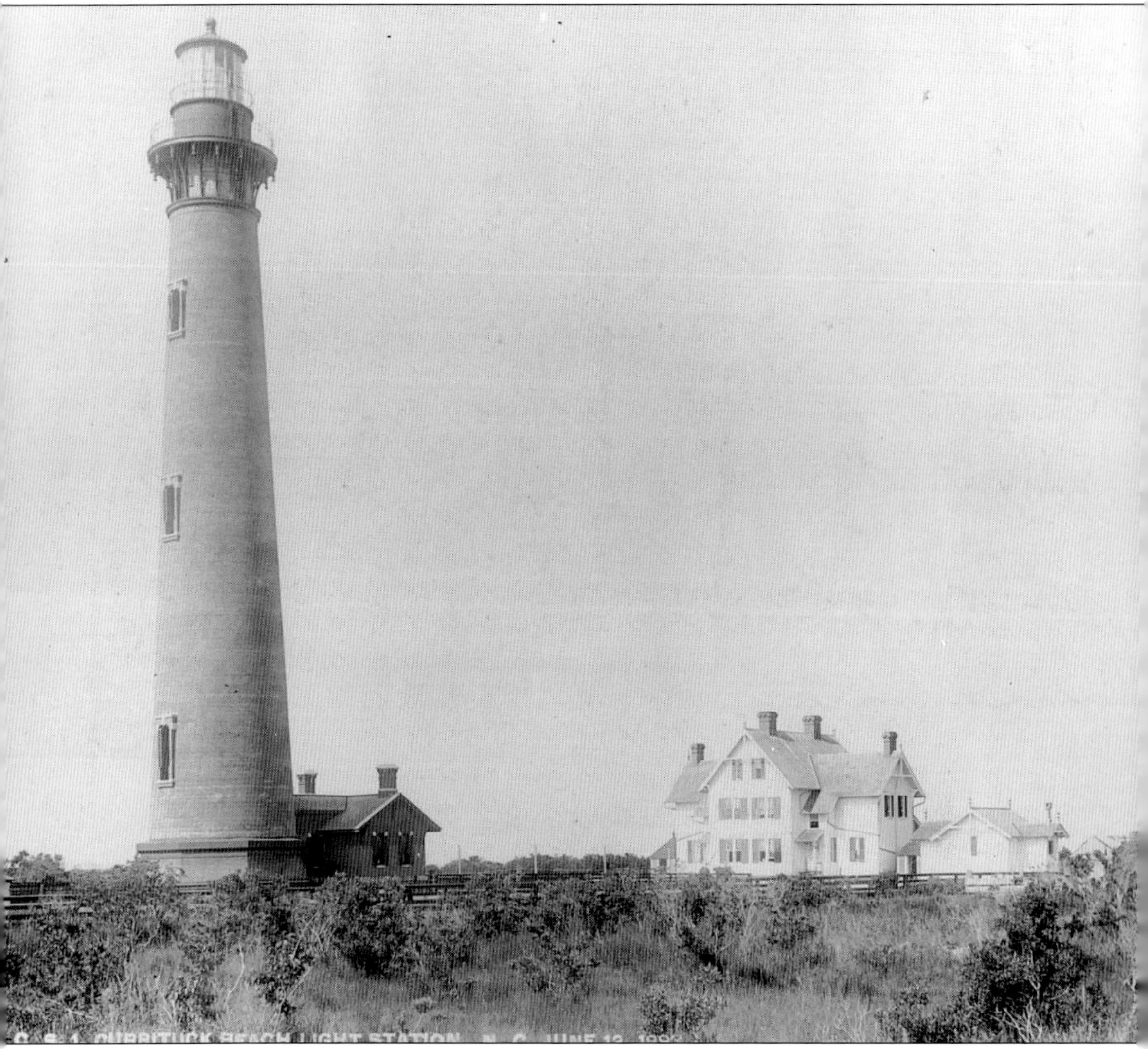

Currituck Lighthouse is a red brick structure that stands 163 feet tall. The light was automated in 1939. (U.S. Coast Guard.)

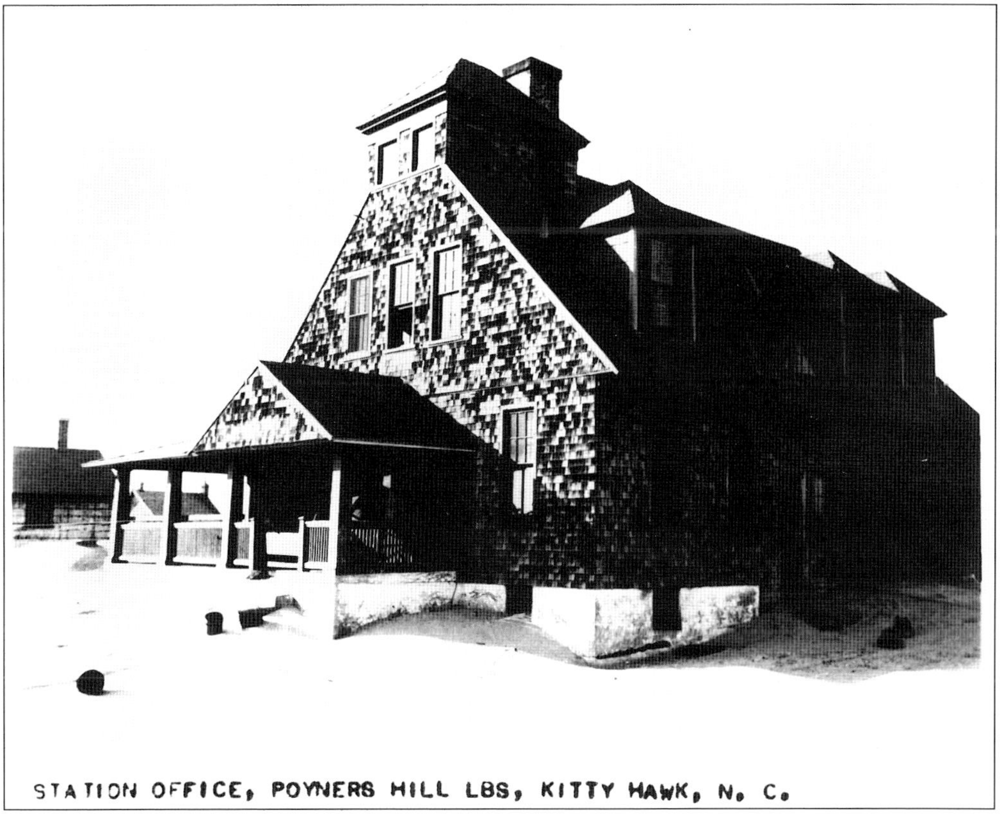

Located 6 miles south of the Currituck Lighthouse, Poyners Hill Lifesaving Station was built in 1878. (U.S. Coast Guard.)

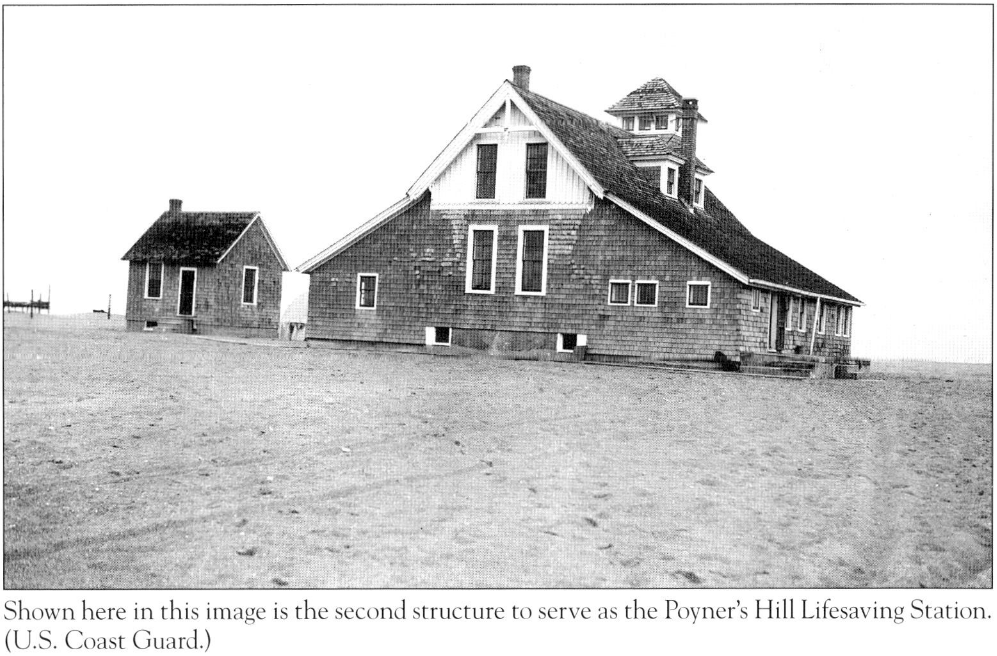

Shown here in this image is the second structure to serve as the Poyner's Hill Lifesaving Station. (U.S. Coast Guard.)

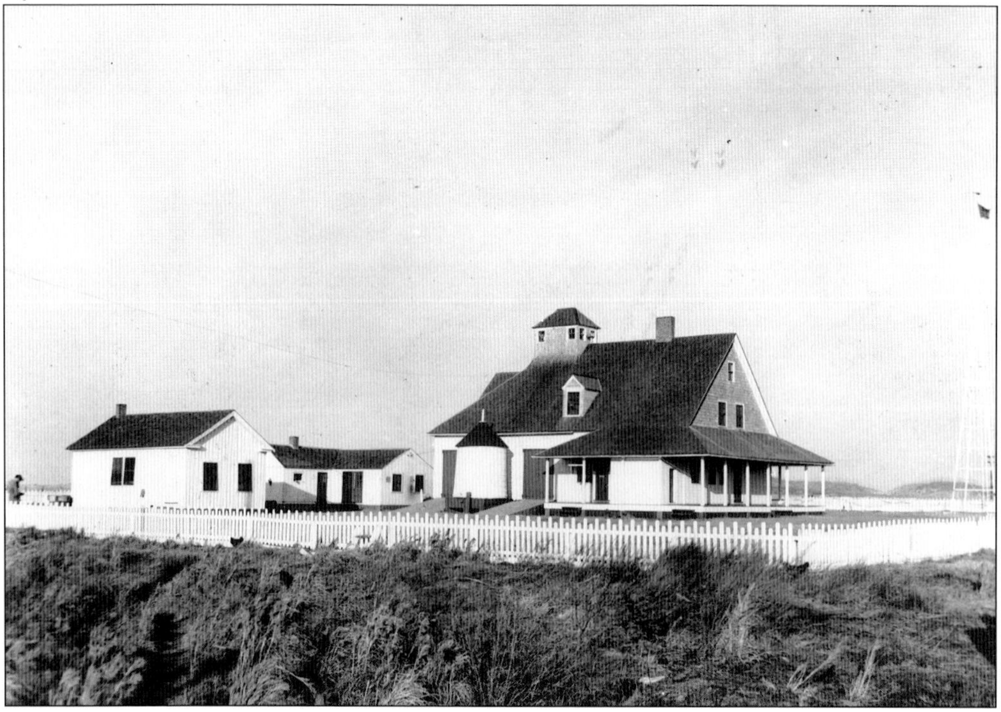

The Caffeys Inlet Lifesaving Station, built in 1920, was patterned after the station farther down the banks at Chicamacamico. (U.S. Coast Guard.)

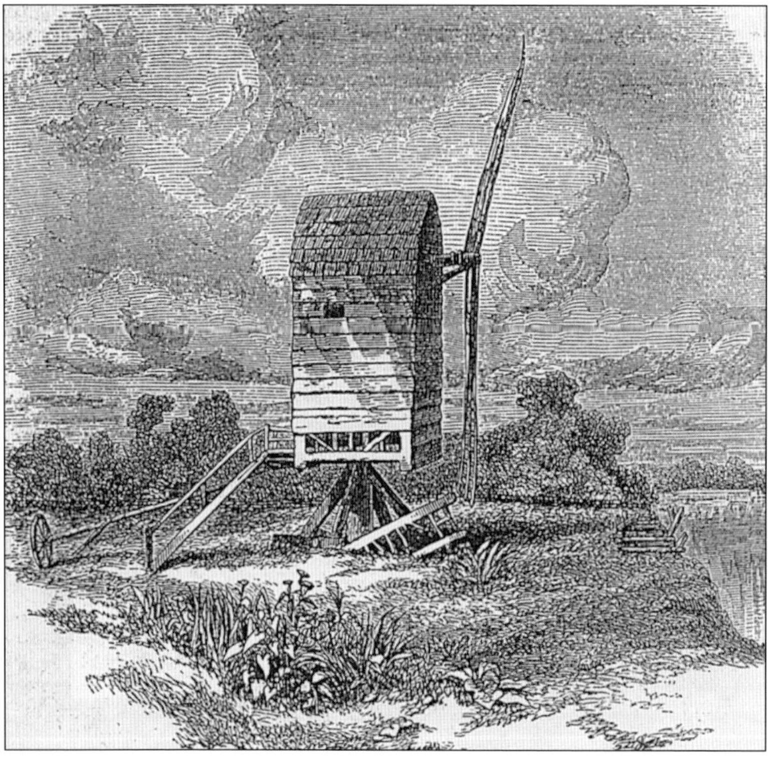

This sketch of a windmill along Currituck Sound appeared in *Harper's Monthly Magazine* in 1859.

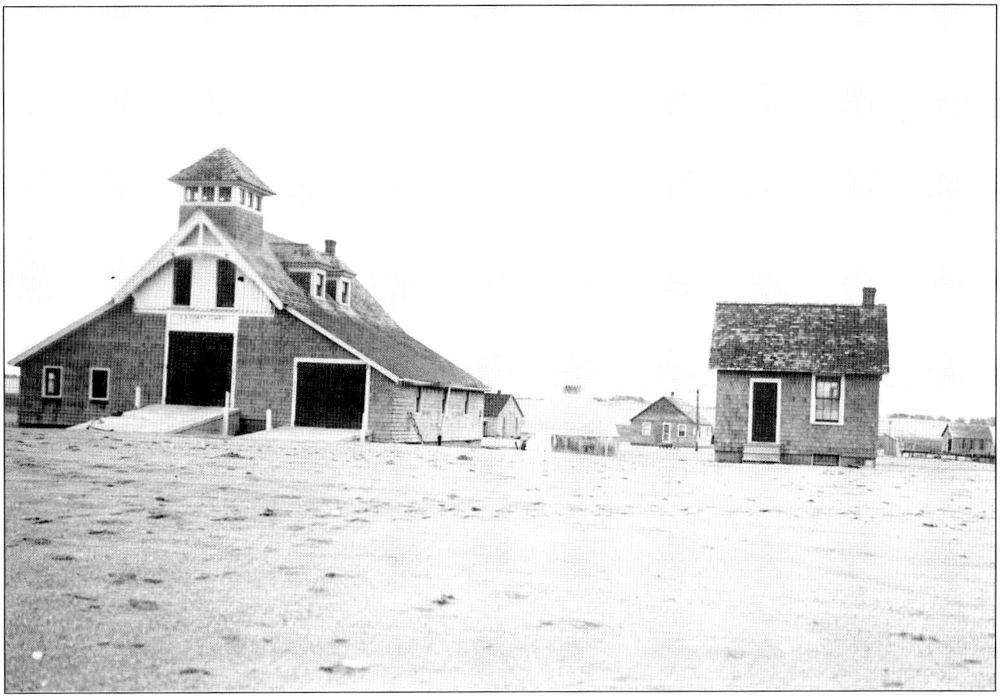

Originally established in 1878, the Lifesaving Station at Paul Gamiels Hill was located 5 miles north of Kitty Hawk. (U.S. Coast Guard.)

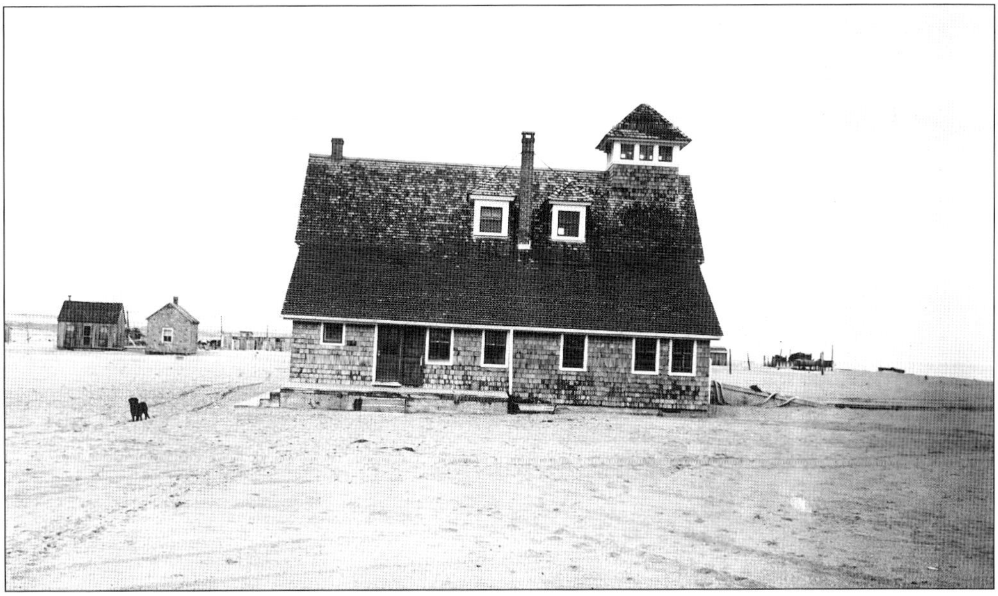

The Paul Gamiels Hill Station appeared as seen in the image above on December 4, 1934. The U.S. Coast Guard abandoned the site in 1949. (U.S. Coast Guard.)

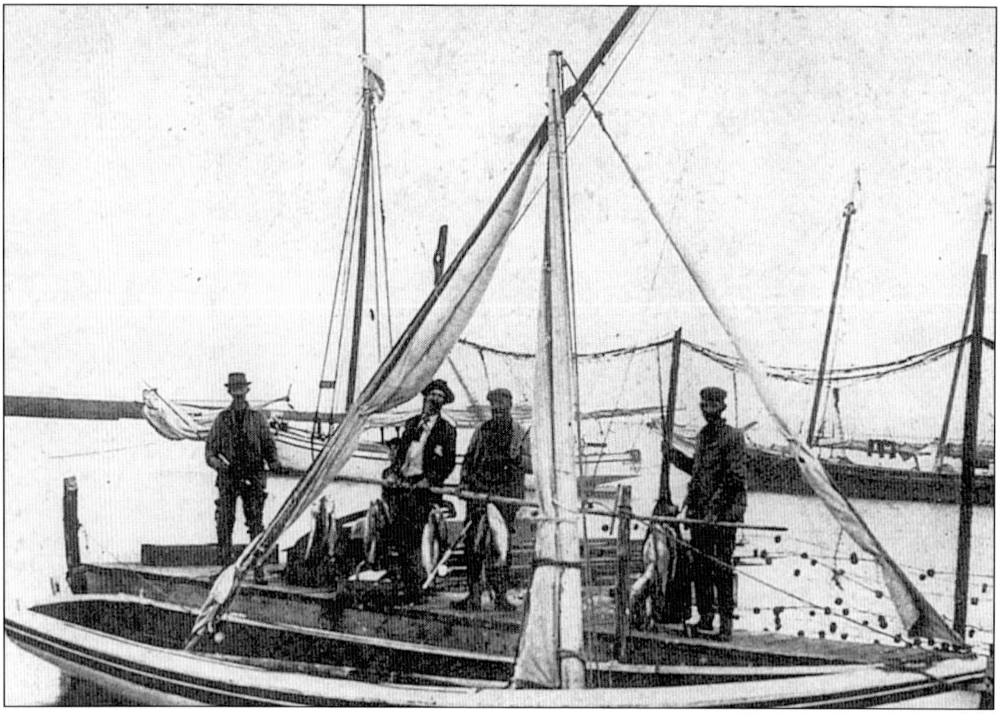

Developed for use in the waters around Roanoke Island, the versatile shad boat was named the official State Historical Boat by the North Carolina General Assembly in 1987.

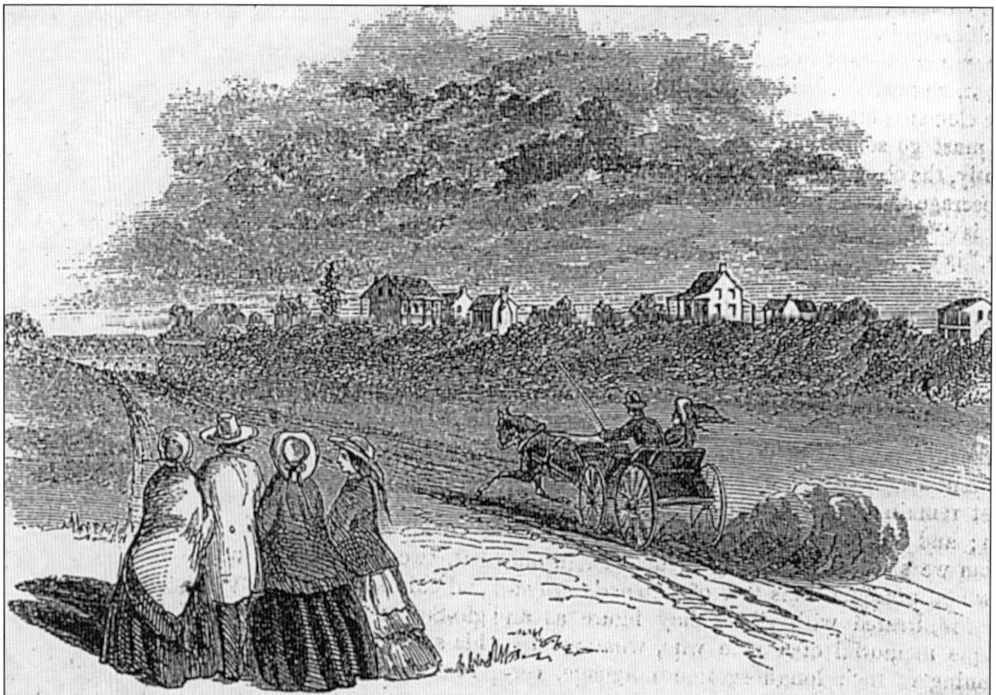

This illustration from *Harper's Magazine* in 1857 shows the resort community at Nags Head.

These men at the Kill Devil Hills Lifesaving Station, in 1903, assisted the Wright Brothers with many of their experiments. (Courtesy Library of Congress.)

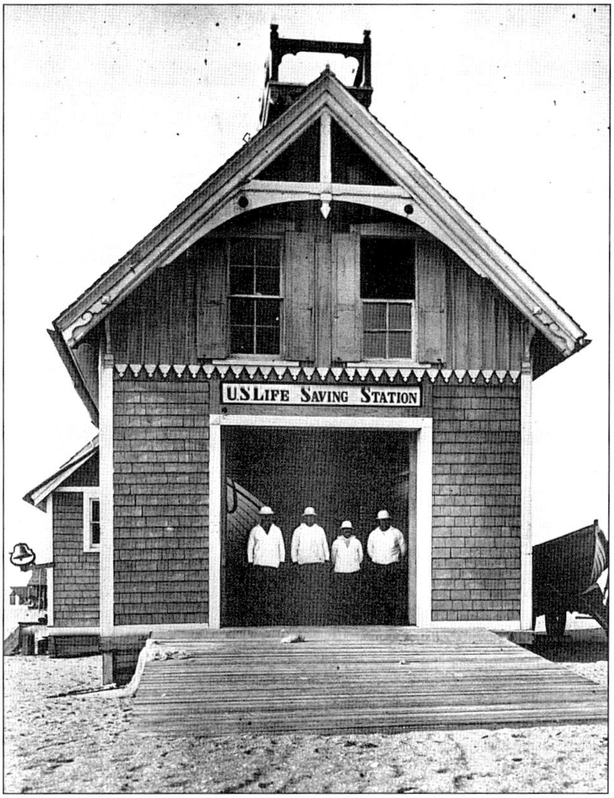

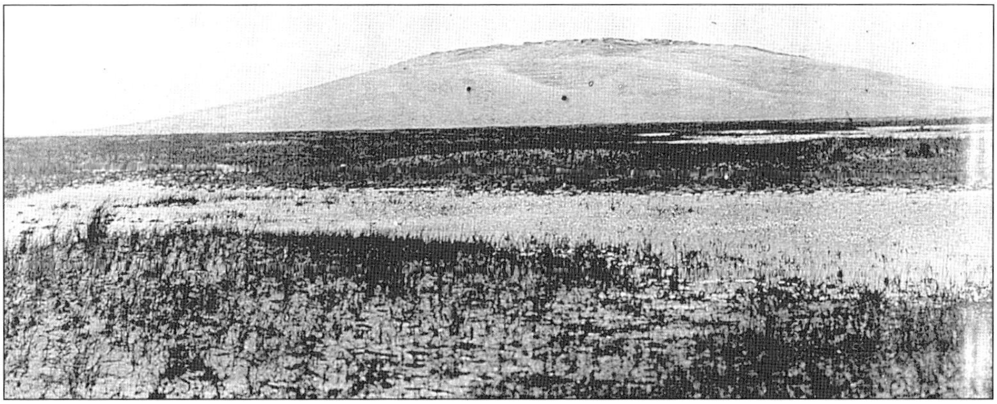

Orville Wright photographed this view of Big Kill Devil Hill in October of 1911. (Courtesy Library of Congress.)

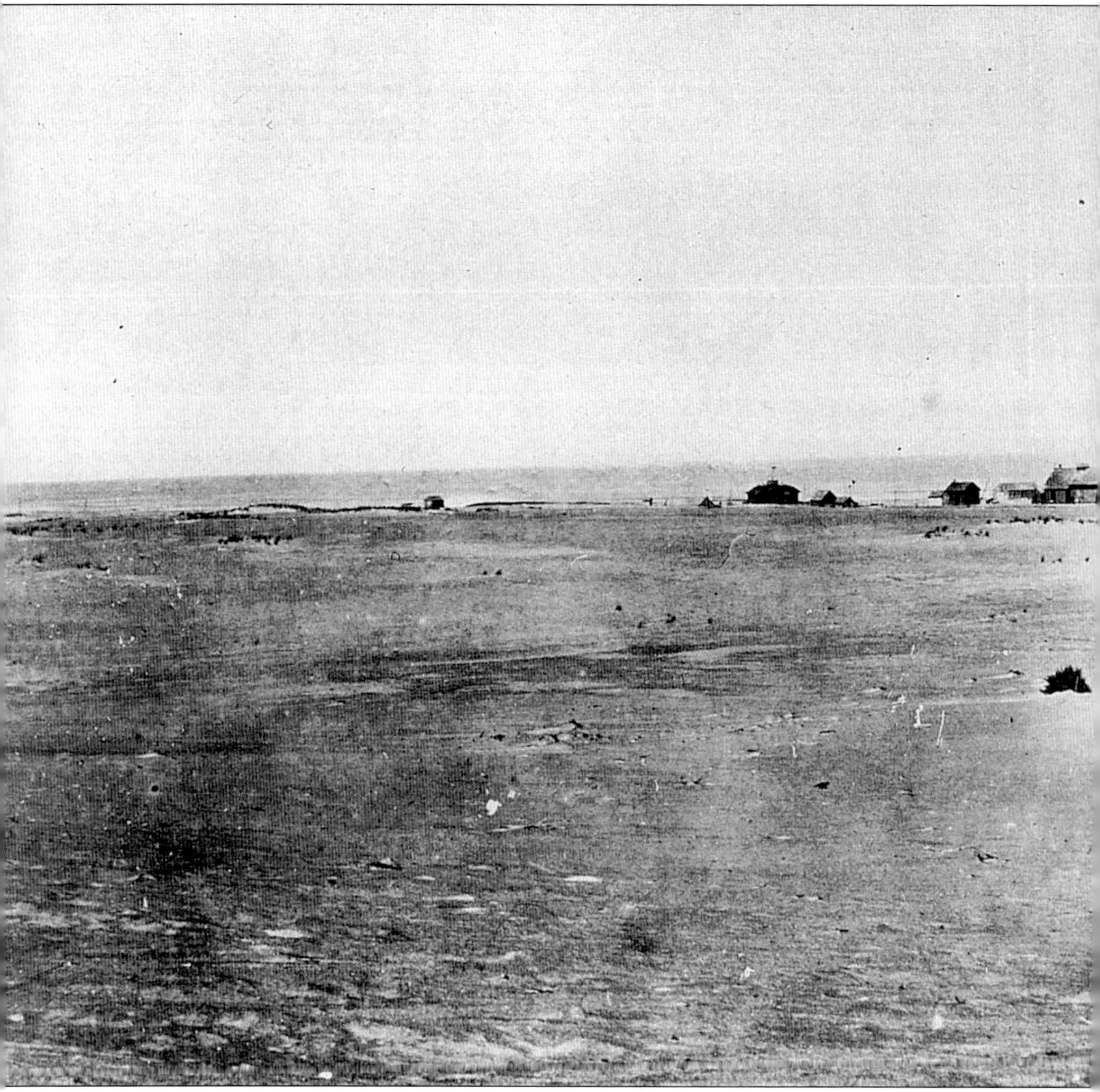

This image portrays how Kitty Hawk Lifesaving Station appeared in the fall of 1900. (Courtesy Library of Congress.)

Orville Wright took this photograph of Tom Tate in October of 1900. The glider, with which the Wright Brothers were experimenting that year, is in the background. (Courtesy Library of Congress.)

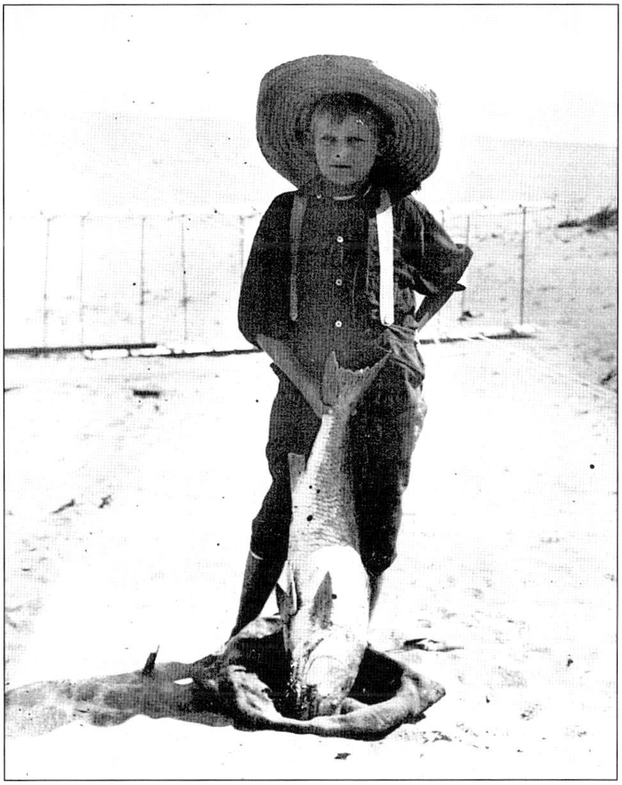

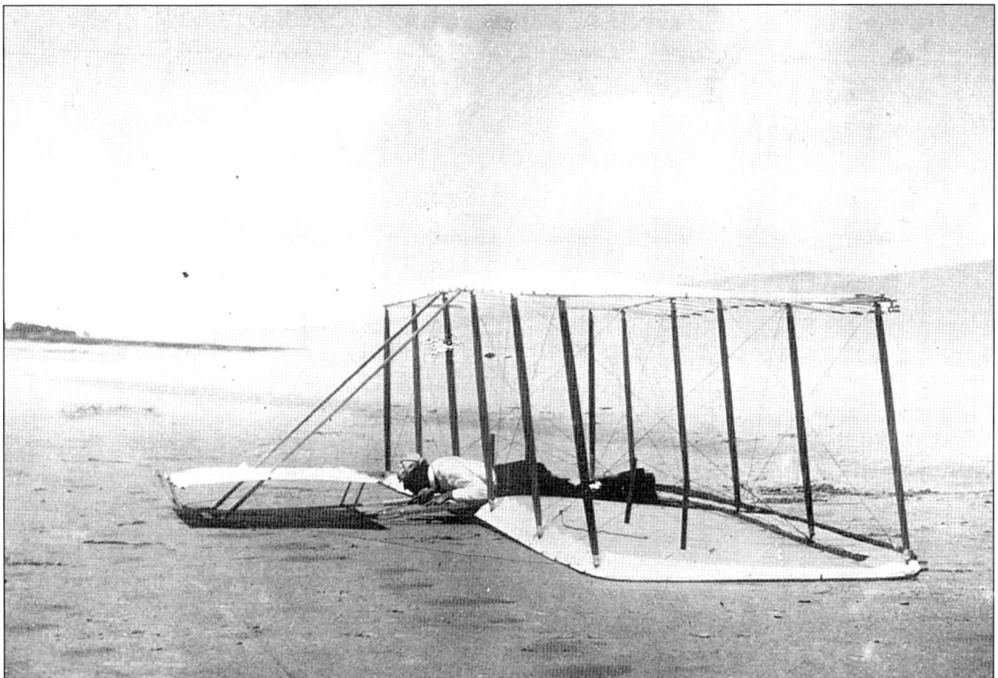

Wilbur Wright is in his glider on the sand at Kill Devil Hills, *c.* 1901. (Courtesy Library of Congress.)

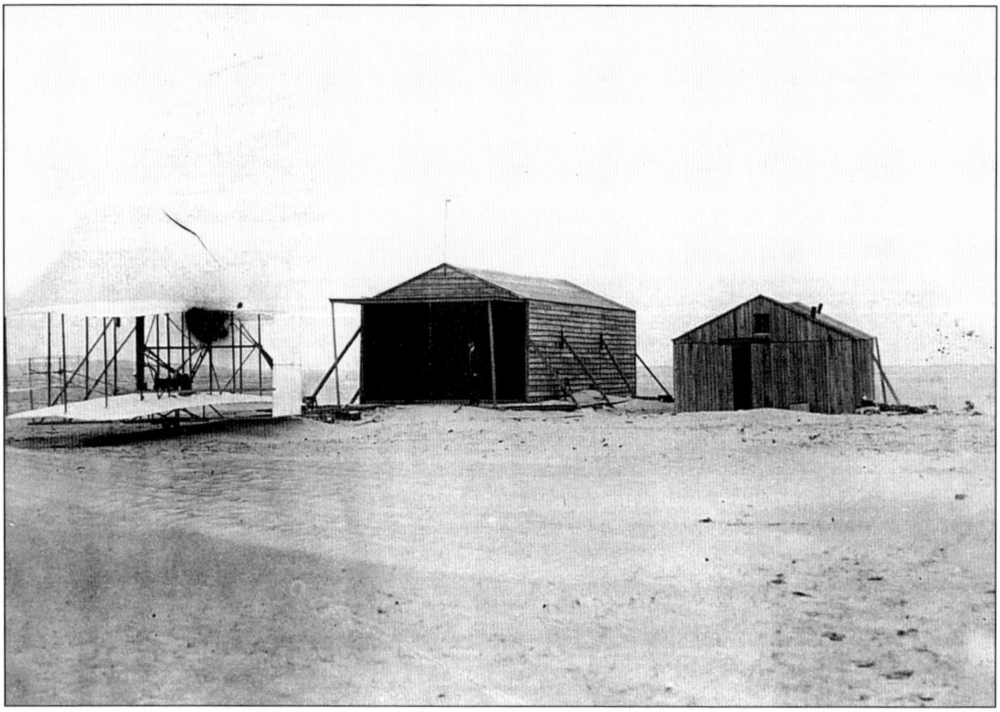

Wilbur Wright stands in his camp in 1903, looking at his flying machine. (Courtesy Library of Congress.)

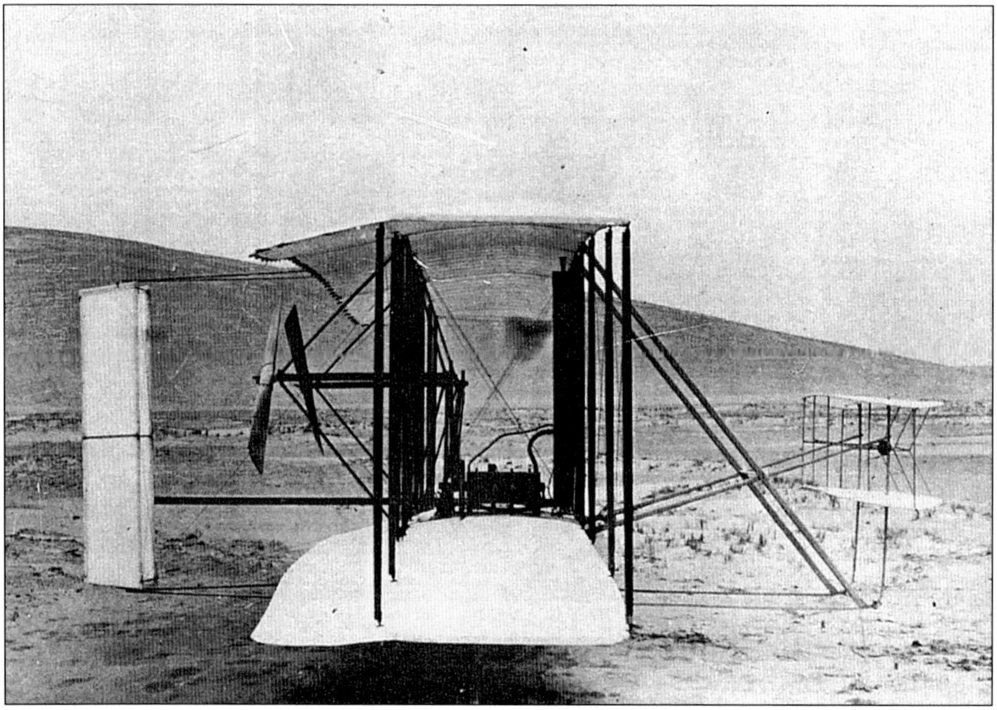

This view shows the side of the Wright Brothers' flying machine at Kill Devil Hills, *c.* 1903. (Courtesy Library of Congress.)

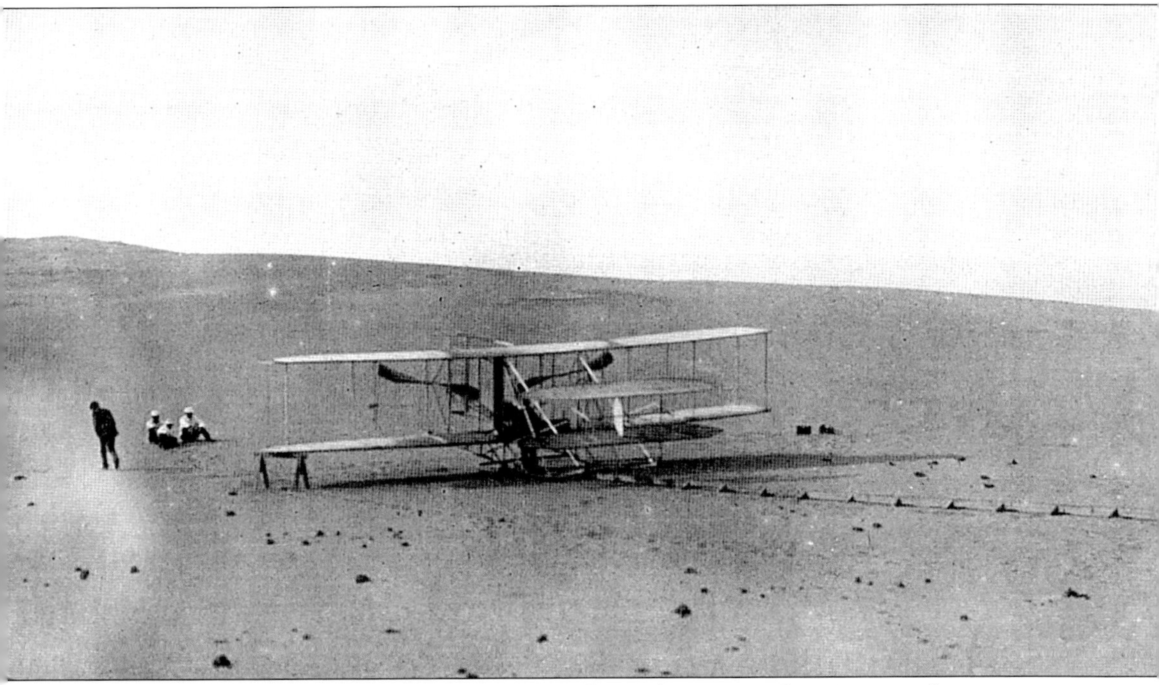

The Wright Brothers returned to Kill Devil Hills in the spring of 1908 to conduct tests on their flying machine. The photograph above was taken May 11, 1908. Three days later, Wilbur Wright crashed this aircraft. (Courtesy Library of Congress.)

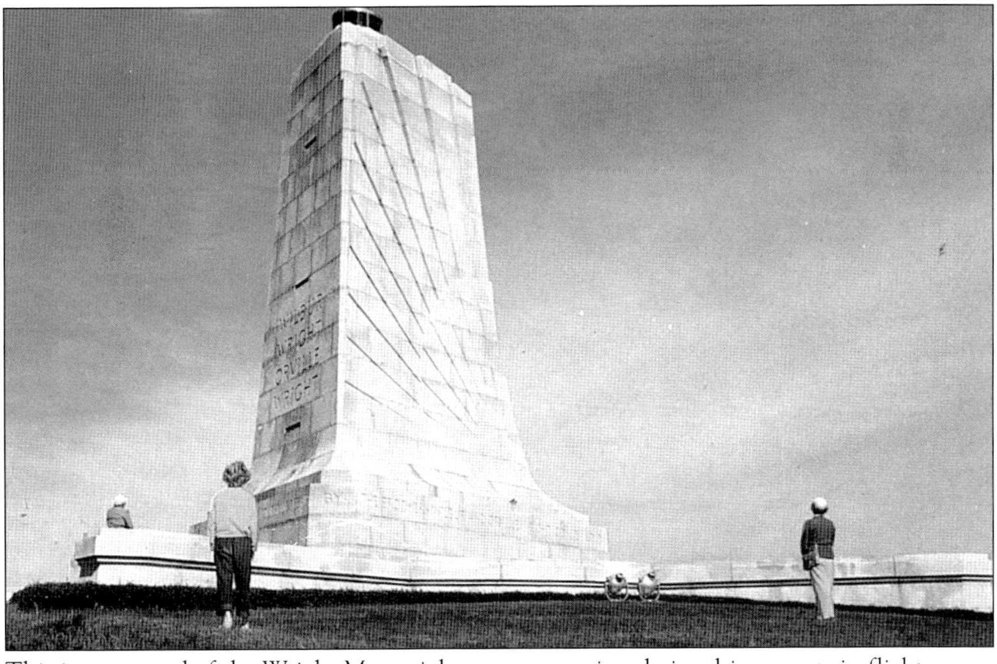

This is a postcard of the Wright Memorial, commemorating their achievements in flight.

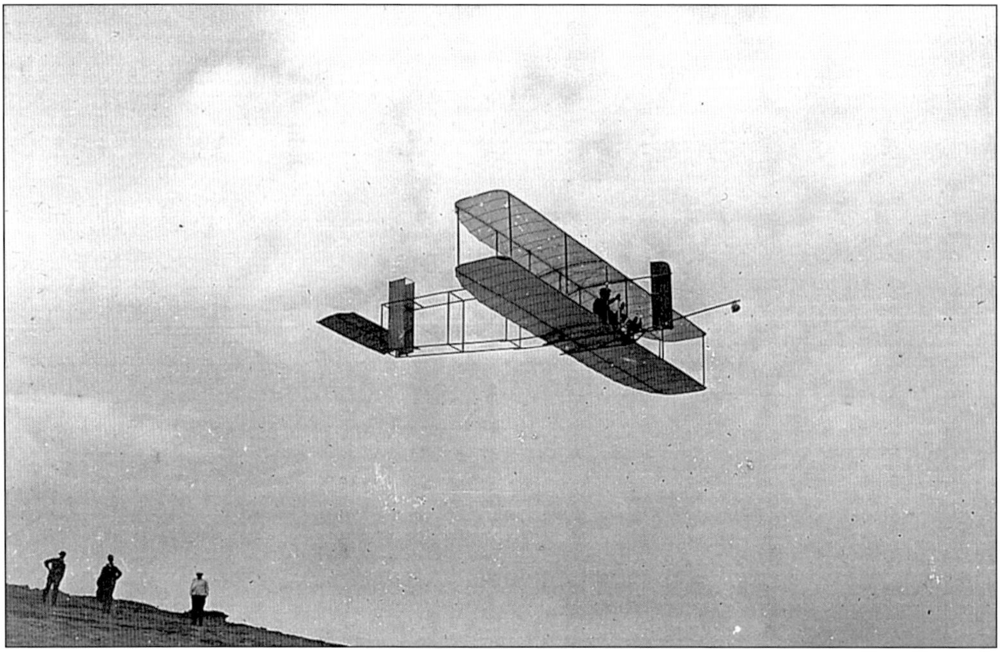

During the glider tests at Kill Devil Hills in October of 1911, Orville Wright made several record-breaking flights on a flying machine, which was unassisted by motor. During the longest flight, Orville managed to stay airborne for 9 minutes, 45 seconds; this record stood for several years. (Courtesy Library of Congress.)

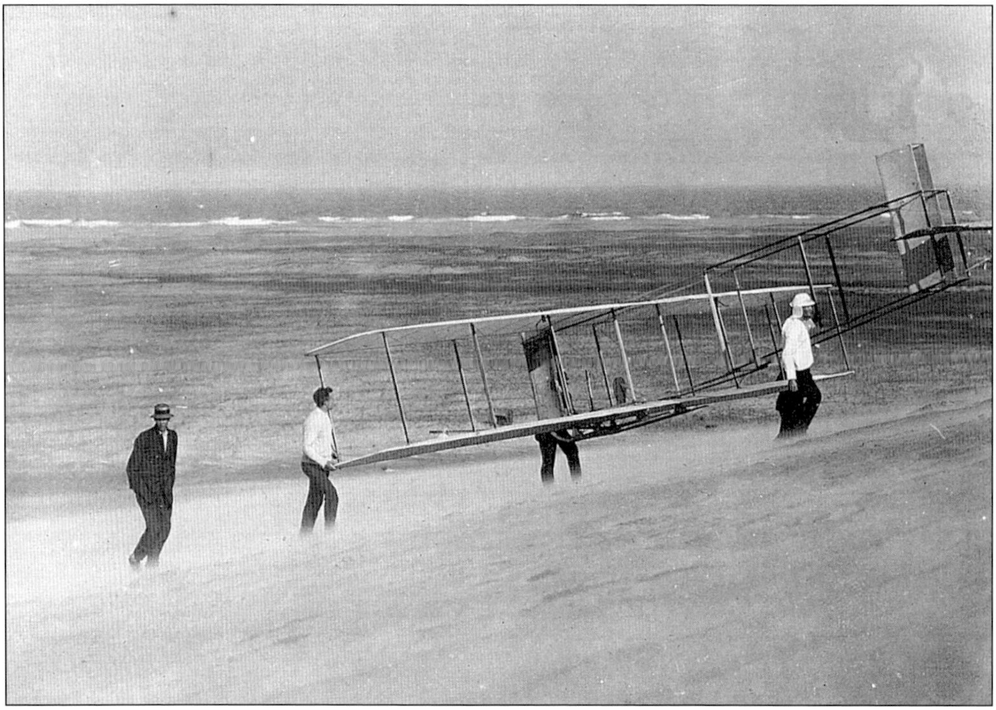

Orville Wright was back on the Outer Banks experimenting with a new glider in 1911. (Courtesy Library of Congress.)

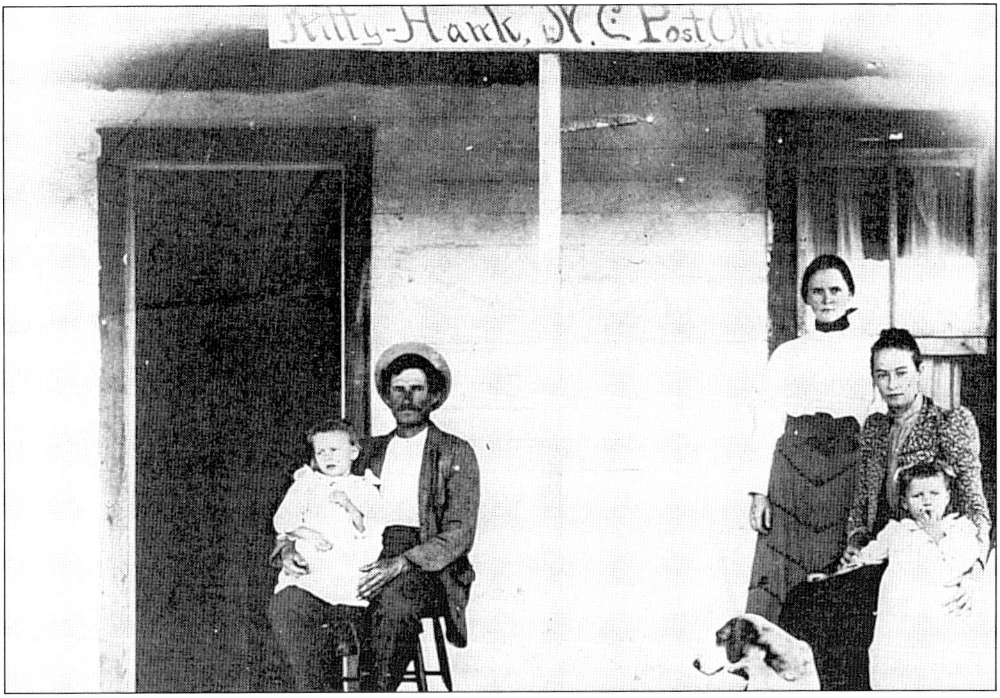

A letter from Bill Tate, who is shown here with his wife, Addie, and their family in 1900, convinced Wilbur Wright to come to the Outer Banks to conduct flight experiments. Tate wrote of the area, "You would find here nearly any type of ground you could wish; you could, for instance, get a stretch of sandy land one mile by five with a bare hill in center 80 feet high, not a tree or bush anywhere to break the evenness of the wind current. This in my opinion would be a fine place; our winds are always steady, generally from 10 to 20 miles velocity per hour." (Courtesy Library of Congress.)

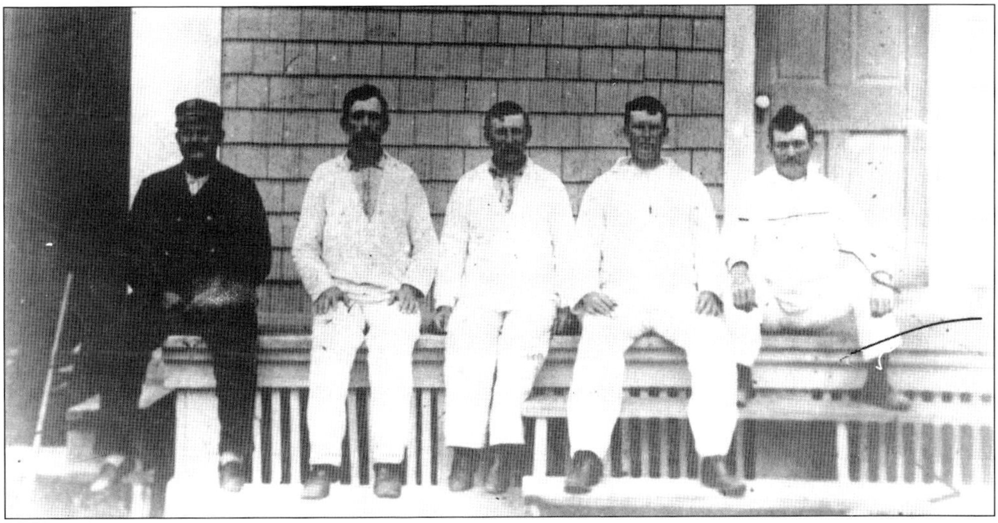

These men were from the Kill Devil Hills Lifesaving Station, c. 1903. Shown here, from left to right, are keeper Jesse Ward, Tom Beacham, unidentified, John Daniels, and Willie Dough. Daniels is the man who took the famous photograph of Orville Wright's first heavier-than-air flight. (U.S. Coast Guard.)

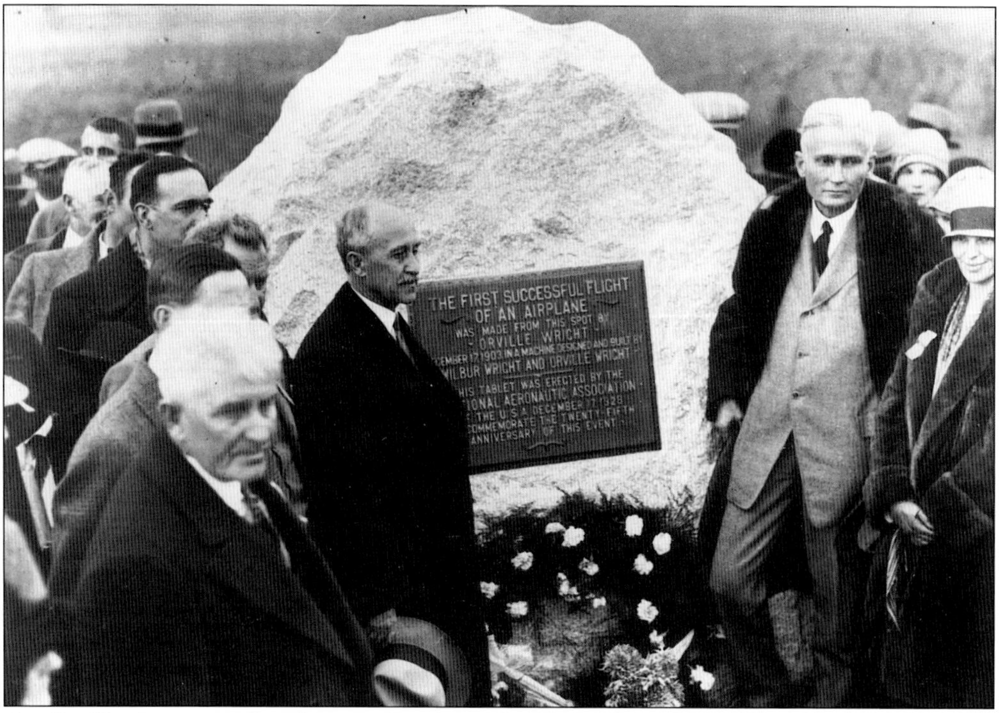

Orville Wright was on hand December 17, 1928, at the dedication of this monument, which marks the site of the first flight. (Courtesy North Carolina Division of Archives and History.)

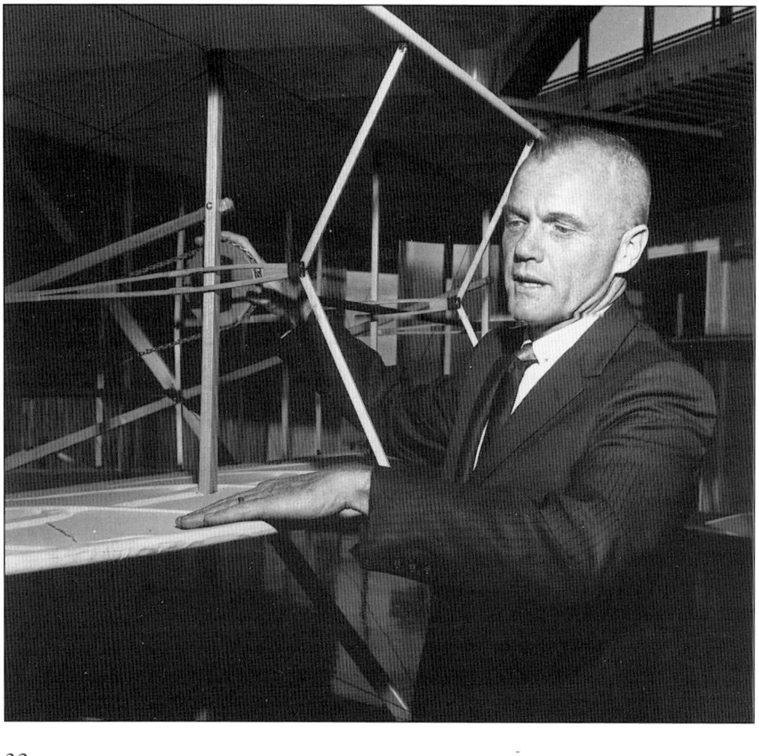

Astronaut John Glenn was one of the many dignitaries on hand at Kitty Hawk for the celebration of the 60th anniversary of the Wright Brothers' historic first flight. (Courtesy North Carolina Division of Archives and History.)

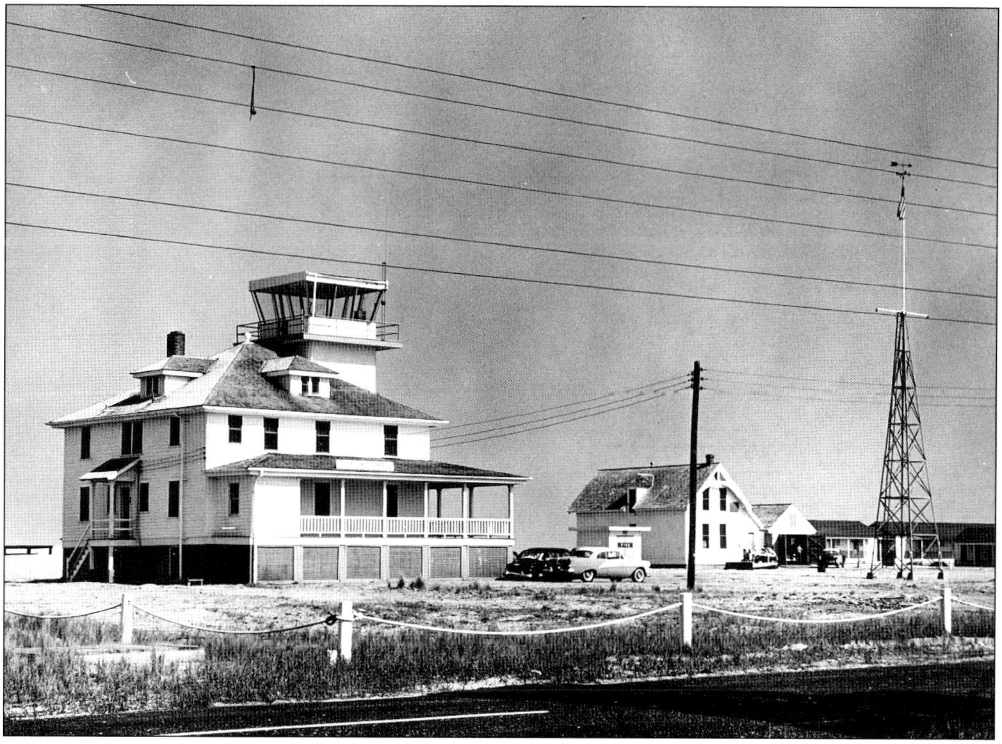

Kill Devil Hills Coast Guard Station was located 4 miles south of Kitty Hawk. (U.S. Coast Guard.)

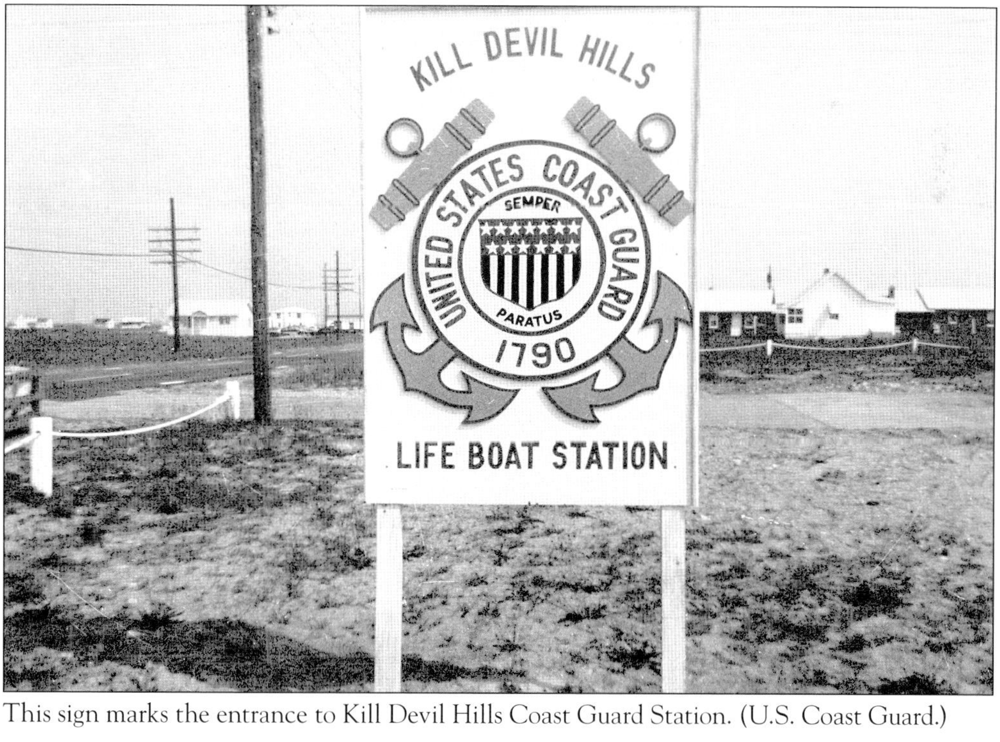

This sign marks the entrance to Kill Devil Hills Coast Guard Station. (U.S. Coast Guard.)

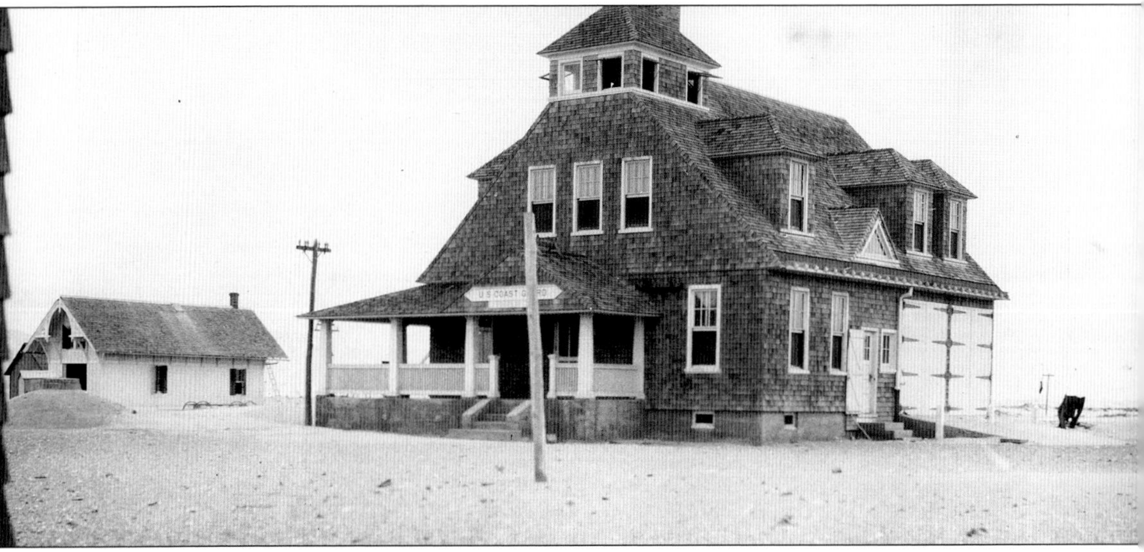

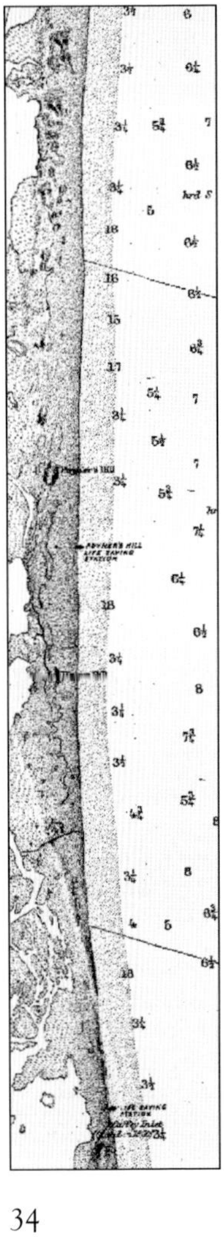

This picture of Nags Head, "Station 174," was photographed on July 18, 1917. (U.S. Coast Guard.)

This chart, which was published in 1879, shows the northern Outer Banks from Currituck Beach to Caffey Inlet Lifesaving Station.

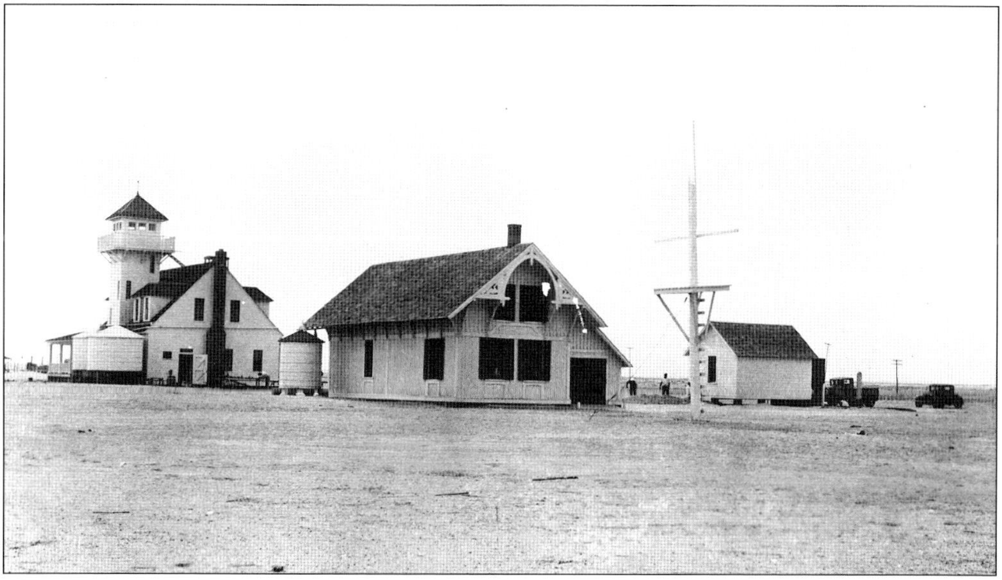

This northeastern view of Nags Head Station was taken on September 20, 1934. (U.S. Coast Guard.)

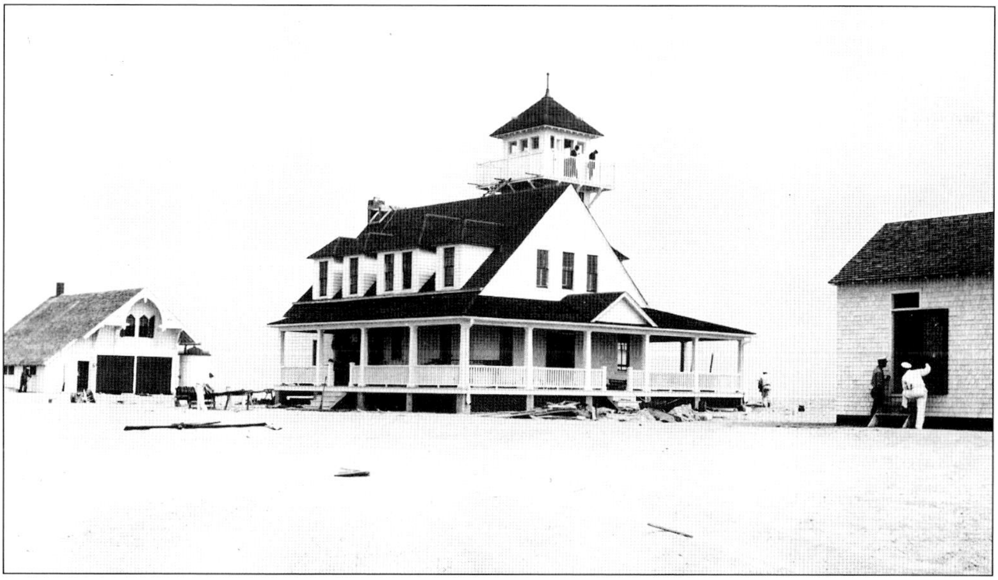

Nags Head Station can be viewed from the southwest in this September 20, 1934 image. (U.S. Coast Guard.)

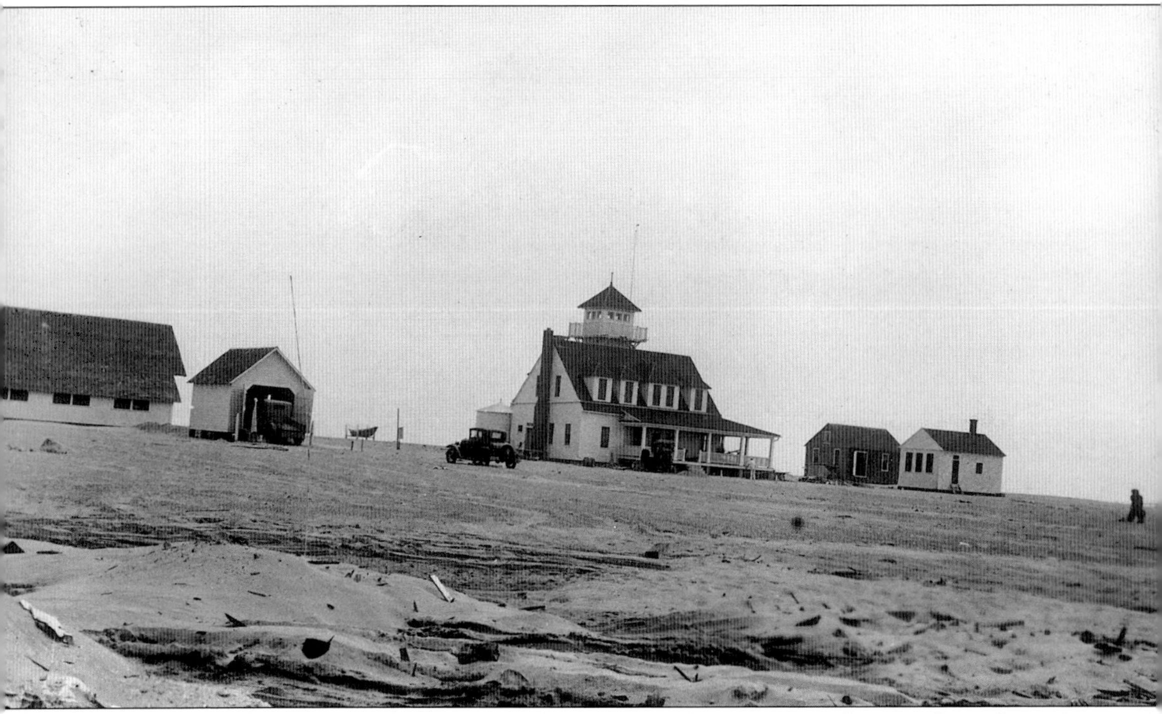

Photographed on September 20, 1934, the Nags Head Station can be seen here from the northwest. (U.S. Coast Guard.)

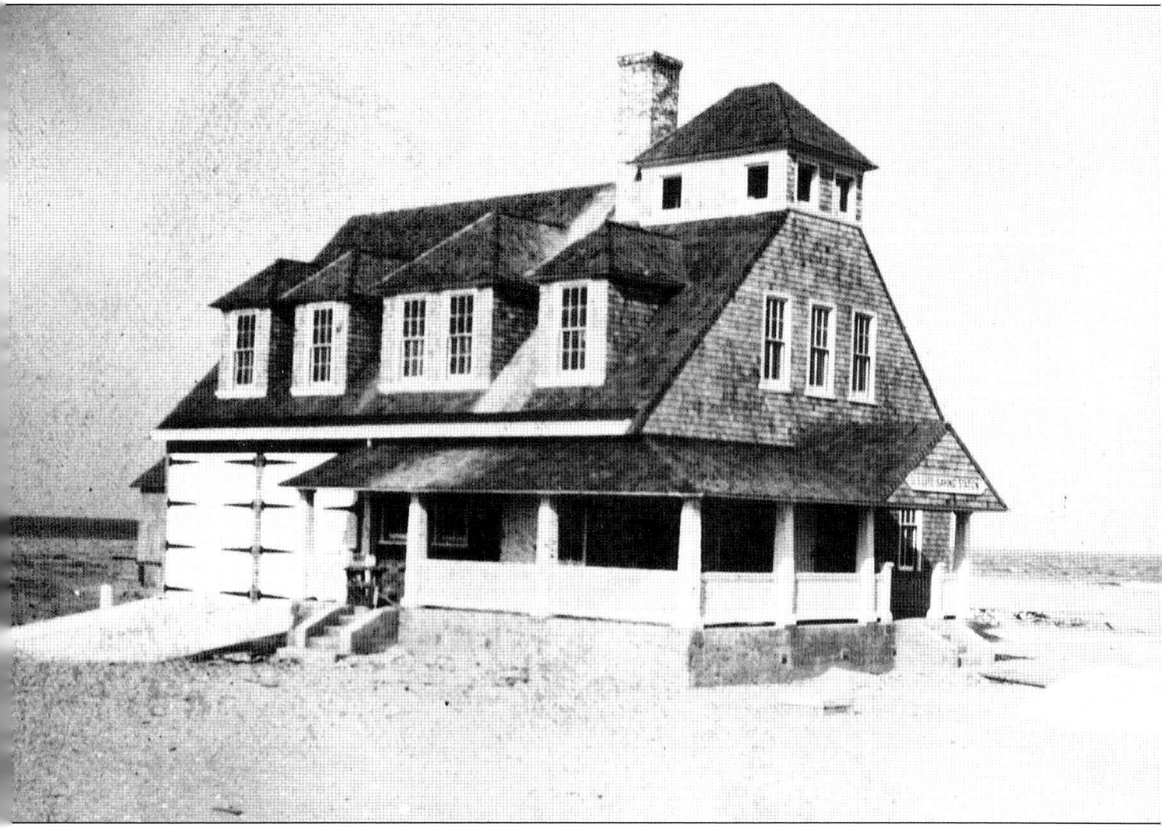

Near this station, Nags Head Station 174, occurred the wreck of the U.S.S. *Huron* during a storm in November 1878. Of her crew of 132 men, only 34 survived. (U.S. Coast Guard.)

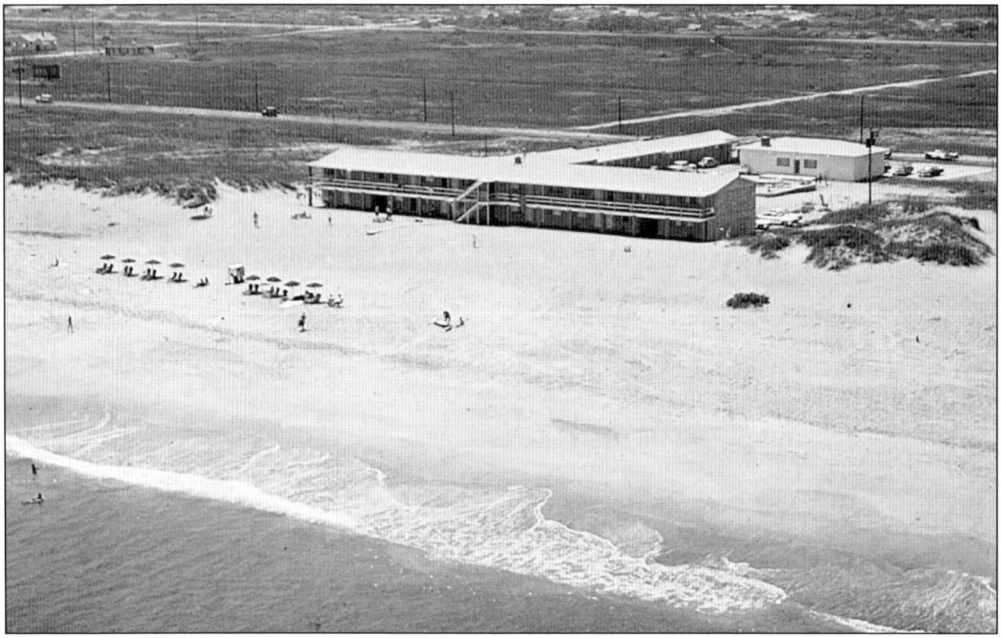

In this birds-eye view, the Outer Banks Motor Lodge stands practically alone at Nags Head.

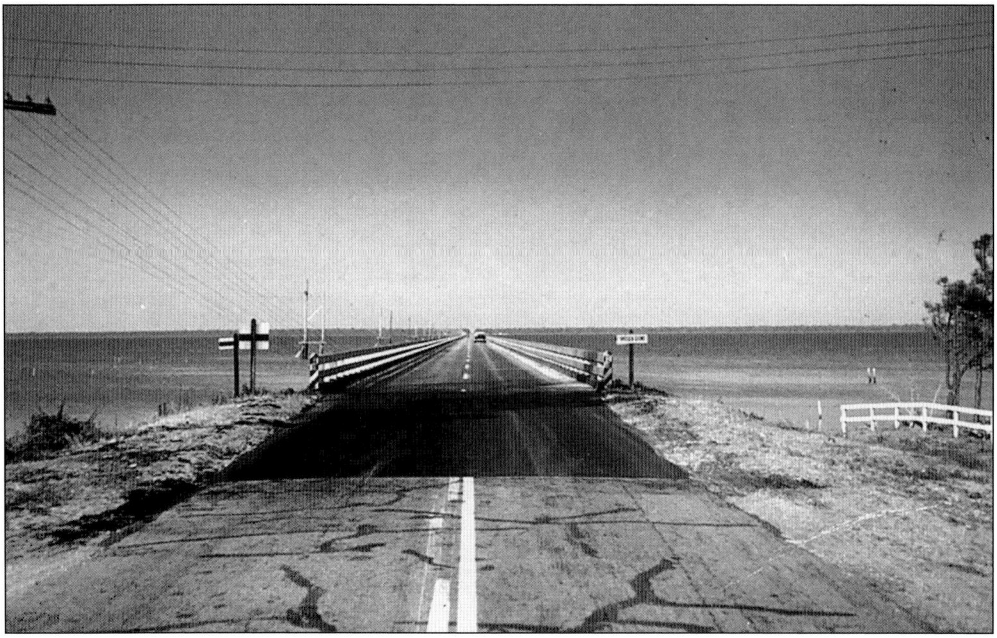

This postcard shows the Currituck Bridge.

NORTH CAROLINA SEA BATHING.

Nag's Head Hotel.

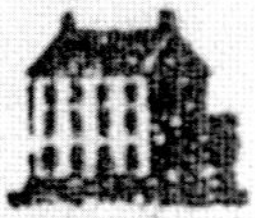

THIS extensive establishment, recently improved, will be opened for the reception of Visitors, superintended by the Junior Partner, A. J. BATEMAN, on the 1st day of July. The Hotel situated in view of the Ocean, presents a magnificent prospect. The great benefits resulting from Sea Bathing and the sea breeze, are becoming more known and appreciated daily. No place can be more healthy or possess a finer climate than Nag's Head. The Bathing is unsurpassed in the United States. We have engaged a good Band of Music, our Ball Room is very spacious and will be opened every evening. Active and efficient assistants have been engaged, and no exertions will be spared to render it in all respects an agreeable and interesting resort. A Rail Road will be completed early in July from the Hotel to the Ocean, that persons preferring a ride to walking may be accommodated.

The steamer Schultz will make a trip every Saturday from Franklin Depot, Va., to Nags' Head, commencing July 12th, immediately after the arrival of the Cars from Norfolk, and returning leave Nags' Head Sunday evening, at 5 o'clock. Passage from Franklin $3, Riddick's Wharf, Winton, &c., $2 50, Edenton to Nags' Head $2. Meals extra. The Schultz will make several Excursions to Nags' Head through the season, due notice of which will be given. The Packet schr. Sarah Porter, Capt. Walker, will make two trips from Edenton, (N. C.,) to Nag's Head each week through the season, leaving Edenton Tuesday and Friday, at 8 o'clock, A. M. The Packet schr. A. Riddick, Capt. Dunbar, will make three trips each week through the season, from Elizabeth City, (N. C.,) to Nag's Head, leaving Elizabeth City immediately after the arrival of the Stage Coach from Norfolk, Va. Passage on each Packet $1, meals extra. Board per day at the Hotel $1 50. By the week at the rate of $1 25. By the two weeks at the rate of $1. By the month at the rate of 75 cents per day. Children and Servants half price. The patronage of the public is very respectfully solicited.

RIDDICK & BATEMAN.

June 11, 1851. 38-2m

This advertisement from an old newspaper extolls the virtues of the Nags Head Hotel.

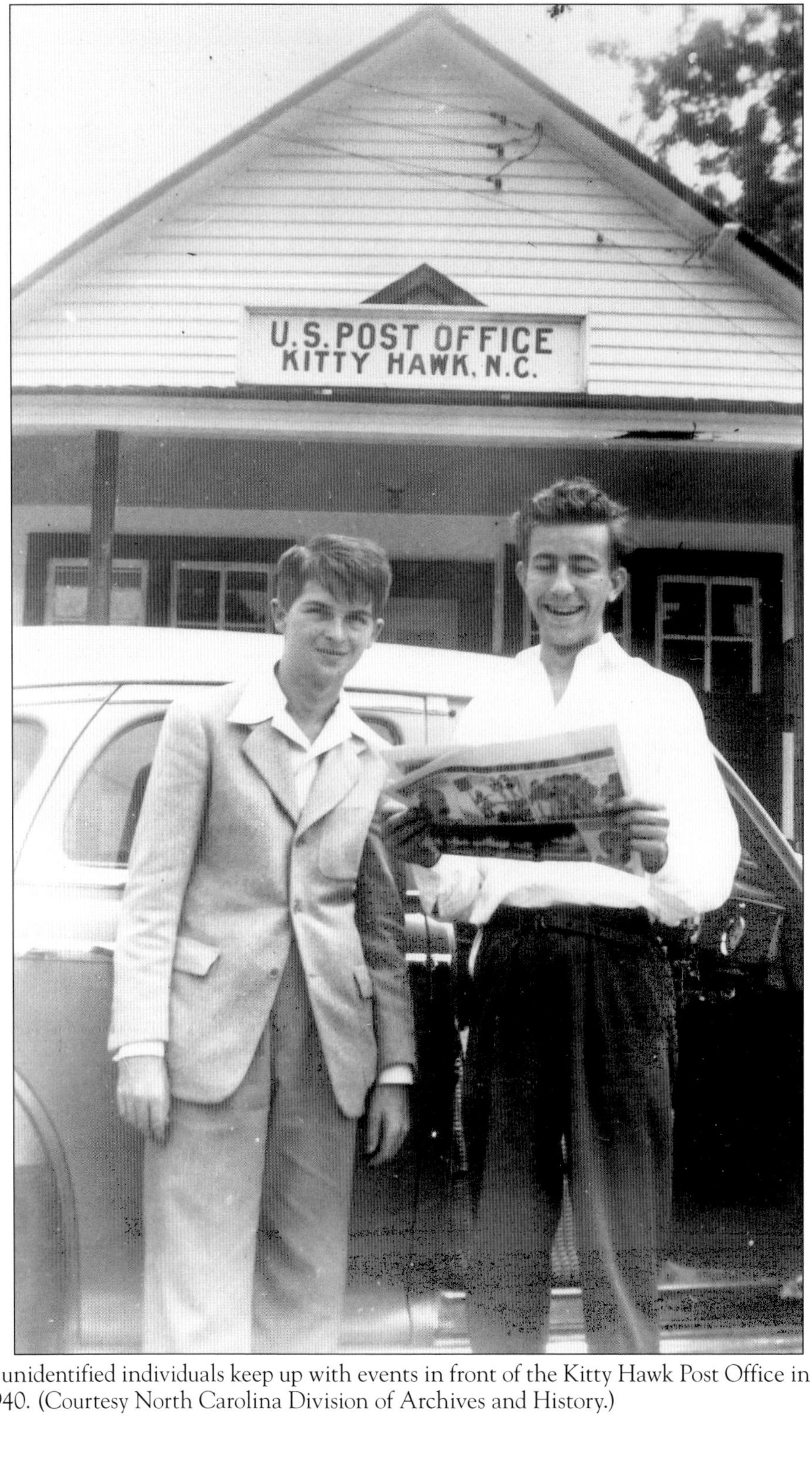

Two unidentified individuals keep up with events in front of the Kitty Hawk Post Office in June of 1940. (Courtesy North Carolina Division of Archives and History.)

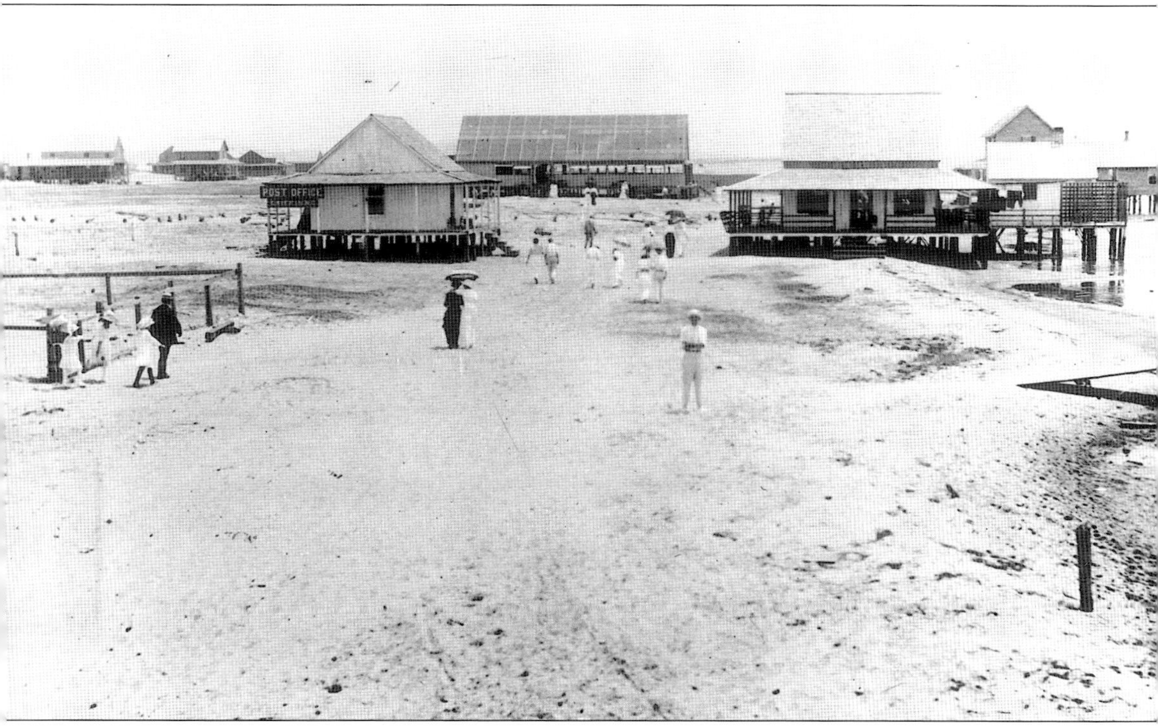

This is a turn-of-the-century postcard view of Nags Head, North Carolina.

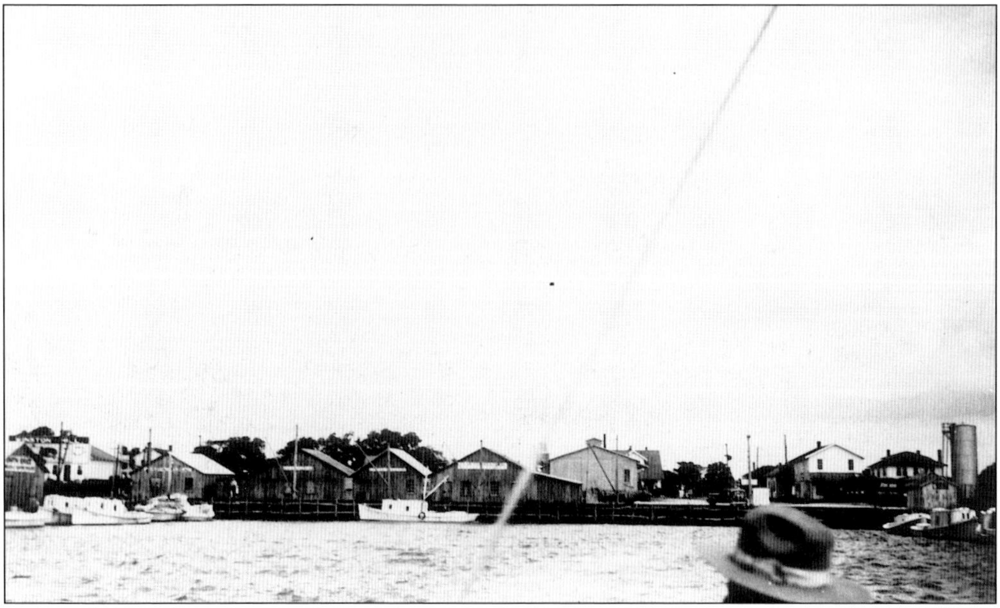

This image of the Manteo waterfront was taken in 1939. (Courtesy North Carolina Division of Archives and History.)

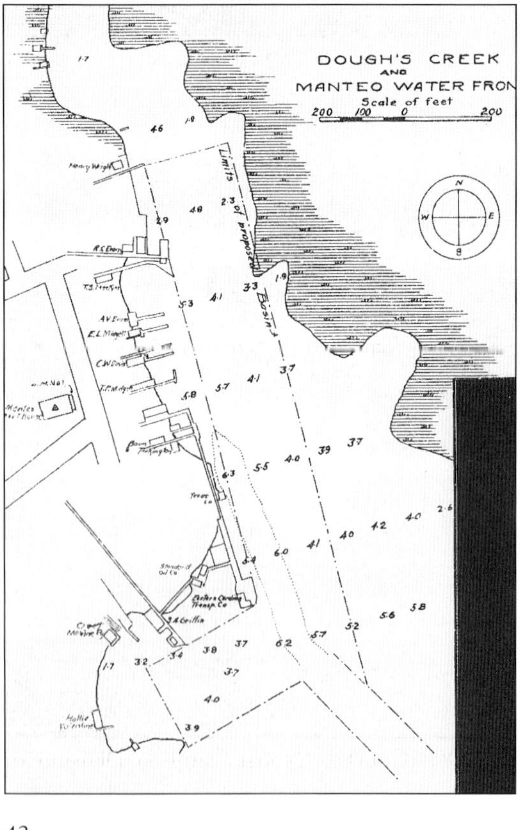

This insert, from a chart of Manteo Bay drawn by Major H.W. Stickle, shows the Manteo waterfront as it appeared in December of 1913.

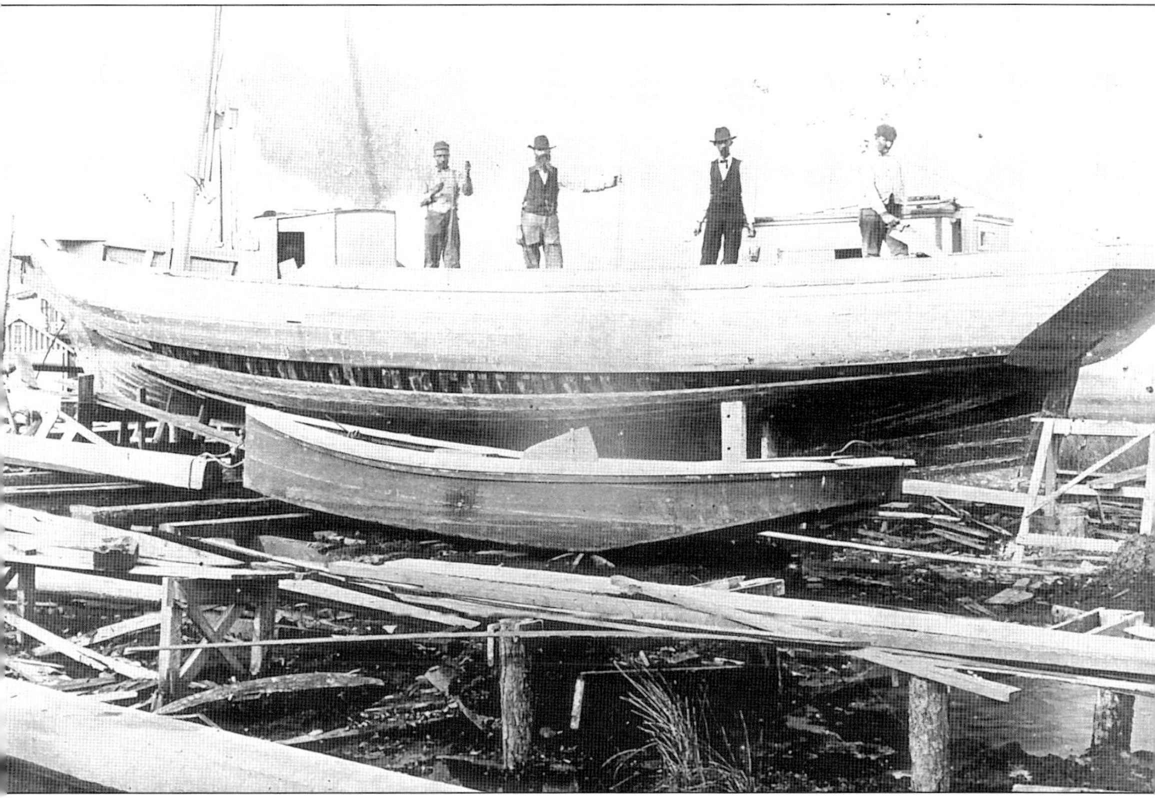

A schooner was under construction at the Creef Boat Works at Wanchese, c. 1898. (Courtesy North Carolina Maritime Museum.)

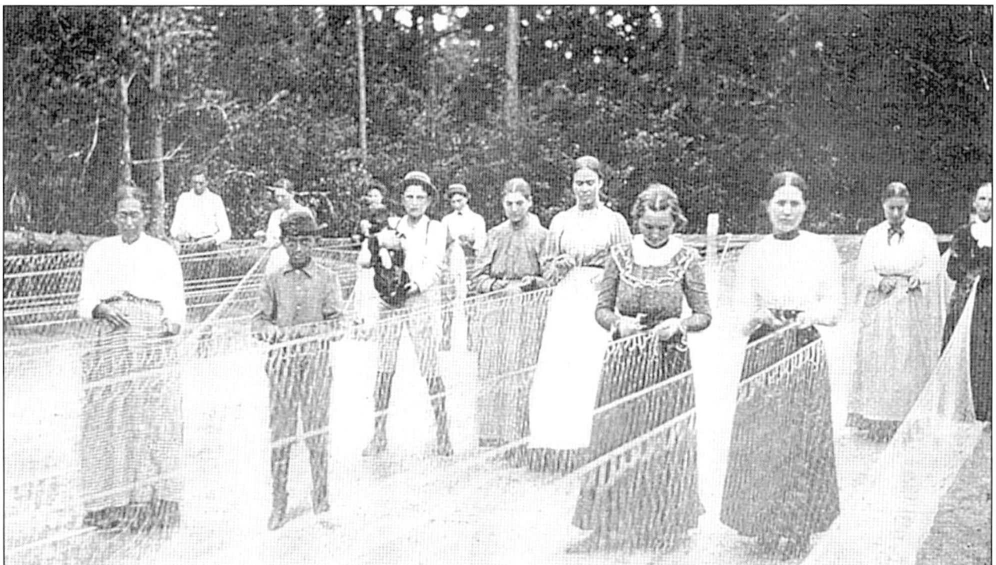

This group mends fishing nets at Manteo in 1906. (Courtesy North Carolina Division of Archives and History.)

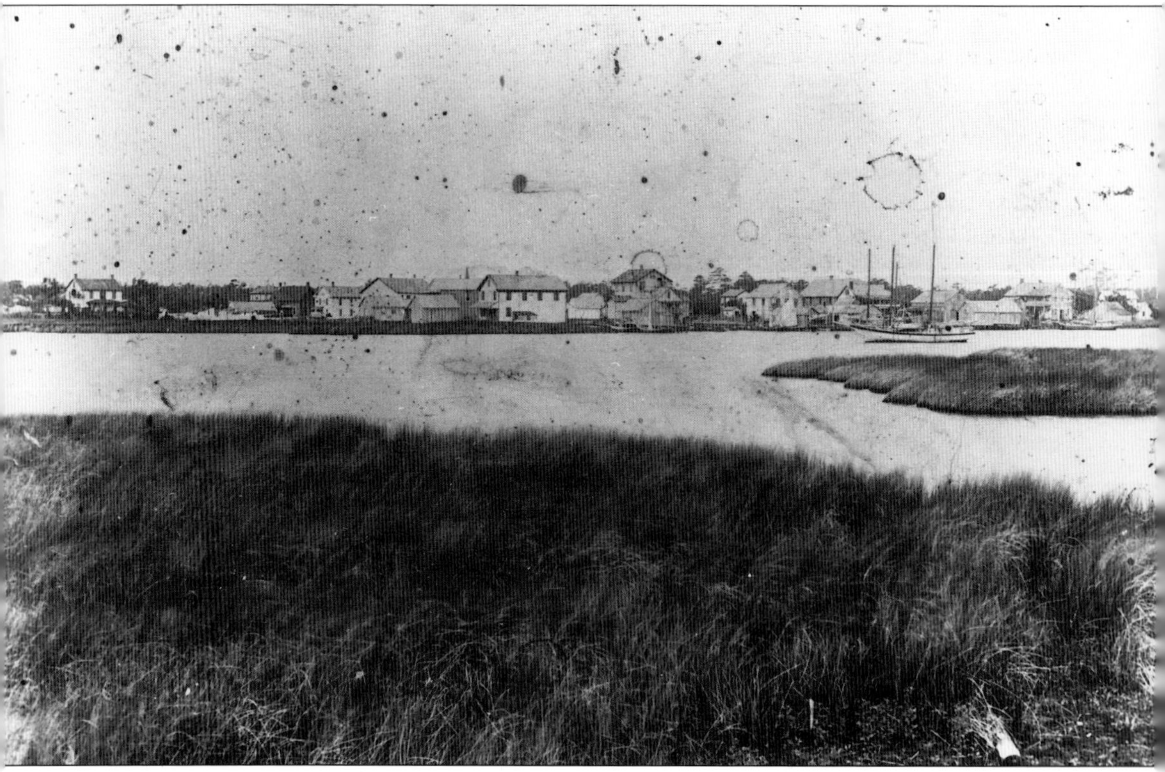

This rare view shows Wanchese on Roanoke Island, *c.* 1900. (Courtesy North Carolina Division of Archives and History.)

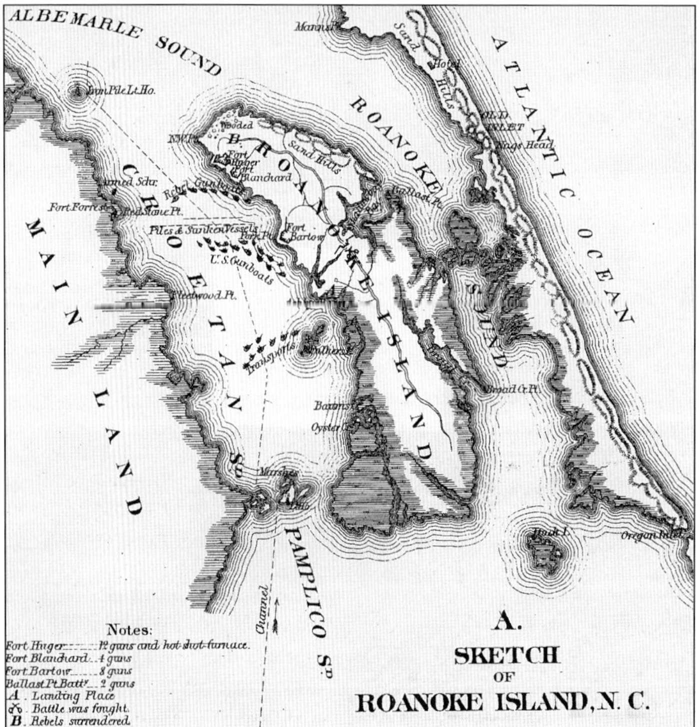

This map, drawn in 1862, shows the Confederate defenses on Roanoake Island.

These men of the Eighth North Carolina Regiment participated in the Battle of Roanoke Island, February 8, 1862. Seen here, from right to left, are Colonel H.M. Shaw, Colonel John R. Murchison, Lieutenant Colonel Rufus A. Barrier, Captain Jonas Cook, Captain Leonard A. Henderson, First Lieutenant Harvey C. McAllister, and Captain W.H. Bagley.

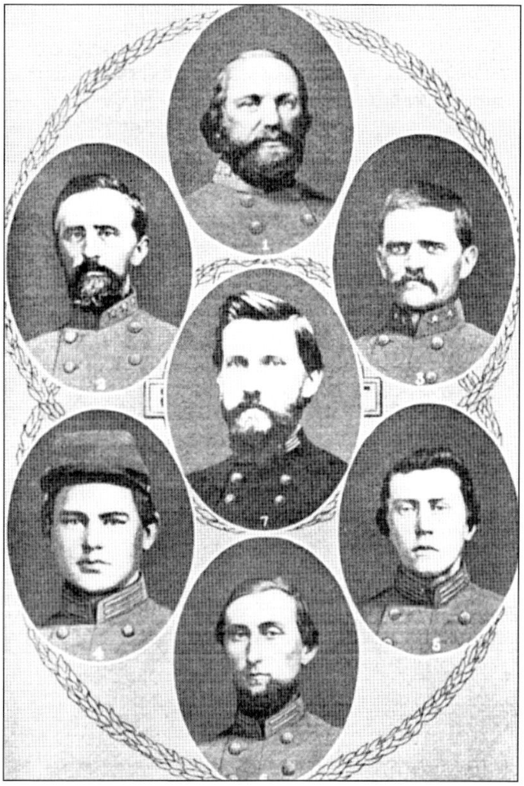

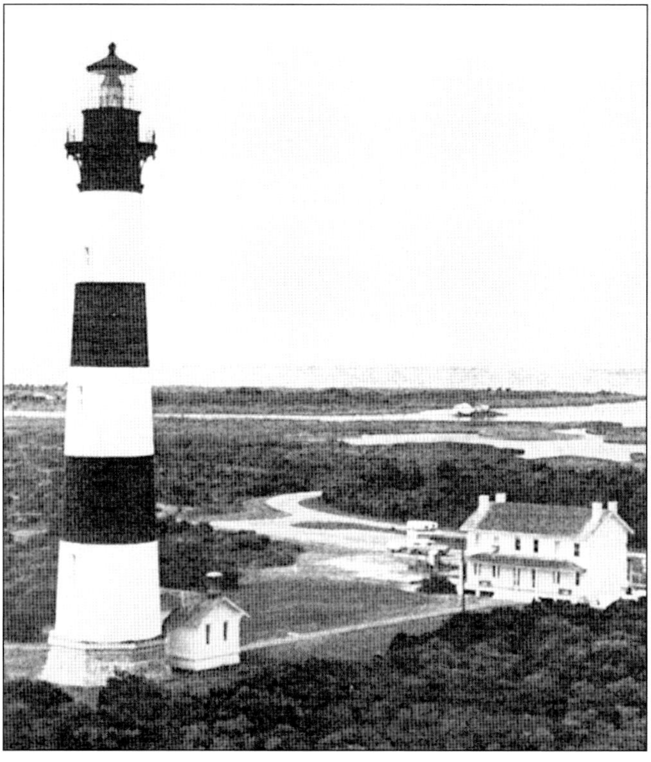

Bodie Island Lighthouse was constructed in 1871. It took less than a year to complete the structure and cost $140,000. In the early days of its existence, the Bodie Island Lighthouse was often damaged by wild geese flying into the glass storm panes. Eventually, screen was put over the glass.

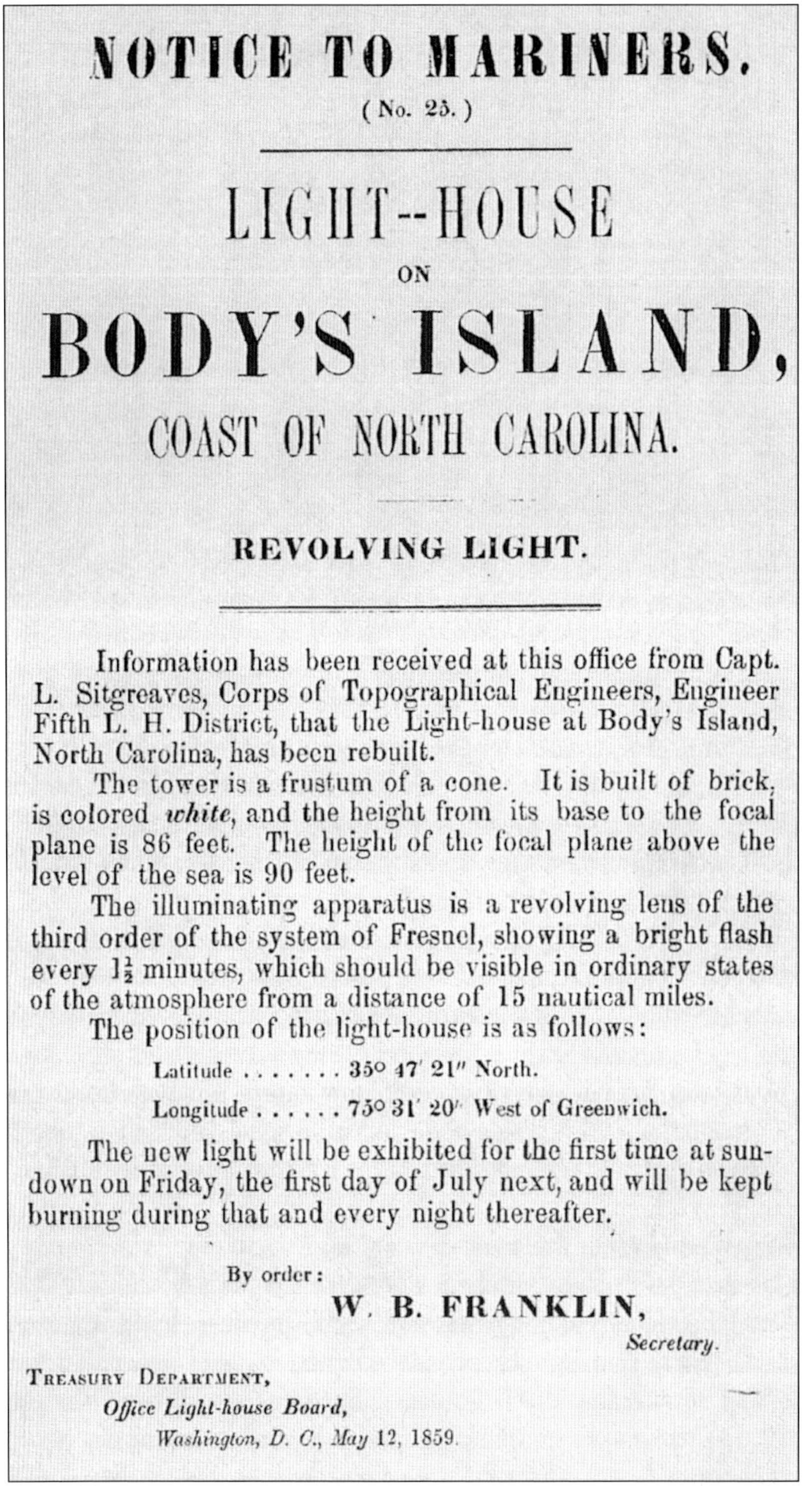

NOTICE TO MARINERS.

(No. 25.)

LIGHT--HOUSE

ON

BODY'S ISLAND,

COAST OF NORTH CAROLINA.

REVOLVING LIGHT.

Information has been received at this office from Capt. L. Sitgreaves, Corps of Topographical Engineers, Engineer Fifth L. H. District, that the Light-house at Body's Island, North Carolina, has been rebuilt.

The tower is a frustum of a cone. It is built of brick, is colored *white*, and the height from its base to the focal plane is 86 feet. The height of the focal plane above the level of the sea is 90 feet.

The illuminating apparatus is a revolving lens of the third order of the system of Fresnel, showing a bright flash every 1½ minutes, which should be visible in ordinary states of the atmosphere from a distance of 15 nautical miles.

The position of the light-house is as follows:

Latitude . . . . 35° 47′ 21″ North.

Longitude . . . . . . 75° 31′ 20″ West of Greenwich.

The new light will be exhibited for the first time at sundown on Friday, the first day of July next, and will be kept burning during that and every night thereafter.

By order:

W. B. FRANKLIN,

Secretary.

TREASURY DEPARTMENT,

Office Light-house Board,

Washington, D. C., May 12, 1859.

This notice contains a description and general information for sailors and mariners about the Bodie Island Lighthouse.

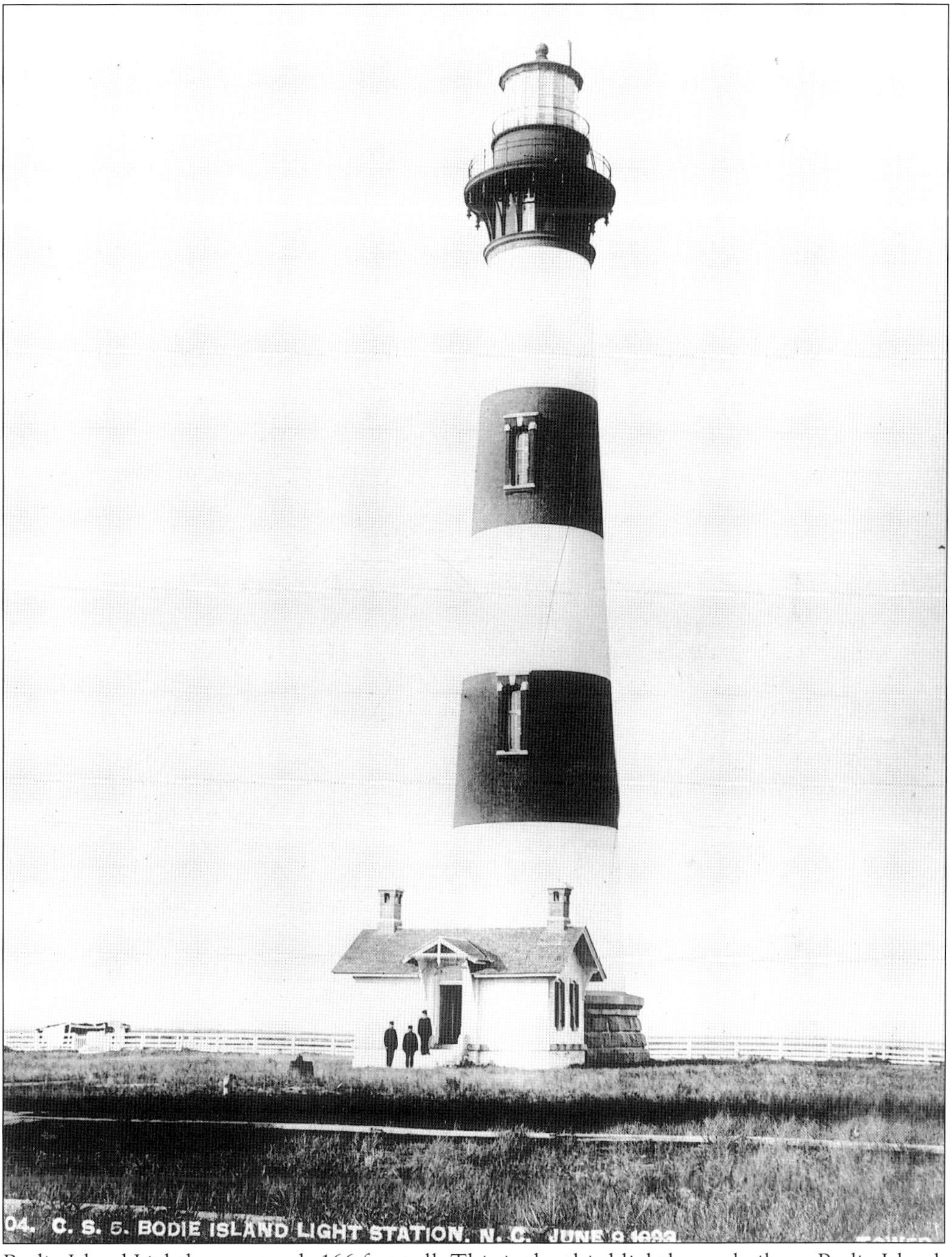

Bodie Island Lighthouse stands 166 feet tall. This is the third lighthouse built on Bodie Island. The first, a 54-foot-tall brick structure, was approved in 1837 and completed in 1848. A year after its construction the tower began listing to one side, thanks to an inadequate foundation. The structure was abandoned in 1859 and eventually fell into the sea.

The second lighthouse at Bodie Island was completed in 1859. The 80-foot-tall brick tower with cast iron lantern and third-order Fresnel lens was destroyed by Confederates in 1861, shortly after the fall of Fort Hatteras. (U.S. Coast Guard.)

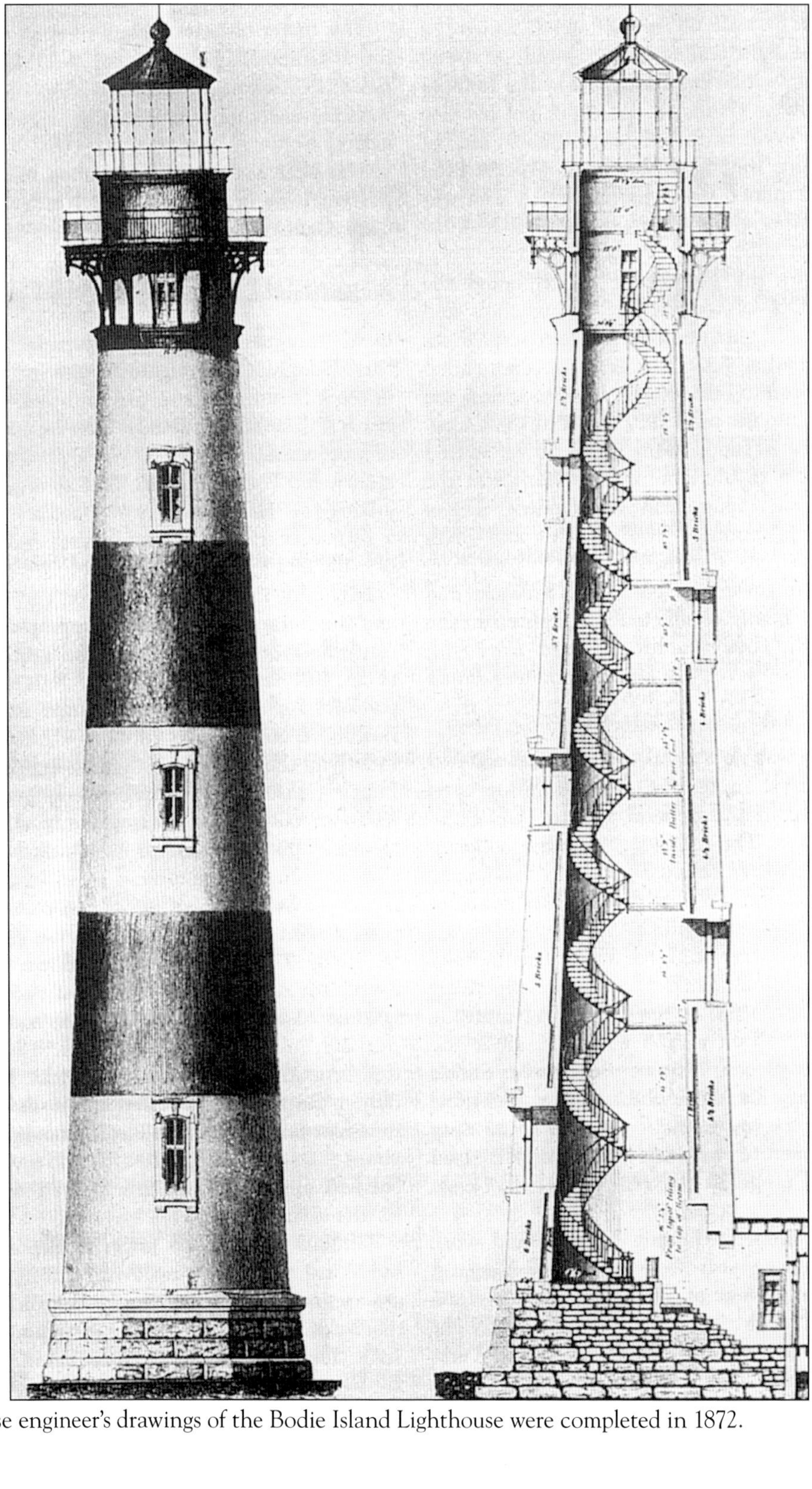

These engineer's drawings of the Bodie Island Lighthouse were completed in 1872.

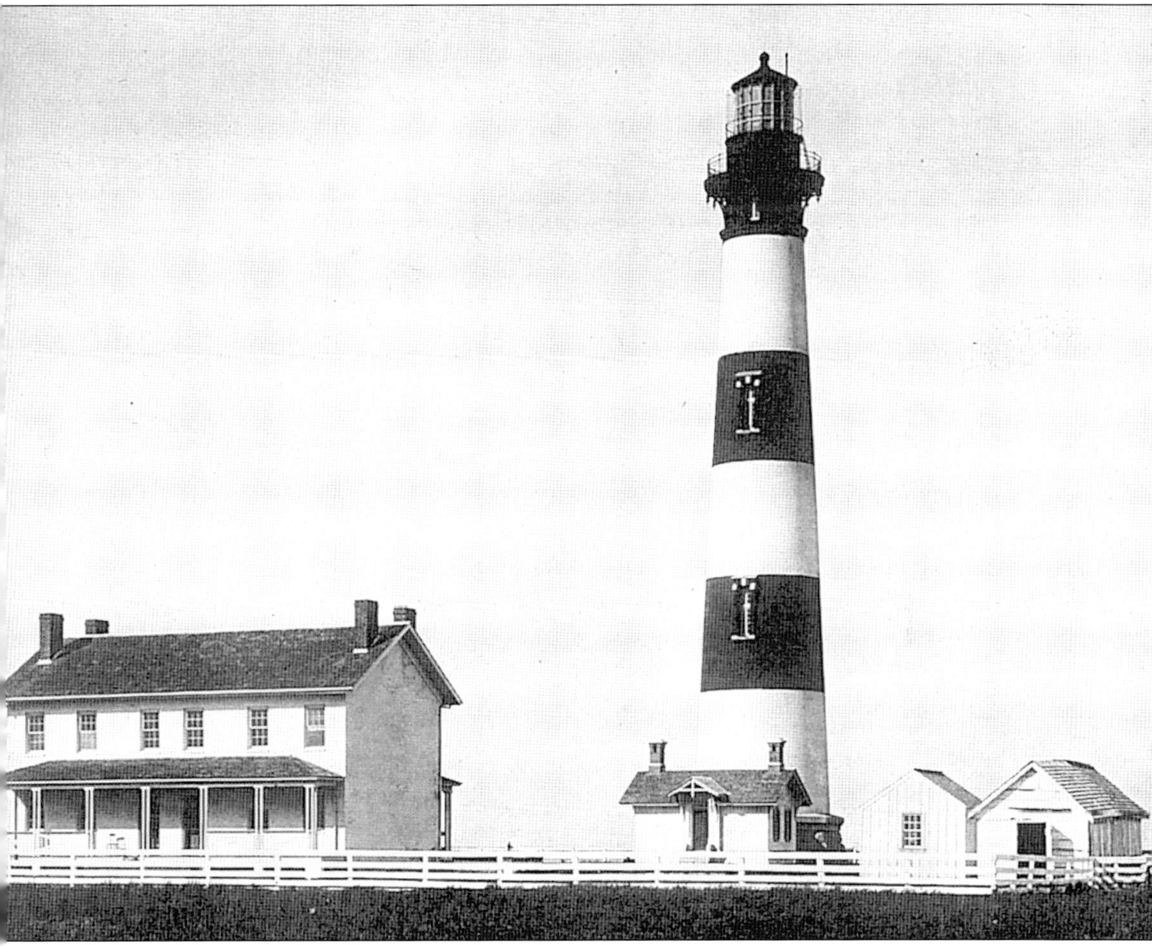

The Bodie Island Lighthouse and Keeper's Quarters were photographed in 1893. (U.S. Coast Guard.)

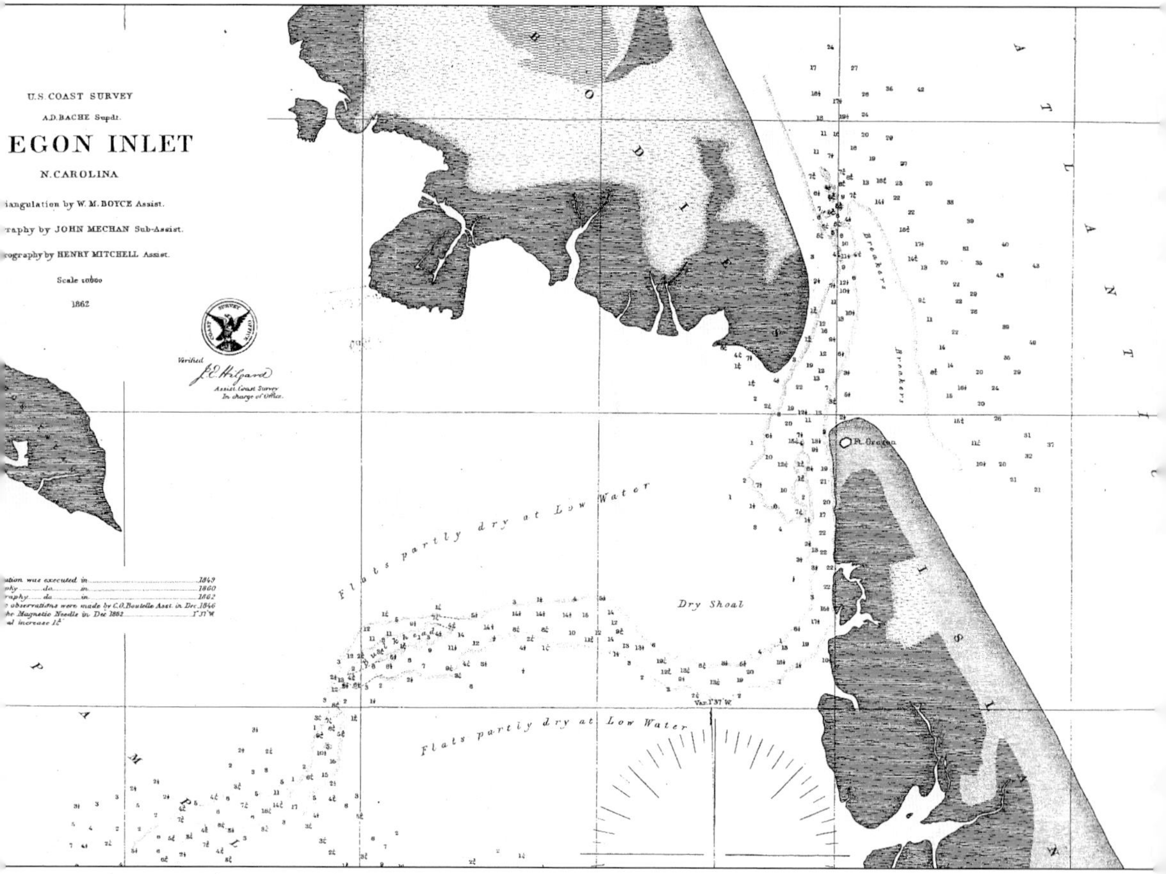

This map of Oregon Inlet was compiled by W.M. Boyce, John Mechan, and Henry Mitchell in 1862. Note the location of Fort Oregon.

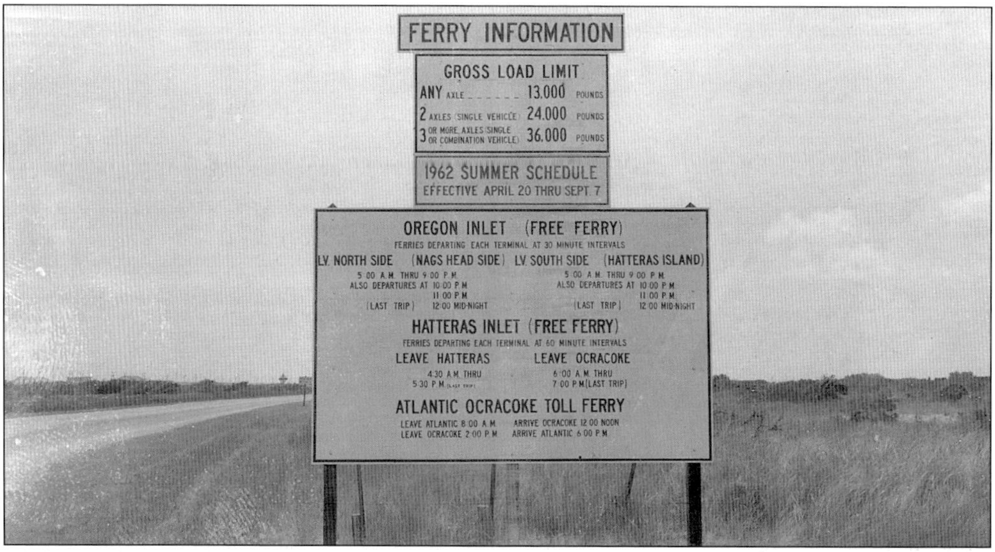

This sign that stood at Whalebone Junction gave information about the ferry crossings along the Outer Banks. (Courtesy NCDOT.)

Two

Oregon Inlet to Hatteras Inlet

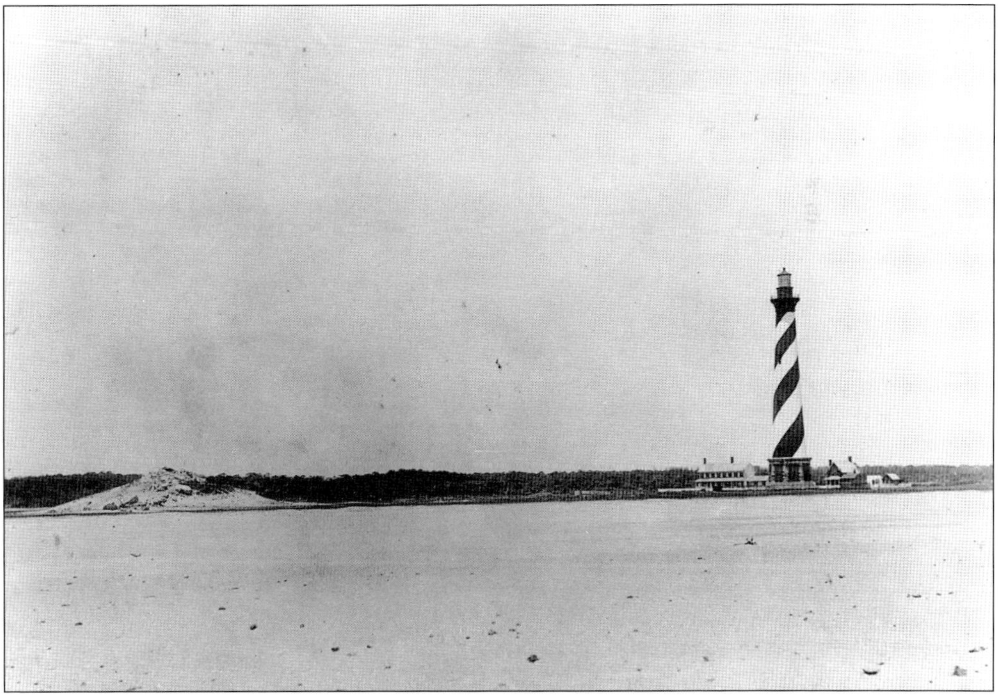

This image of the Cape Hatteras Lighthouse shows its condition as photographed on May 30, 1898. This candy-striped tower is probably one of the most recognized landmarks along the Outer Banks. (U.S. Coast Guard.)

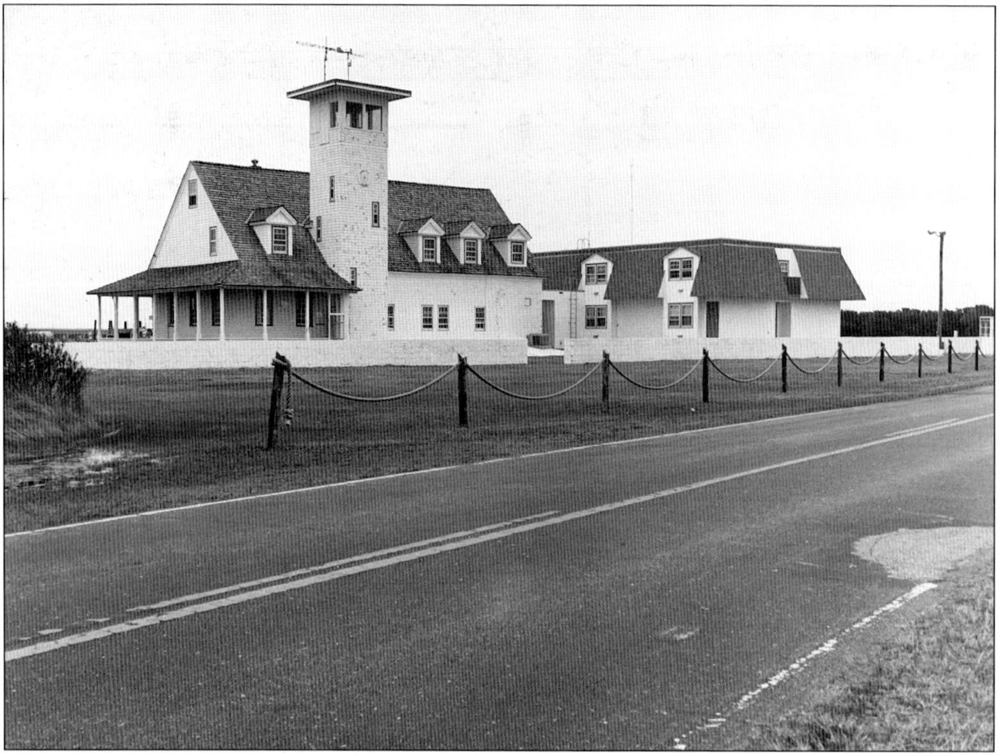

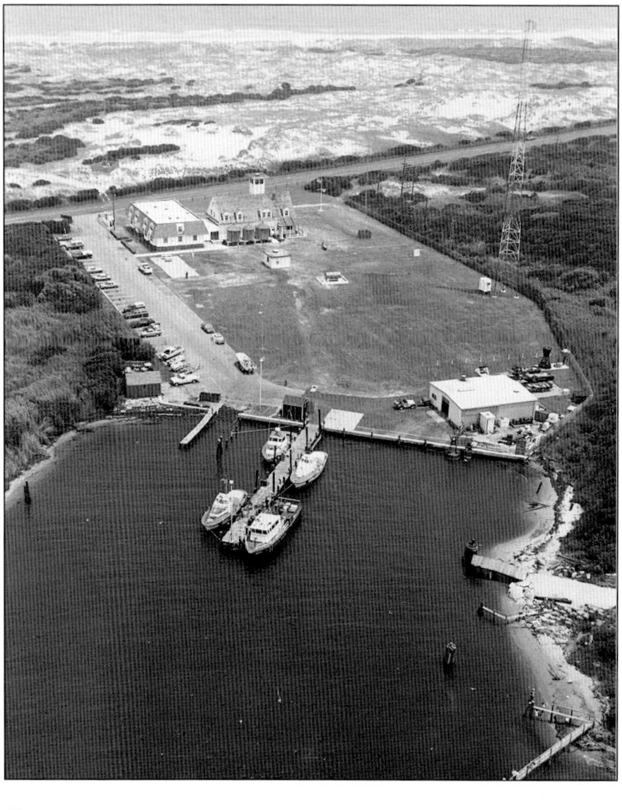

Oregon Inlet Coast Guard Station can be seen here. (U.S. Coast Guard.)

This aerial view shows the Oregon Inlet Coast Guard Station. (U.S. Coast Guard.)

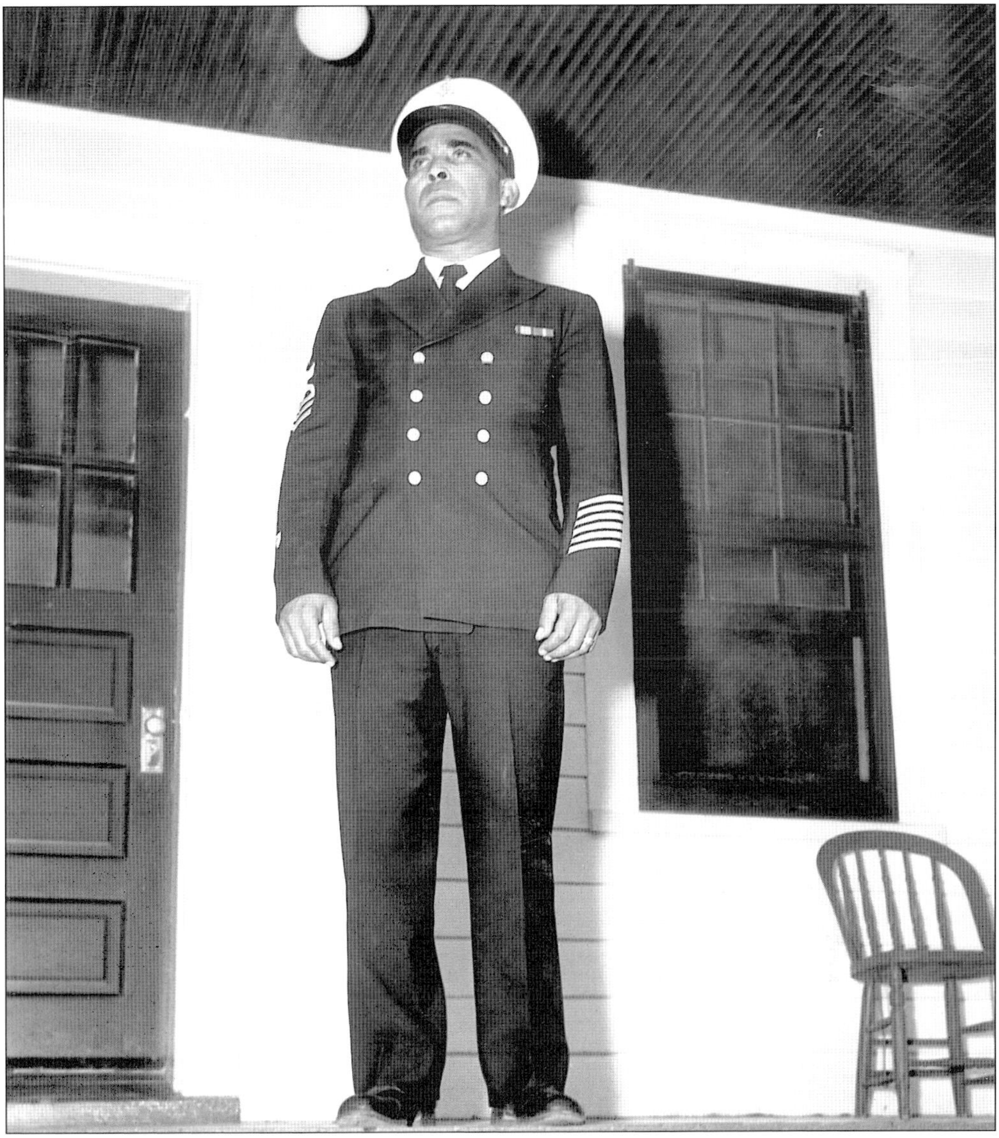

Maxie Berry C.B.M. served for 25 years at Pea Island. His father, Joseph Berry, retired as a surfman in 1917 after serving 13 years at Pea Island. (U.S. Coast Guard.)

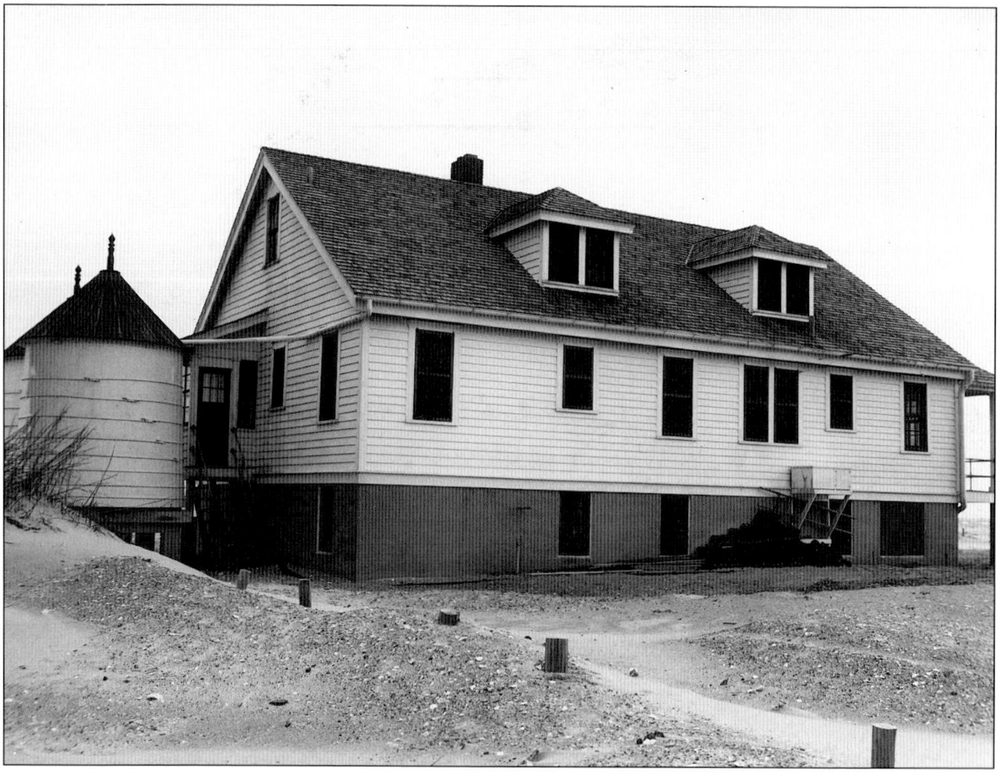

For nearly all of its existence, an all African-American crew manned the Pea Island Lifesaving Station until it closed in 1947. (U.S. Coast Guard.)

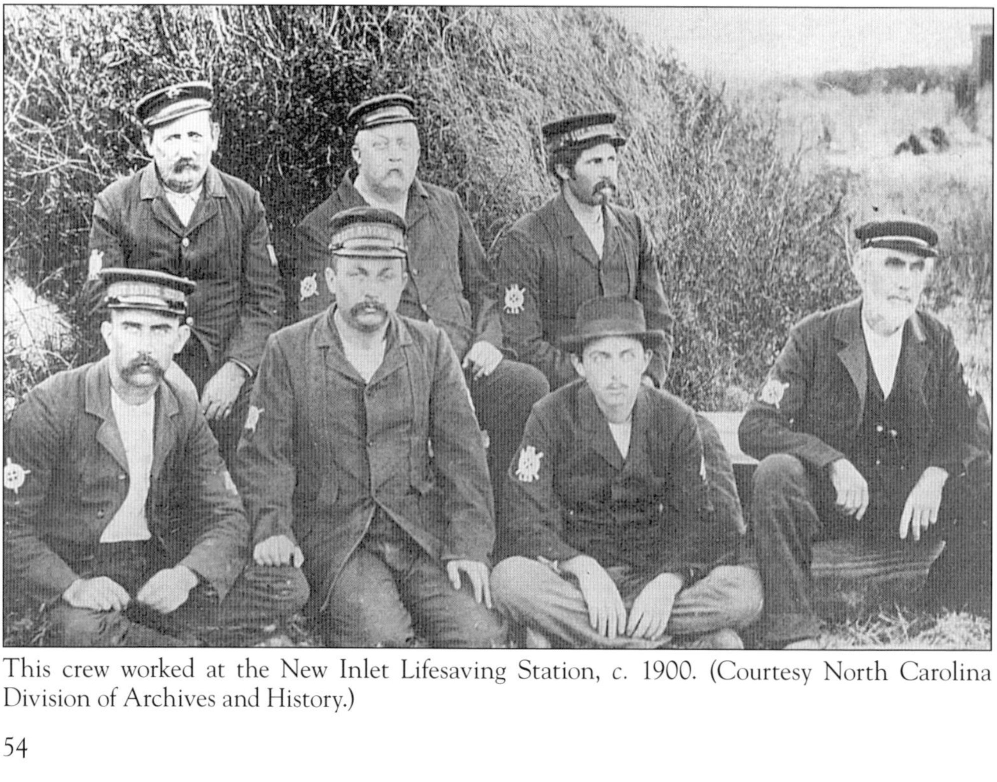

This crew worked at the New Inlet Lifesaving Station, *c.* 1900. (Courtesy North Carolina Division of Archives and History.)

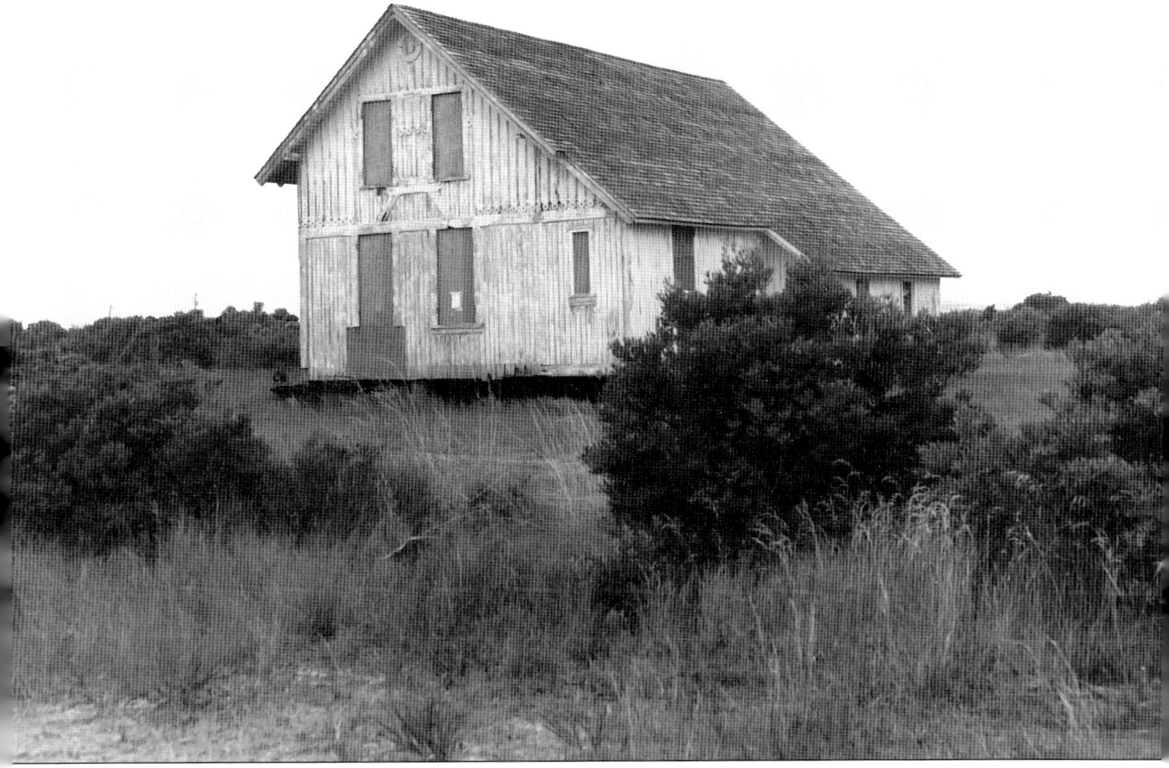

The first Chicamacomico Lifesaving Station was built in 1874. Upon completion of the new station, the old structure was converted into a boathouse. (U.S. Coast Guard.)

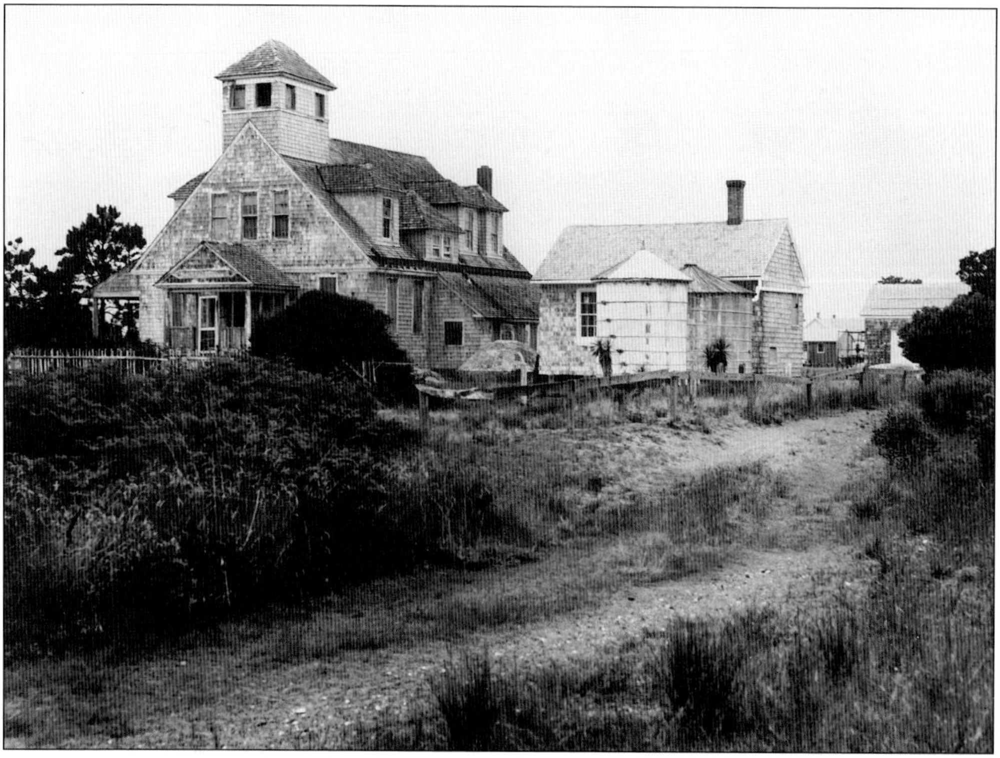

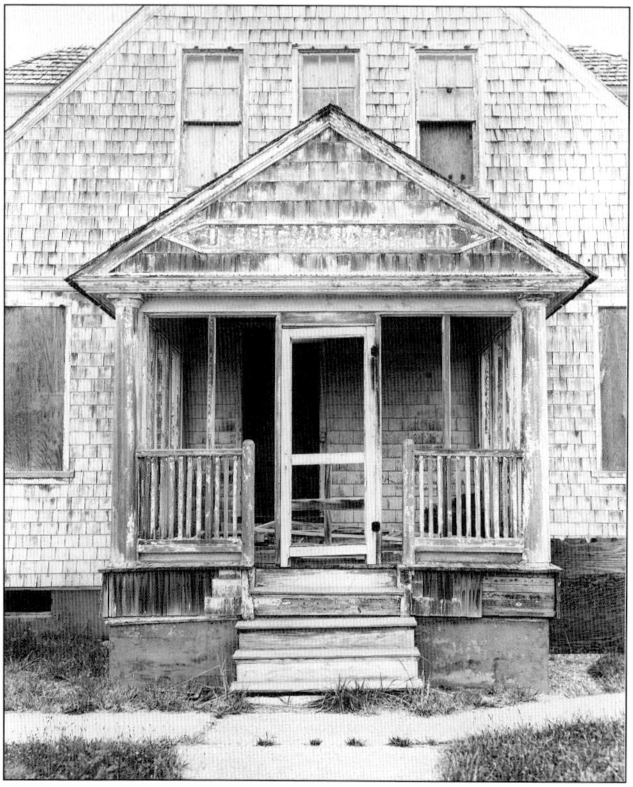

The second Chicamacomico Lifesaving Station was built in 1911 and replaced an earlier structure. This station was designed by architect Victor Mendelhoff. (U.S. Coast Guard.)

The entrance of Chicamacomico Lifesaving Station appears weathered here, before the restoration began. (U.S. Coast Guard.)

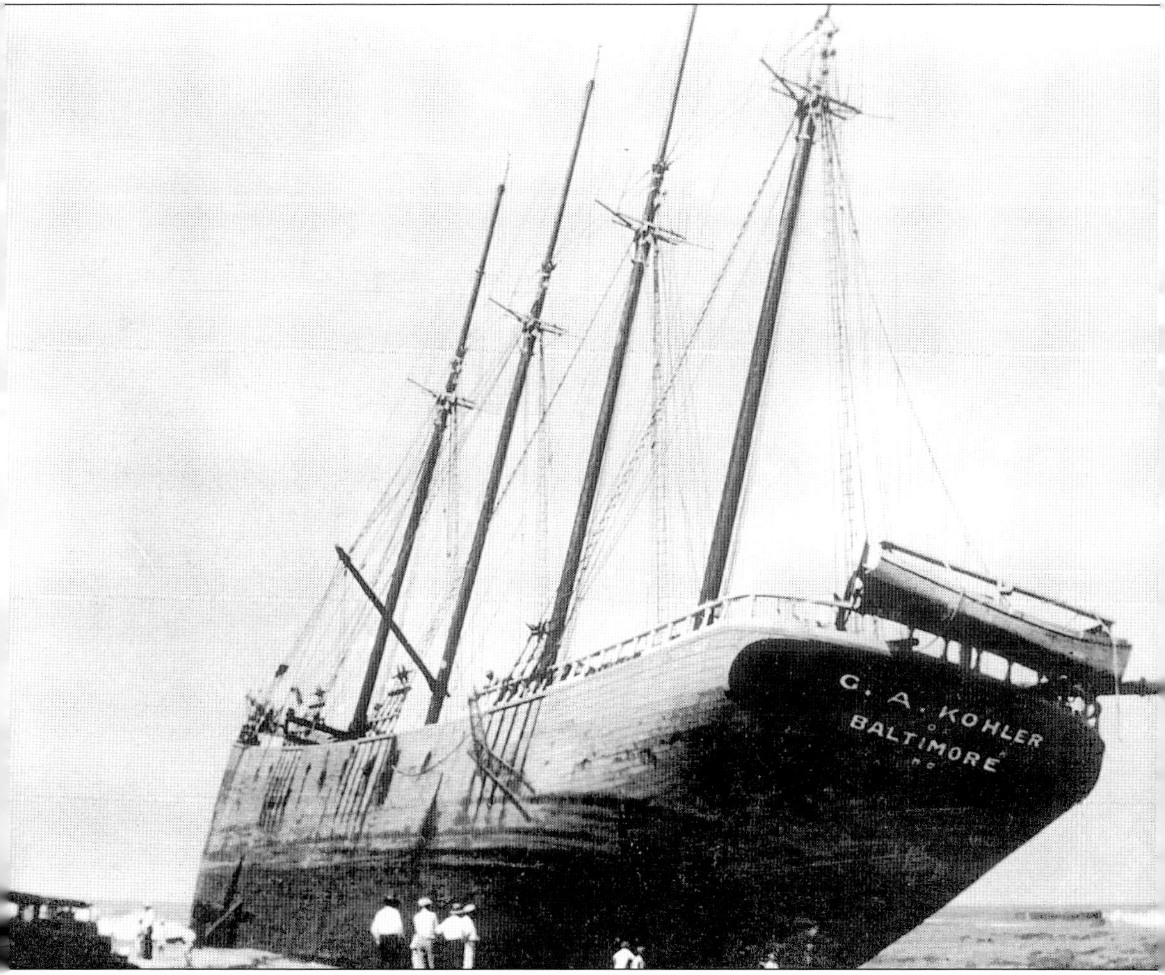

The G.A. *Kohler* wrecked on the beach a mile below the Shoal Station during a hurricane on August 2, 1933. Everyone on board was rescued, but the ship was stranded high up on the beach, where it became a tourist attraction of sorts. The ship was destroyed in the early 1940s for scrap iron. (Courtesy Museum of the Albemarle.)

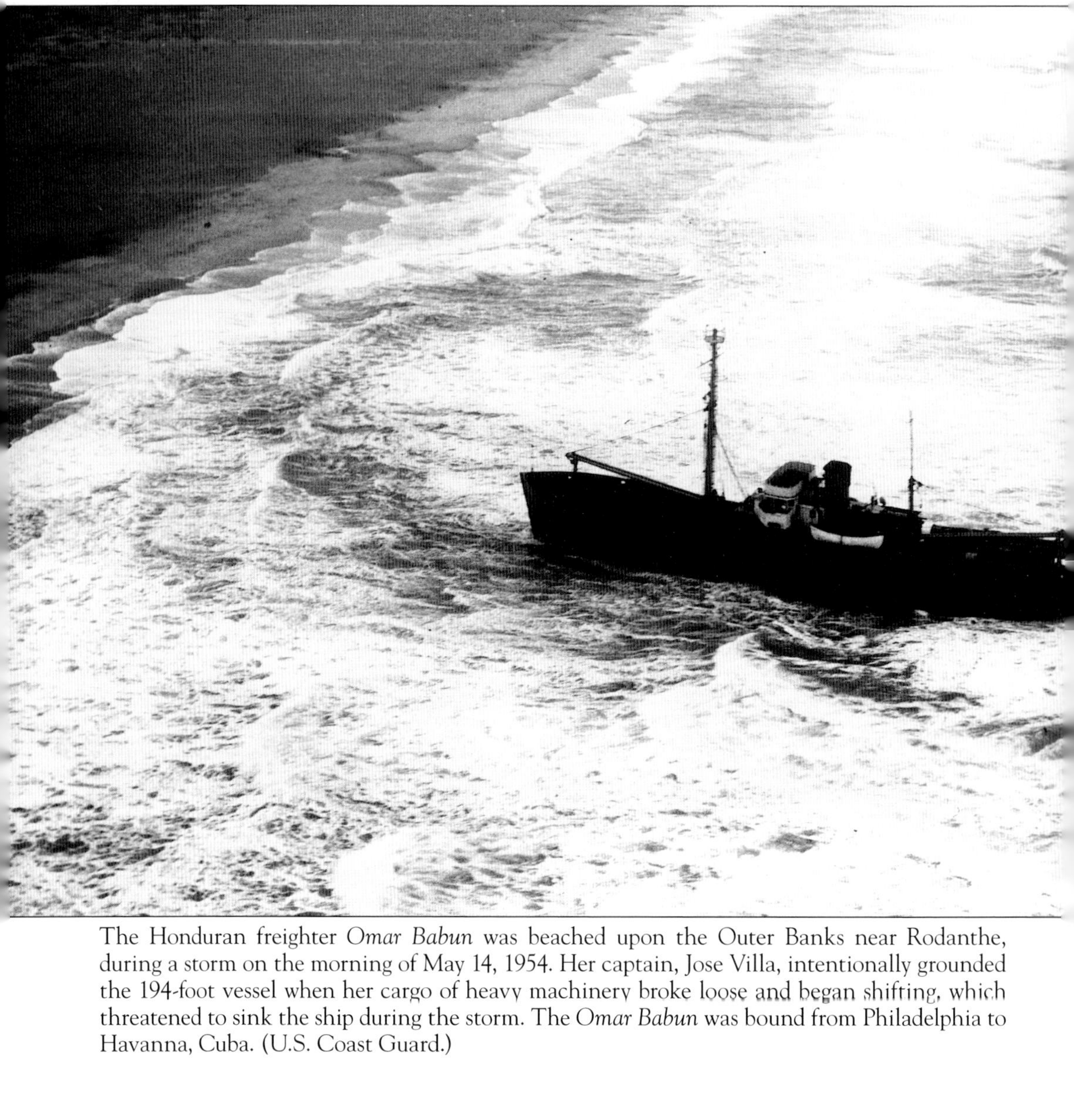

The Honduran freighter *Omar Babun* was beached upon the Outer Banks near Rodanthe, during a storm on the morning of May 14, 1954. Her captain, Jose Villa, intentionally grounded the 194-foot vessel when her cargo of heavy machinery broke loose and began shifting, which threatened to sink the ship during the storm. The *Omar Babun* was bound from Philadelphia to Havanna, Cuba. (U.S. Coast Guard.)

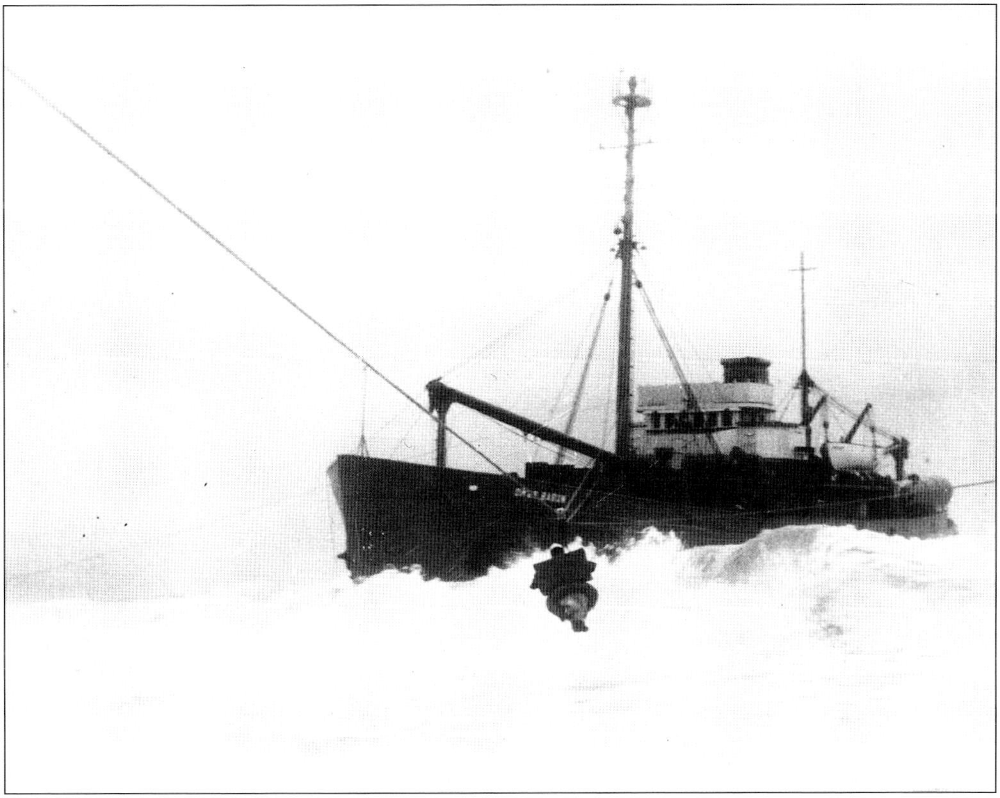

Thanks to the efforts of the U.S. Coast Guard, all 14 crewmen were rescued from the *Omar Babun*. (U.S. Coast Guard.)

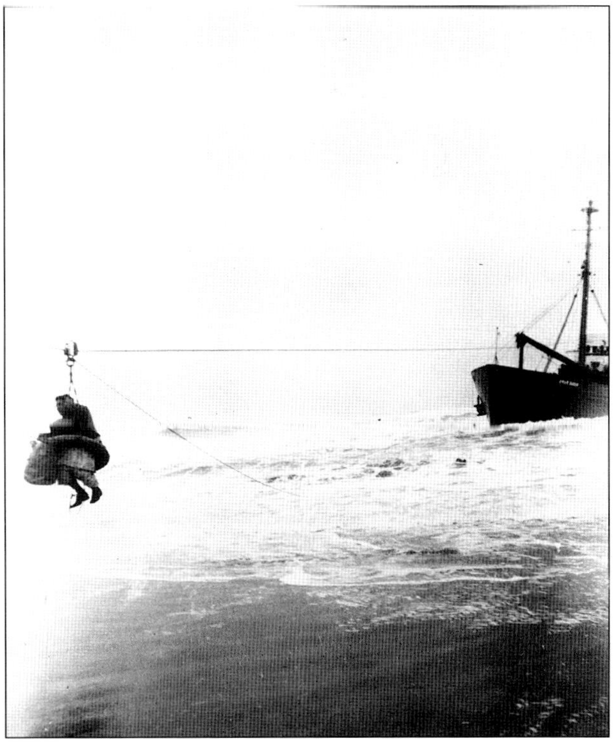

A crewman from the *Omar Babun* rides to safety above the pounding surf. (U.S. Coast Guard.)

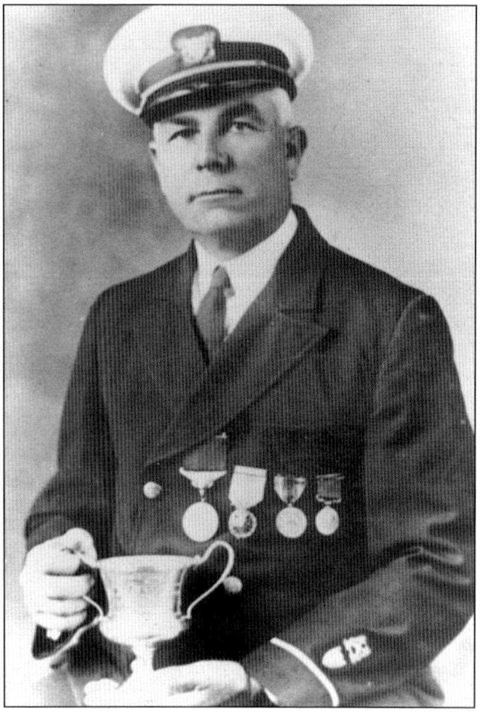

Captain John Allen Midgett of the Chicamacomico Coast Guard Station received the British Gold Lifesaving Medal and the Grand Cross of the American Cross of Honor for the heroism he demonstrated in the rescue of the crew of the British tanker *Mirlo*, August 16, 1918. (Courtesy North Carolina Division of Archives and History.)

Kapitanleutnant Droscher, the commander of the German *U-117* during World War I, is shown here. (North Carolina Division of Archives and History.)

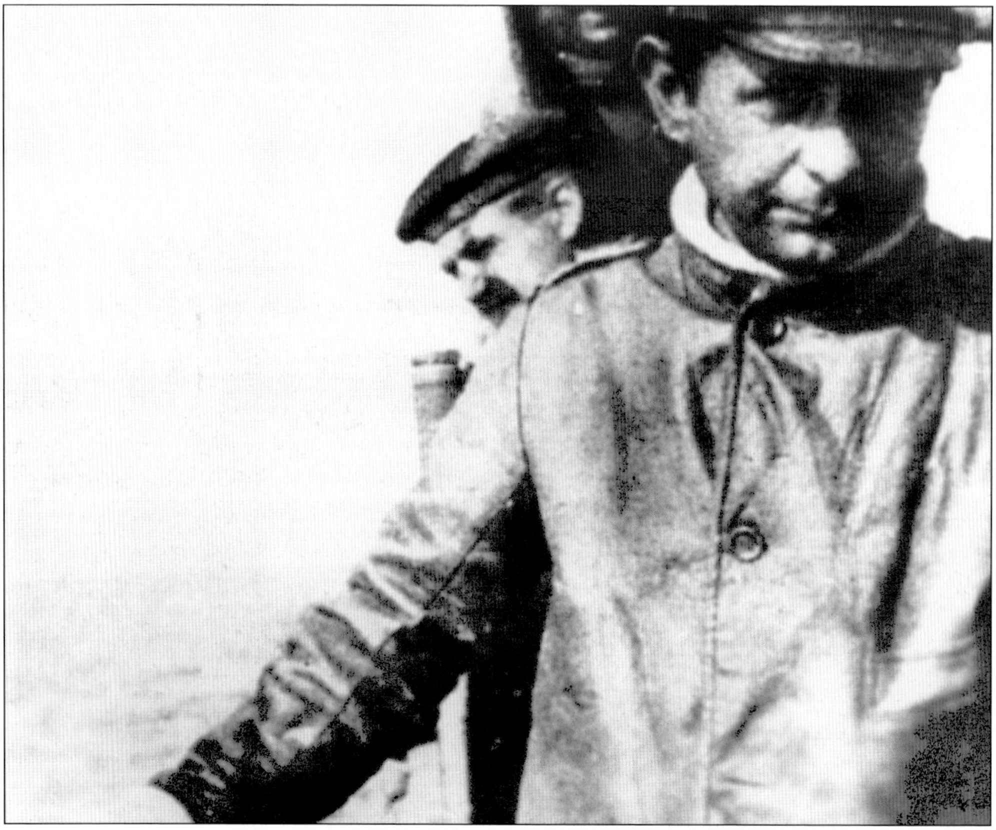

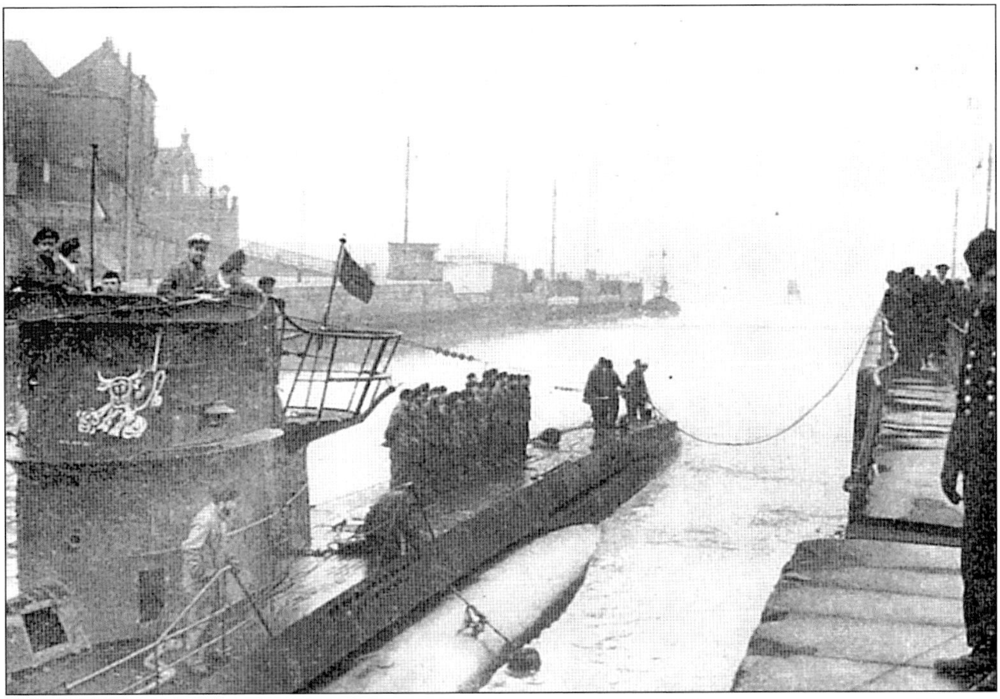

The U.S.S. *Roper* sank the *U-85*, a German submarine of World War II, approximately 15 miles off Oregon Inlet on April 14, 1942.

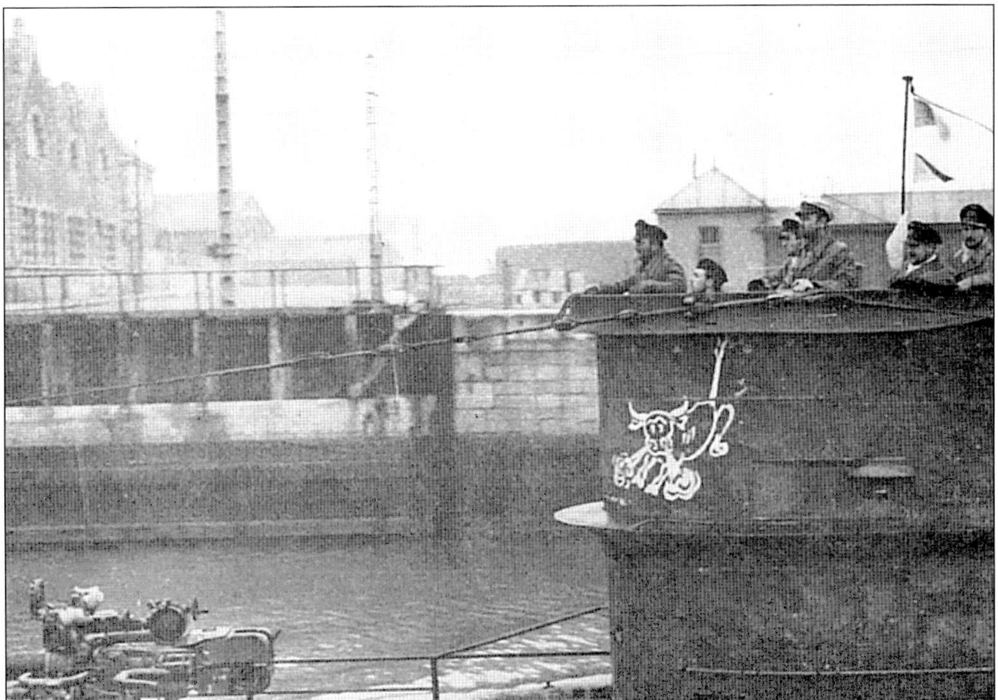

In this photograph and the one above, the *U-85* is in port in St. Nazaire, France. Her captain, Kapitanleutnant Eberhard Gregor, is the man wearing the white hat.

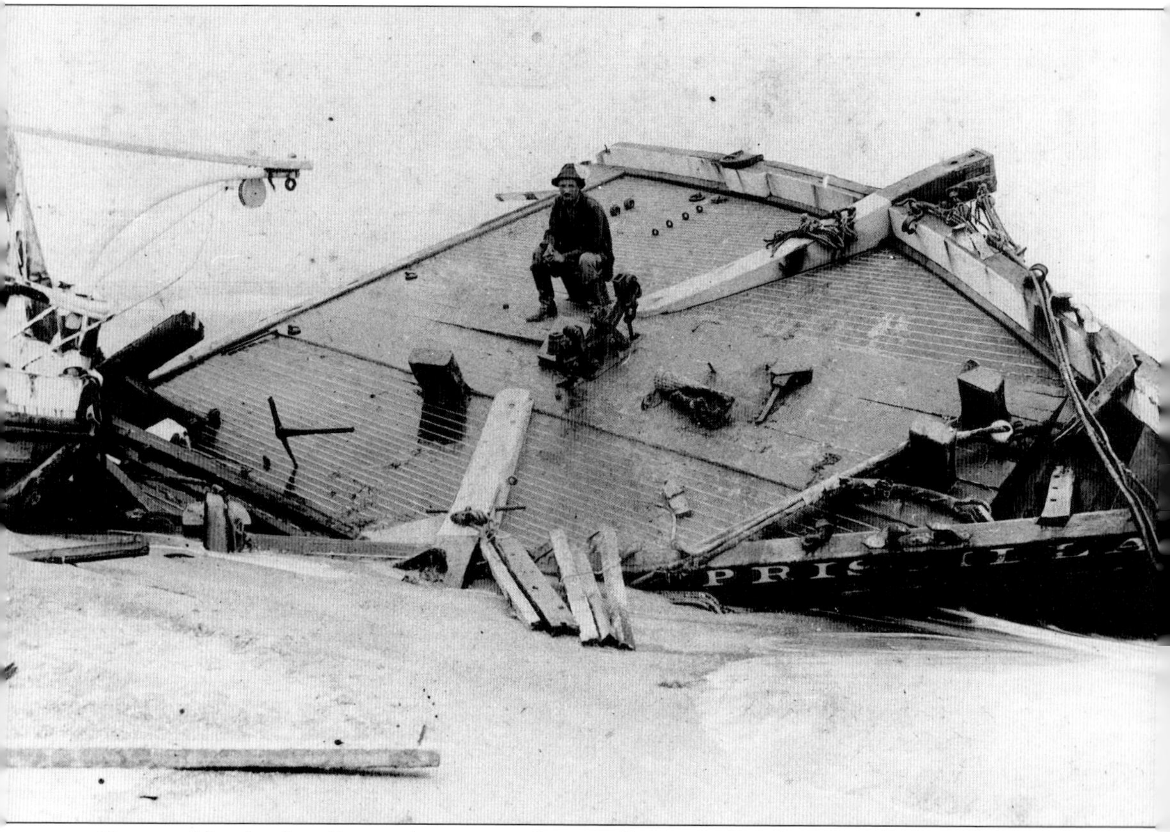

Damaged by the San Ciriaco hurricane, the *Priscilla* ran aground on the Outer Banks near the Gull Shoal Lifesaving Station on the morning of August 18, 1899. Captain Benjamin Springsteen lost his wife, two sons, and his cabin boy in the ferocious surf. Fortunately, the few men who remained were saved from a similar fate when surfman Rasmus Midgett happened upon the site while on routine patrol from the Gull Shoal Station. Midgett single-handedly rescued the crewmen of the *Priscilla*, a feat that earned him the Gold Lifesaving Medal of Honor. (Courtesy North Carolina Division of Archives and History.)

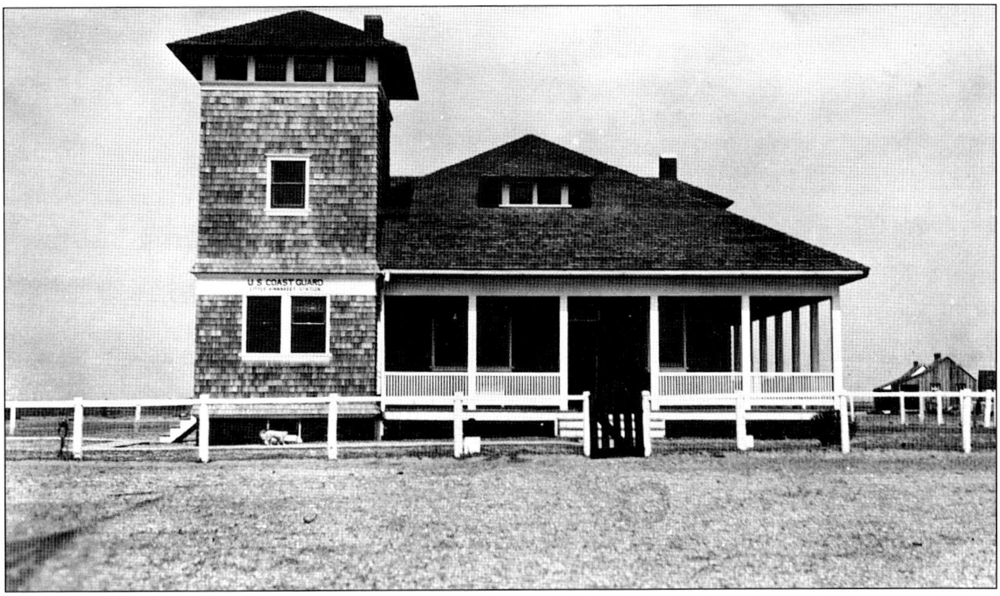

The Little Kinnakeet Station is seen from the east in this March 9, 1934 photograph. (U.S. Coast Guard.)

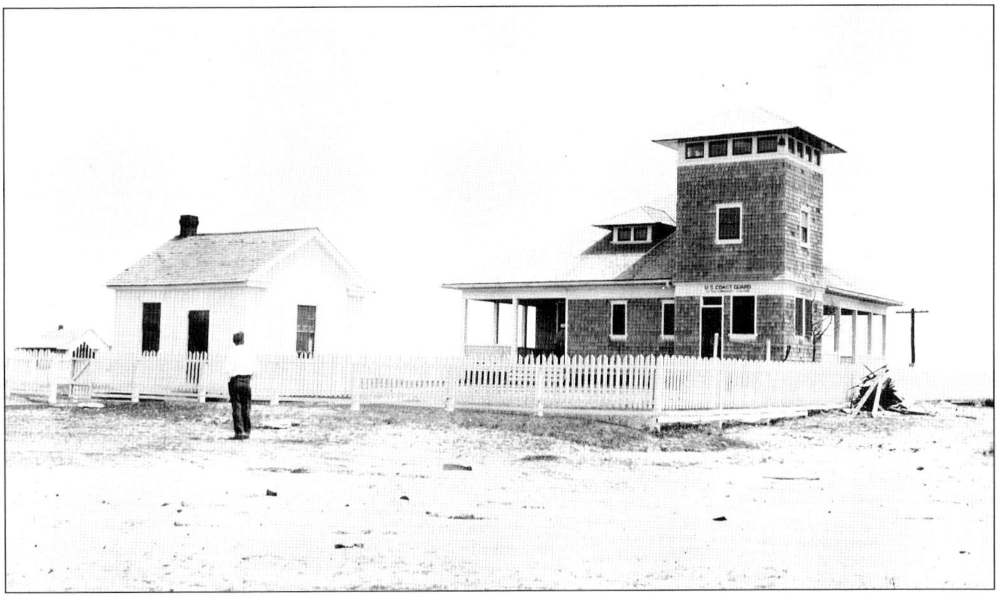

Another view of the station at Little Kinnakeet, this one looks from the southwest. (U.S. Coast Guard.)

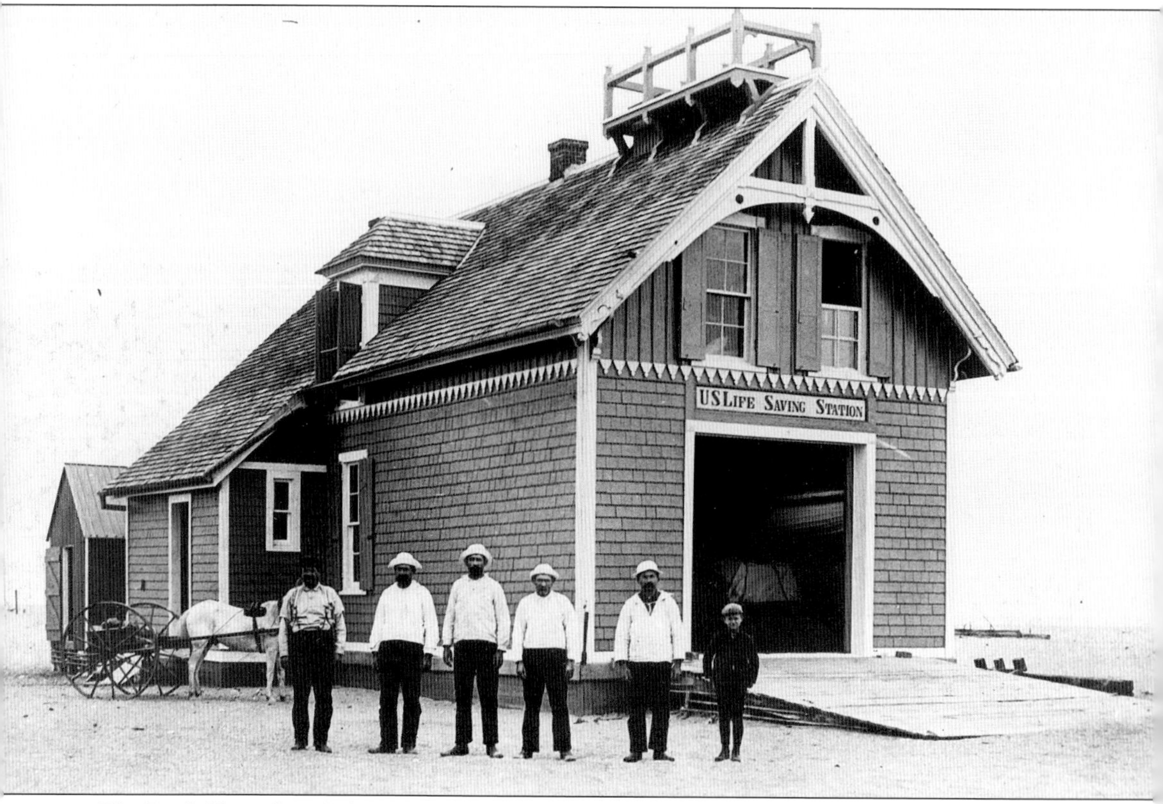

The Little Kinnakeet Lifesaving Station appears in this *c.* 1895 photograph. The original station at this site was erected in 1874. (U.S. Coast Guard.)

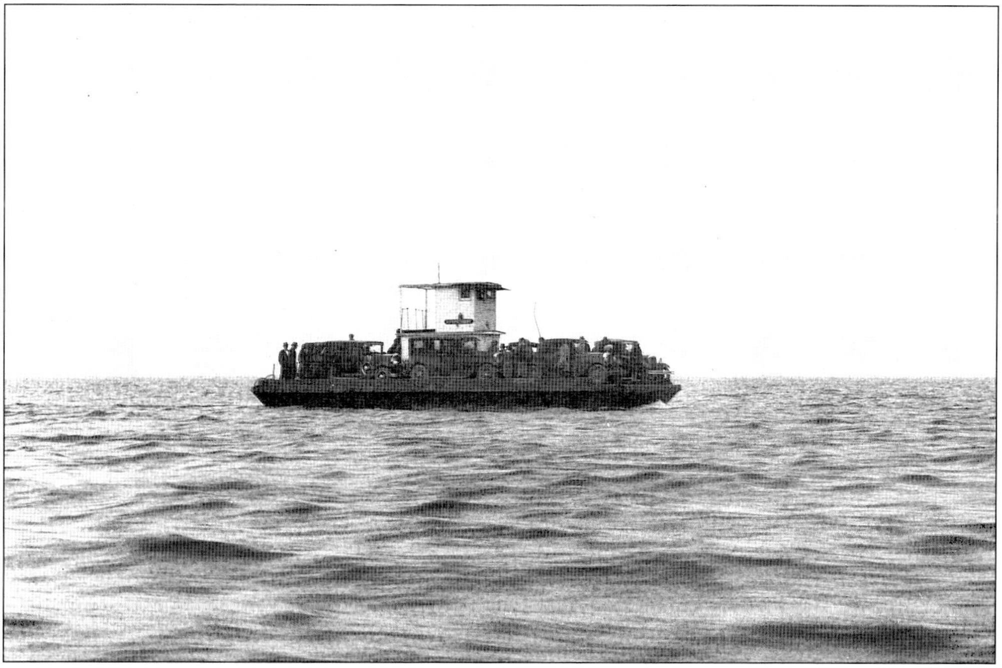

This view shows one of the early ferries transporting vehicles across Oregon Inlet. (Courtesy North Carolina Department of Transportation.)

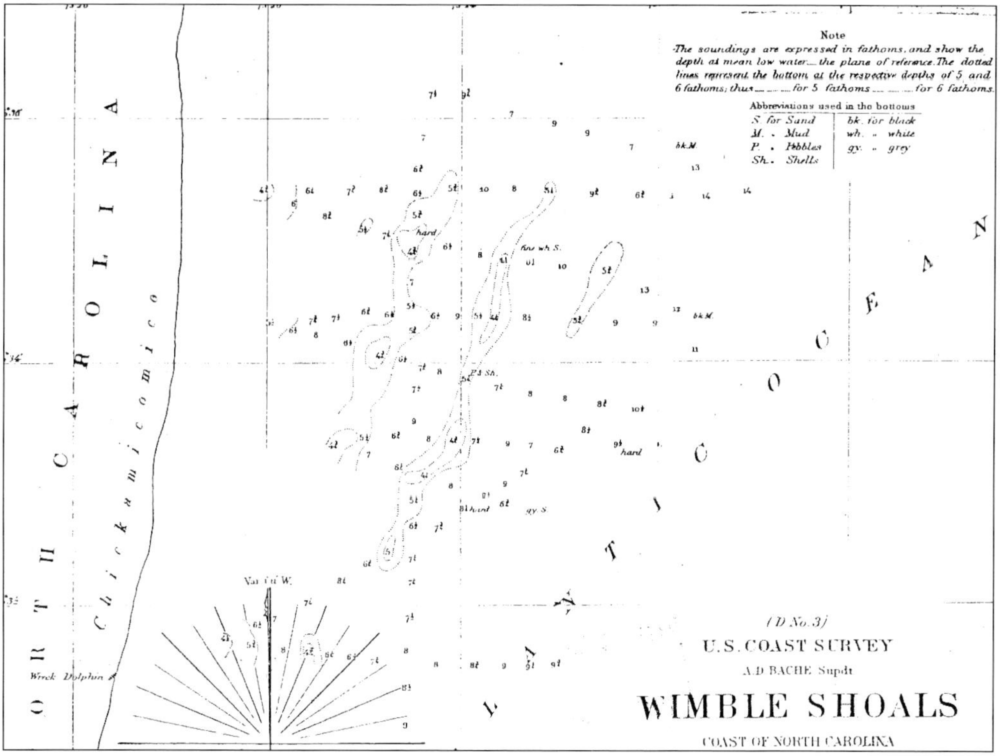

Lieutenant T.S. Craven compiled this chart of Wimble Shoals in 1854. Note the location of the "Wreck Dolphin" on the beach at Chicamacomico.

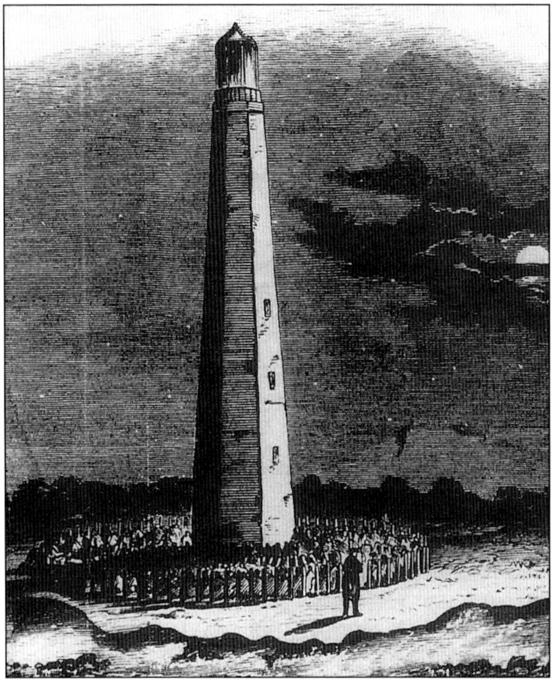

This group of Union soldiers is encamped around the base of the Cape Hatteras Lighthouse in 1861. (Courtesy North Carolina Division of Archives and History.)

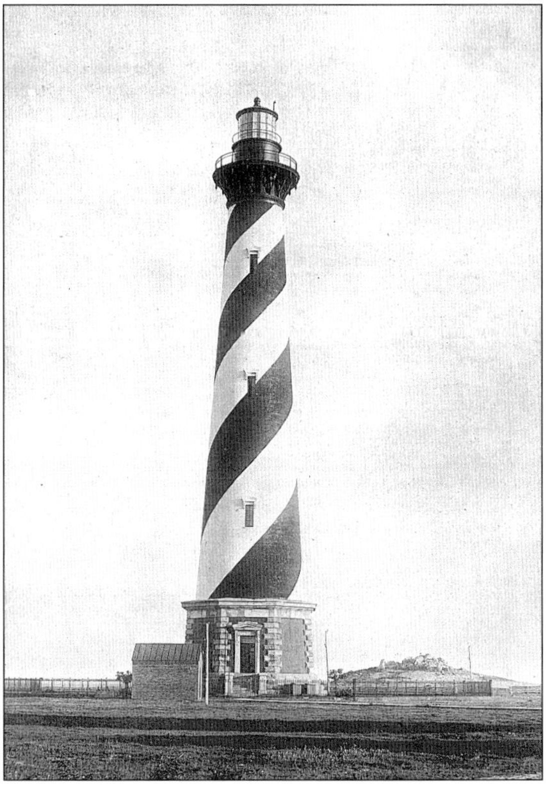

This view of the lighthouse at Cape Hatteras, taken *c.* 1885, shows a pile of rubble in the background, which is the remains of the first Cape Hatteras Lighthouse. The first lighthouse was destroyed in 1871.

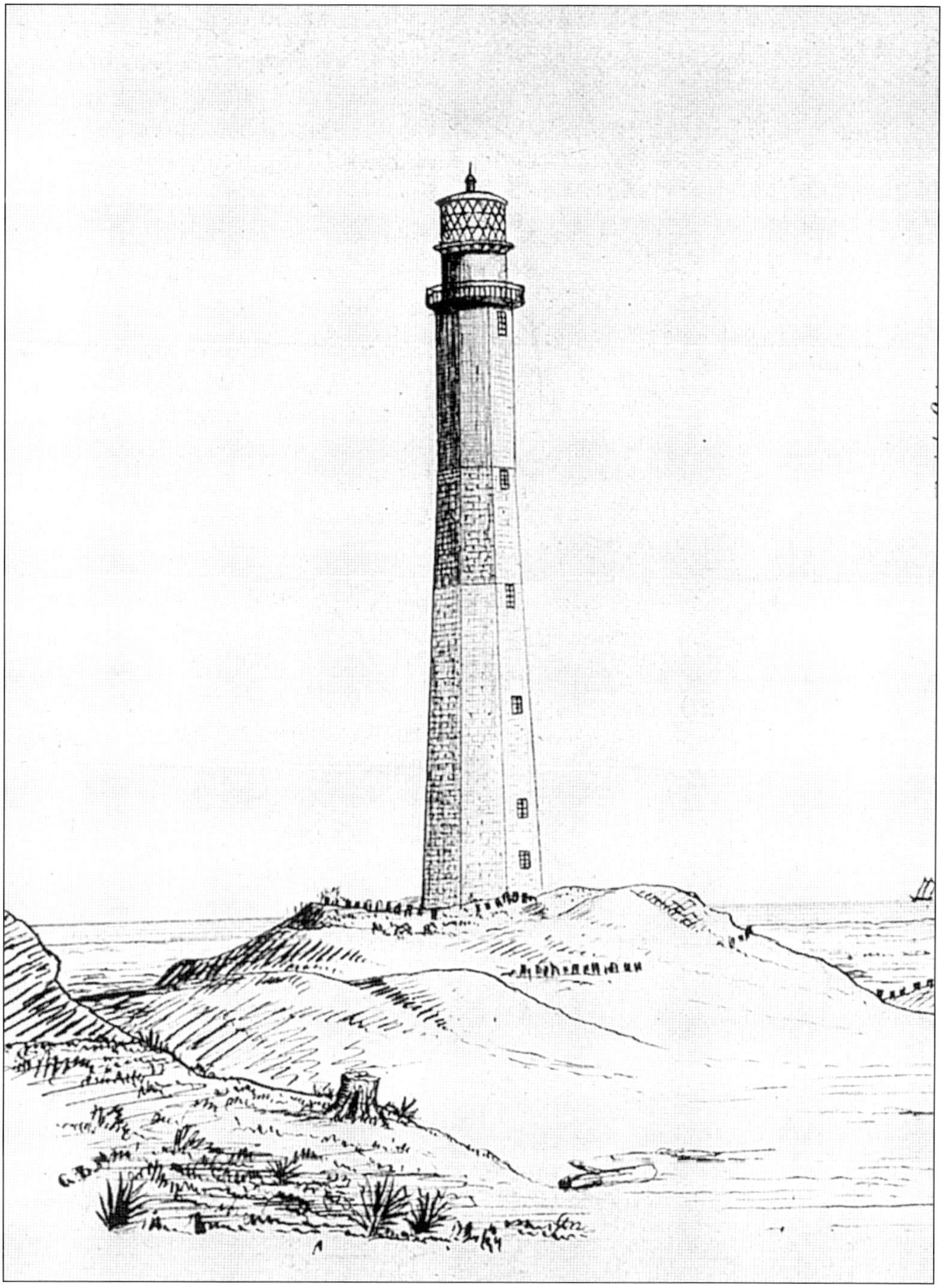

George B. Nicholson, assistant engineer of the Fifth Lighthouse District, drew this sketch of the first Cape Hatteras lighthouse in November of 1870. The original lighthouse was completed in 1802. It stood 100 feet above the ground and was constructed of white stone on the bottom and red stone on top. William Tatham described it as "an architectural eyesore" in 1806 and suggested painting it red. In 1854, the U.S. Lighthouse Board completed an addition to the tower to expand its height to 150 feet.

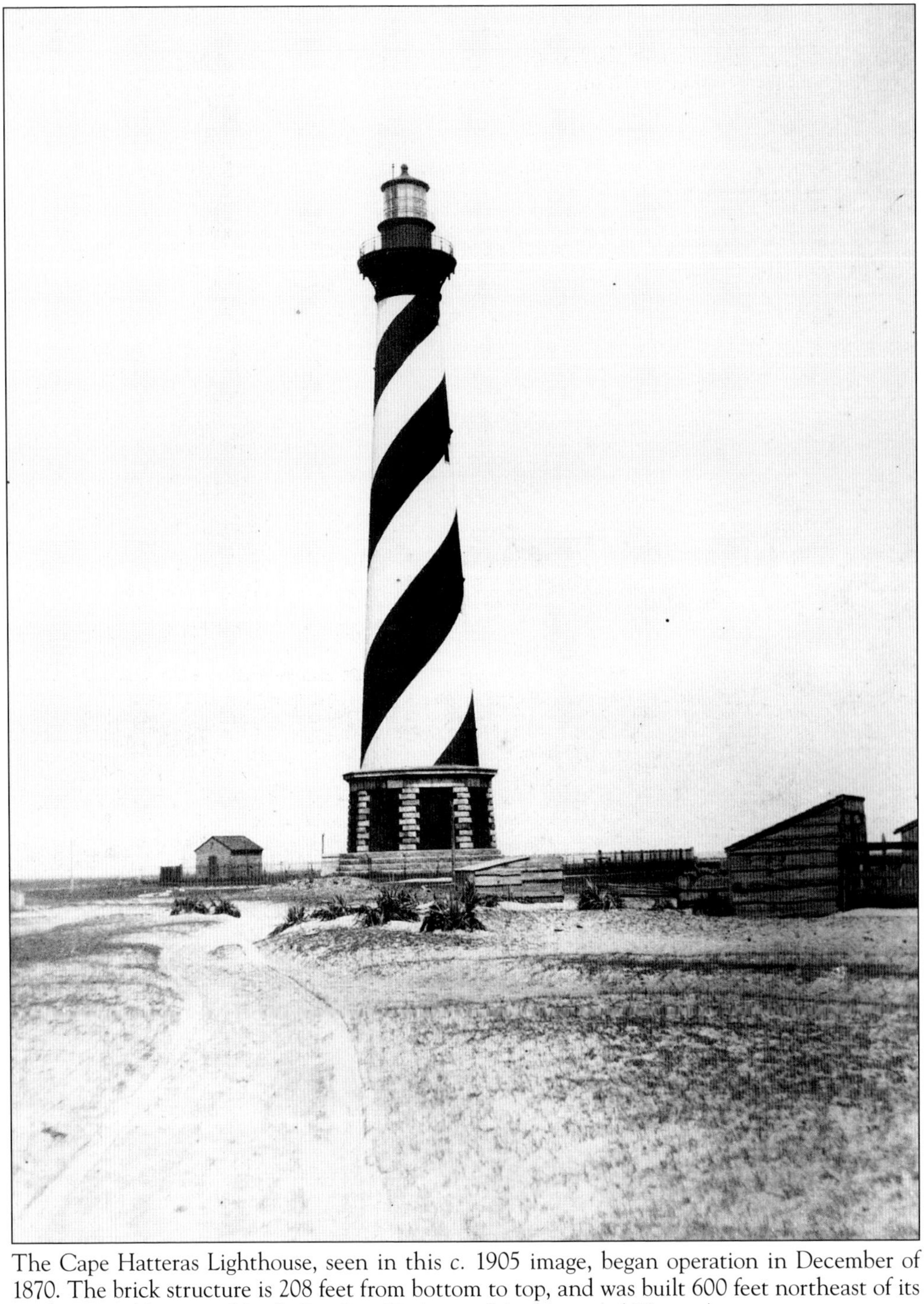

The Cape Hatteras Lighthouse, seen in this *c.* 1905 image, began operation in December of 1870. The brick structure is 208 feet from bottom to top, and was built 600 feet northeast of its predecessor. (Courtesy North Carolina Division of Archives and History.)

A Union soldier sketched a picture of the first Cape Hatteras Lighthouse in 1862. (Courtesy North Carolina Division of Archives and History.)

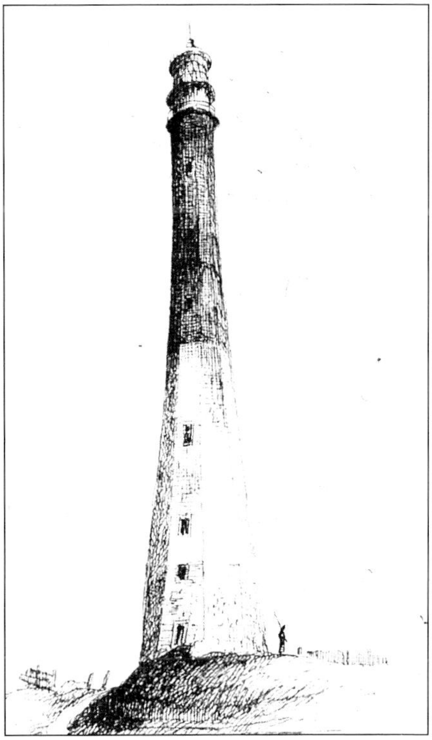

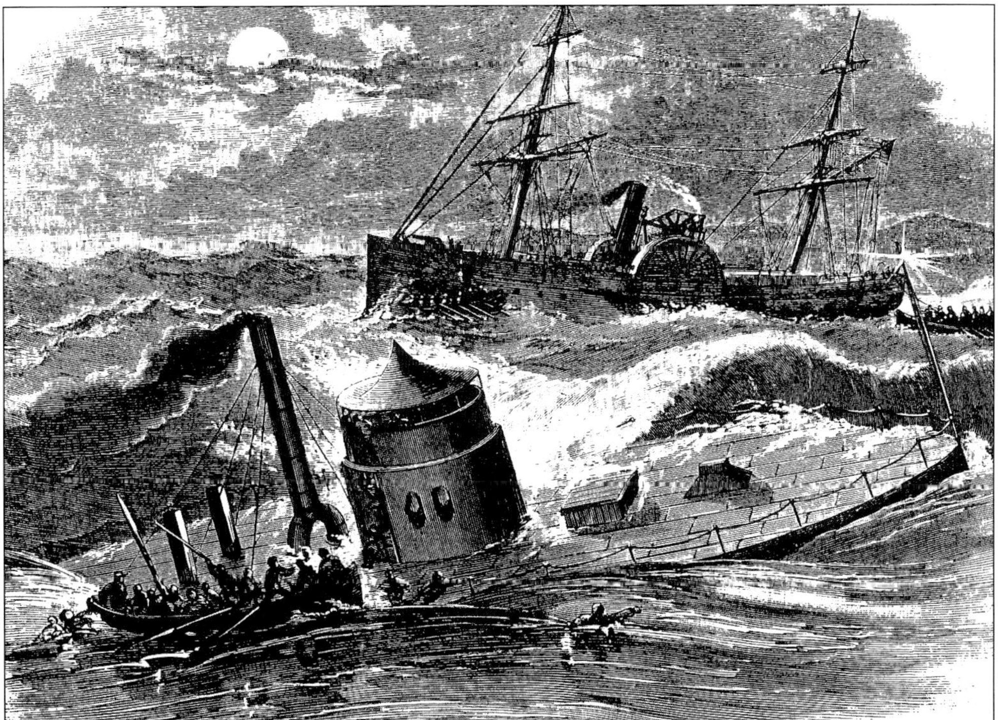

This engraving from *Harper's Weekly* shows the final moments of the USS *Monitor*. The famous ironclad went down in a storm off Cape Hatteras on December 30, 1862.

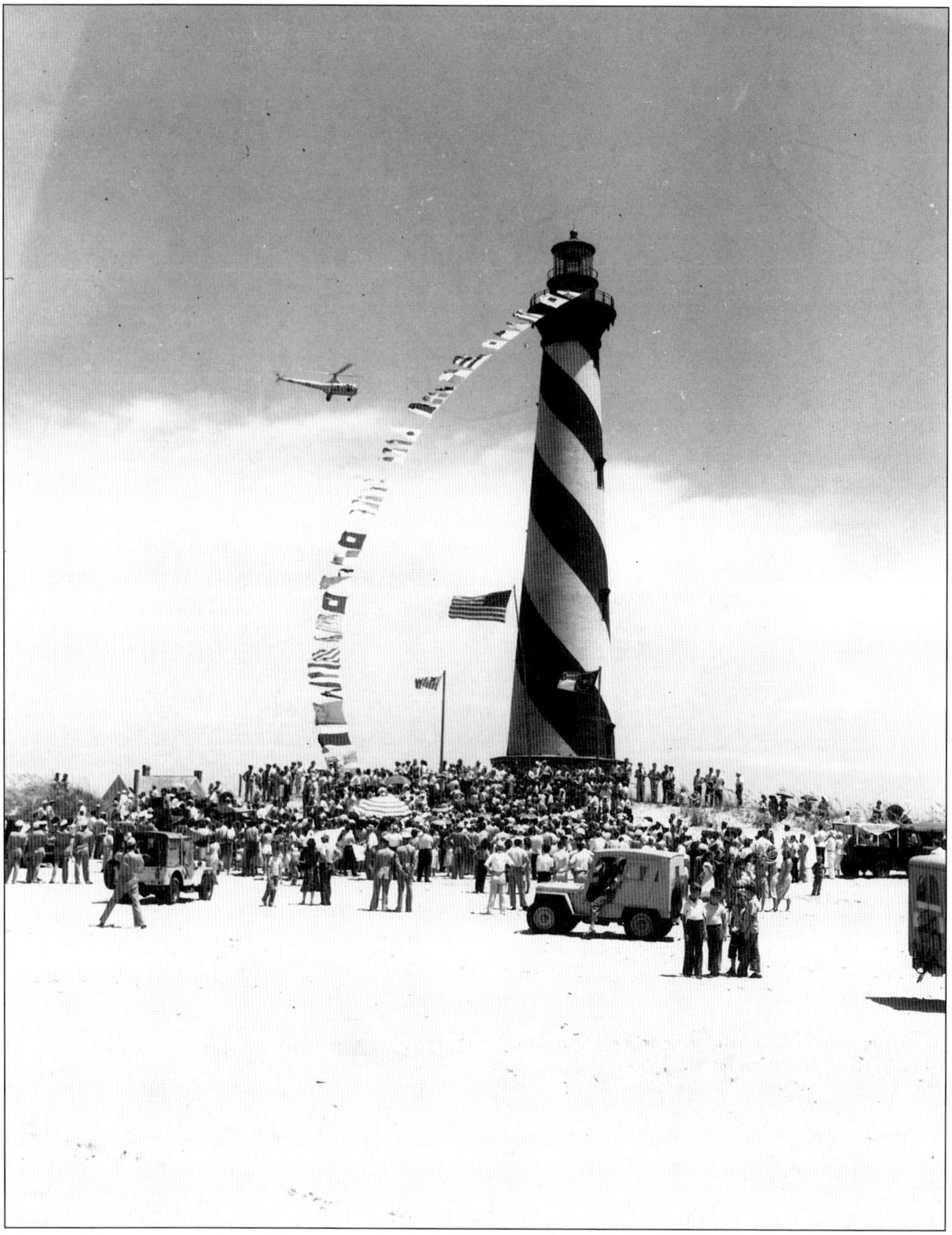

This celebration at Cape Hatteras was captured in this 1956 photograph. (North Carolina Division of Archives and History.)

Due to the encroachment of the ocean, the Cape Hatteras Lighthouse, seen in this 1900 photograph, is scheduled to be moved in the summer of 1999. A similar problem with erosion led to the construction of the Buxton Woods Light Tower in 1936 and the abandonment of the Cape Hatteras Lighthouse, which everyone thought would shortly thereafter fall into the sea. Instead, the erosion problem corrected itself, and the Cape Hatteras Lighthouse was reactivated in January of 1950. (U.S. Coast Guard.)

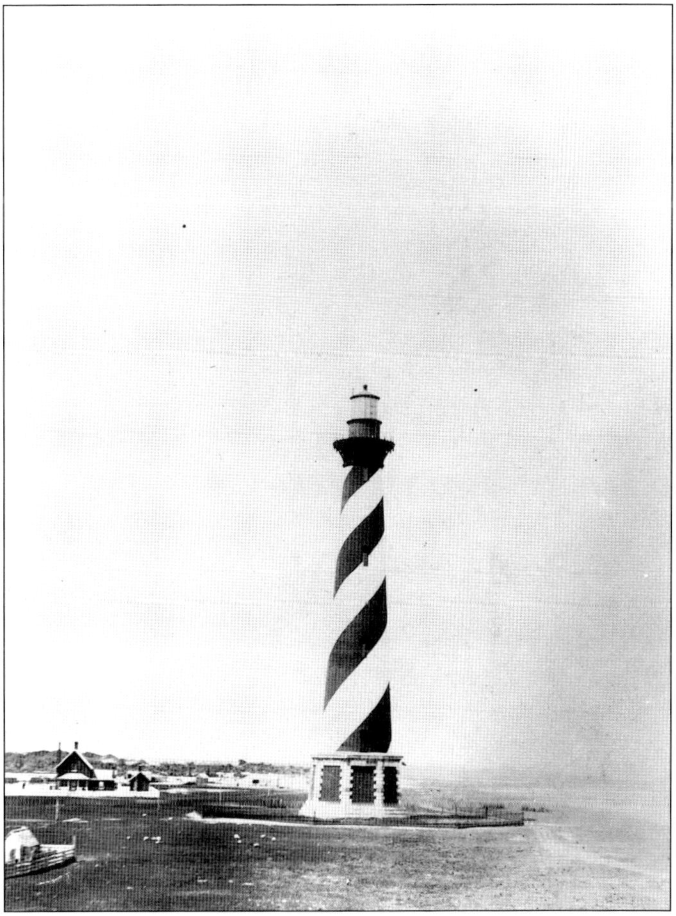

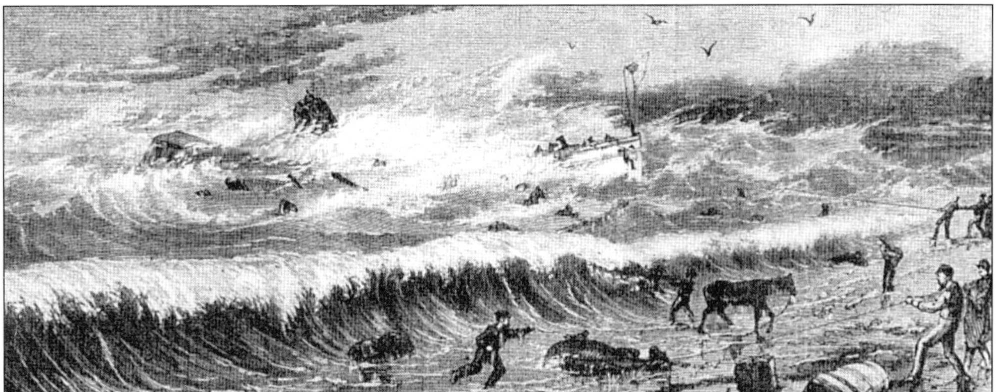

The *Pocohantas* was one of several Union ships to be wrecked at Hatteras in January of 1862. (Courtesy North Carolina Division of Archives and History.)

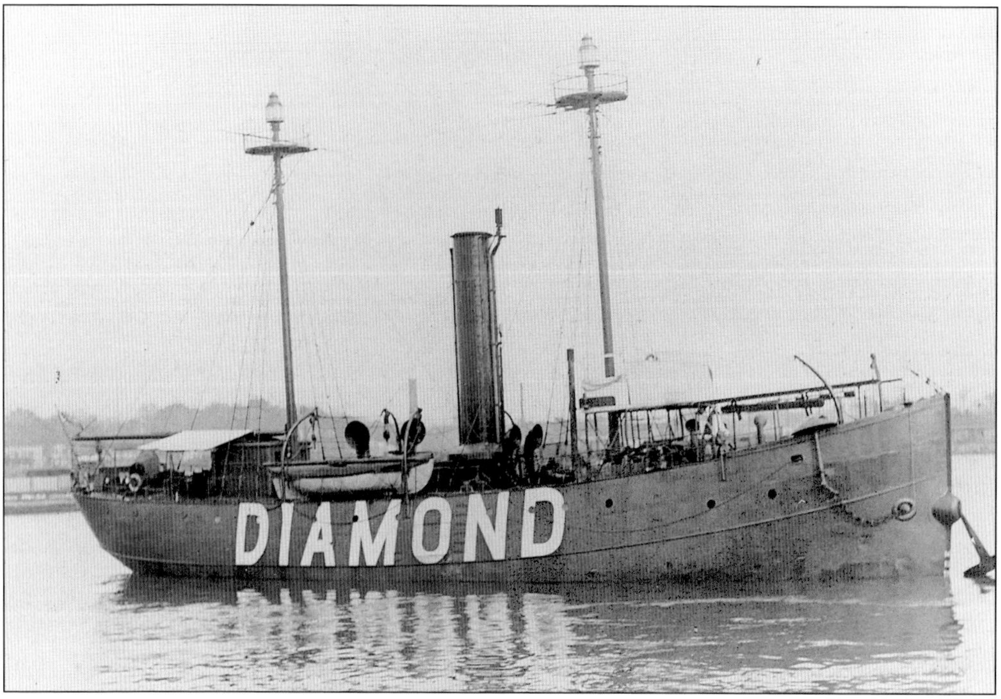

The second *Diamond Shoals Lightship* was placed in the treacherous Diamond Shoals in 1897. Its predecessor anchored there in 1824 and only served three years before it was wrecked by a hurricane in 1827. (U.S. Coast Guard.)

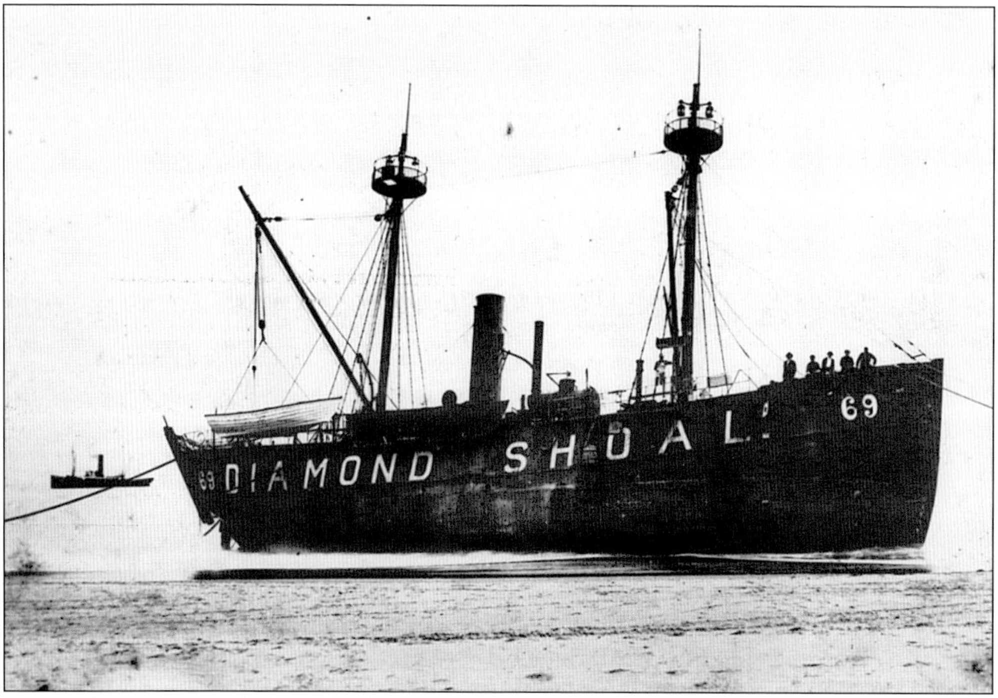

Diamond Shoals Lightship came ashore a mile west of Creeds Hill during the San Ciriaco hurricane in August of 1899. (Courtesy North Carolina Division of Archives and History.)

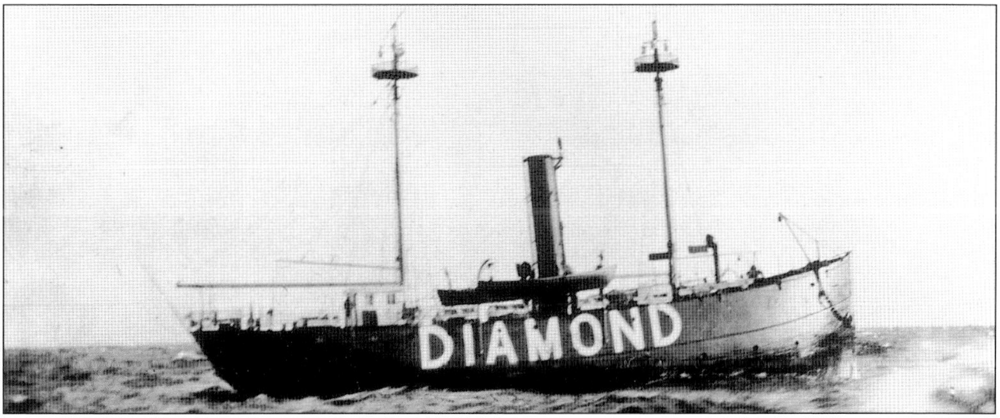

The *Diamond Shoals Lightship* was sunk by the *U-140* on August 6, 1918. The lightship reportedly drew the ire of the German commander by wiring the news of an attack upon a freighter by an enemy submarine. The *U-140* fired six shots at the lightship at approximately 3:25 p.m. from a distance of approximately 2 miles. According to a statement from the U.S. Coast Guard, "Two shots passed between the smokestack and the mainmast, two shots struck on the port side filling the spar deck with water, and under the wireless antenna. At 3:30 all hands were ordered in the starboard boat, which was launched and pulled away from the ship." Figuring that he had silenced the *Diamond Shoal Lightship*, Fregattenkapitan Waldemar Kophamel went off in pursuit of other prizes. Its work complete, the *U-140* returned to the lightship and fired seven shots into her, sinking her to the bottom. "At the time the last shots were fired the lightships men including the mate (in charge), engineer, cook, three firemen, four seamen and two radio operators, the latter Navy personnel. All escaped without injury. While the lightship was sunk, reports indicated that the wireless message she had sent out resulted in about 25 other vessels taking refuge in Lookout Bight and escaping possible attack." (U.S. Coast Guard.)

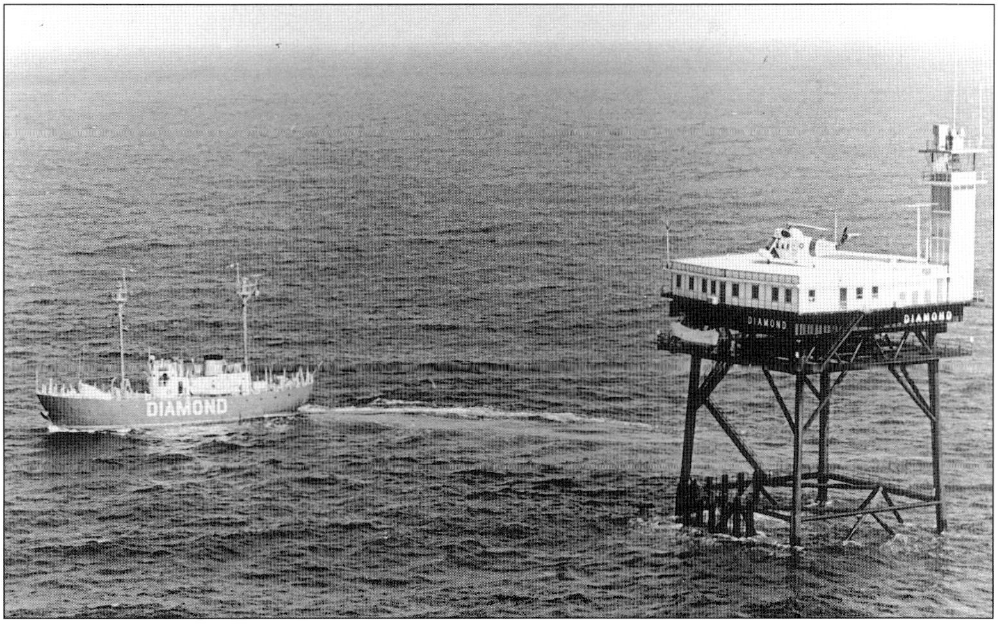

The *Diamond Shoals Lightship* was replaced by the Diamond Shoals Light Tower in 1967. The tower stands 54 feet above the water and can be seen 17 miles away. (U.S. Coast Guard.)

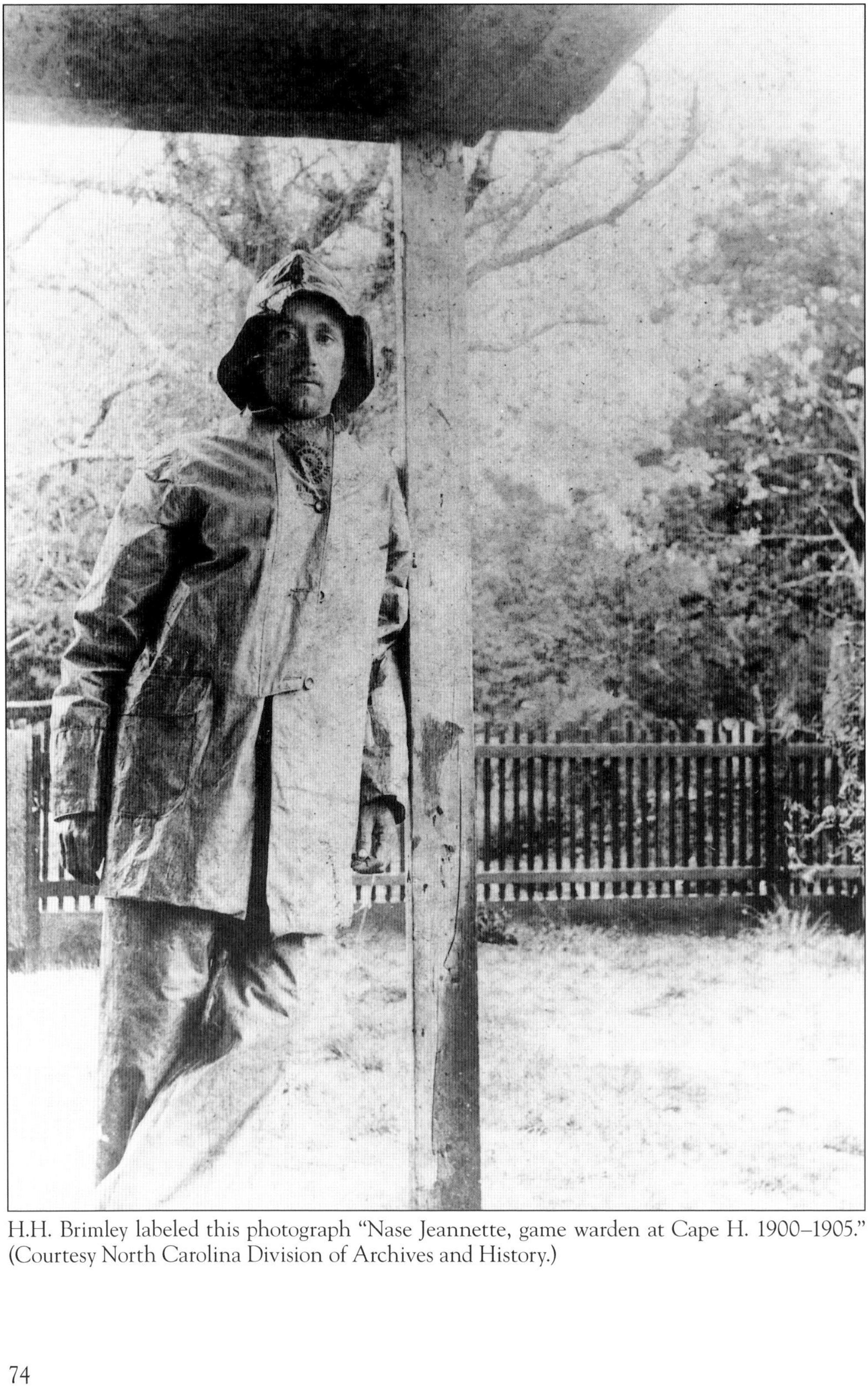

H.H. Brimley labeled this photograph "Nase Jeannette, game warden at Cape H. 1900–1905." (Courtesy North Carolina Division of Archives and History.)

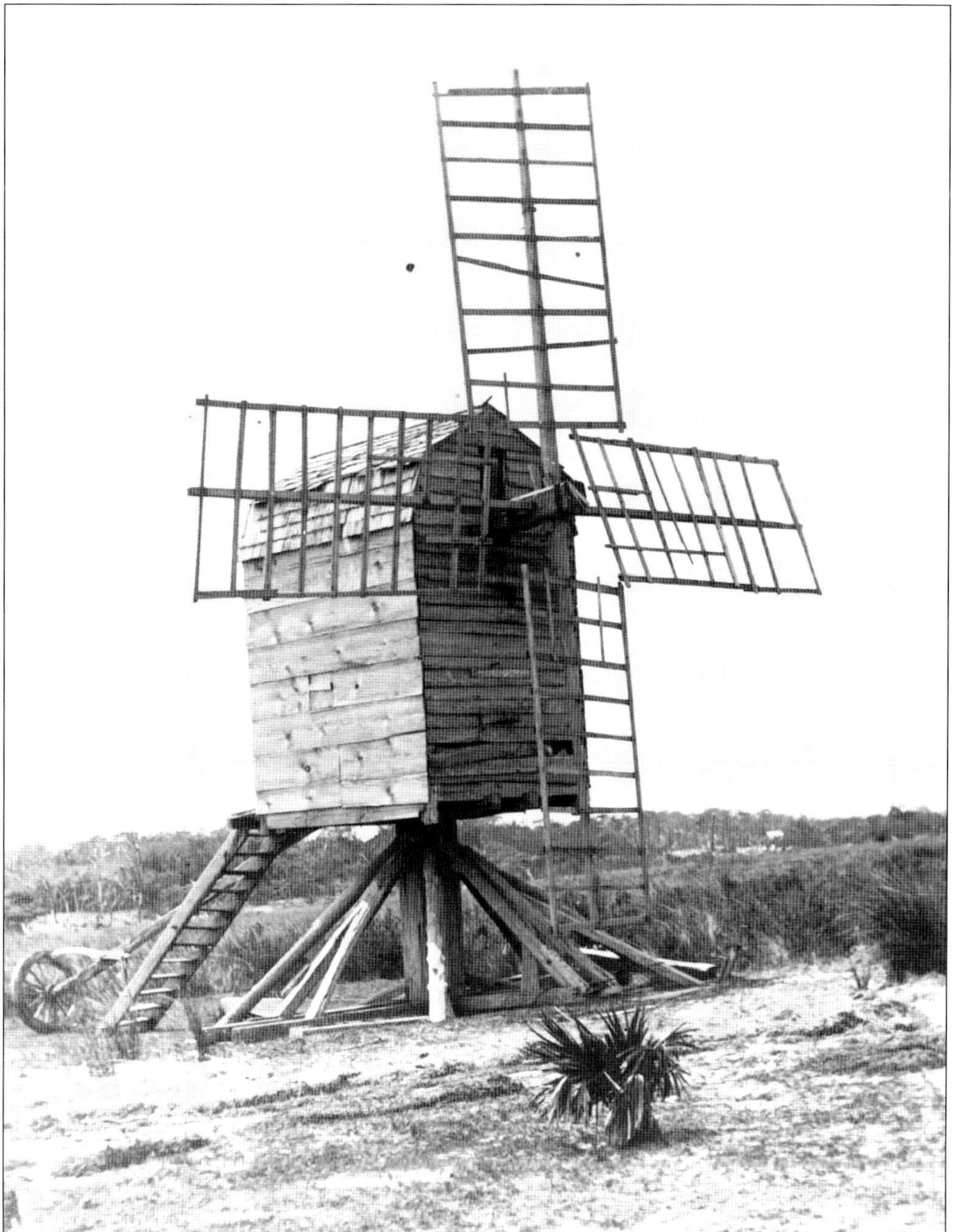

Captain Ben Midgett's Mill, a "corn grinding windmill," stood near Cape Hatteras. H.H. Brimley captured this structure on film in 1900. (Courtesy North Carolina Division of Archives and History.)

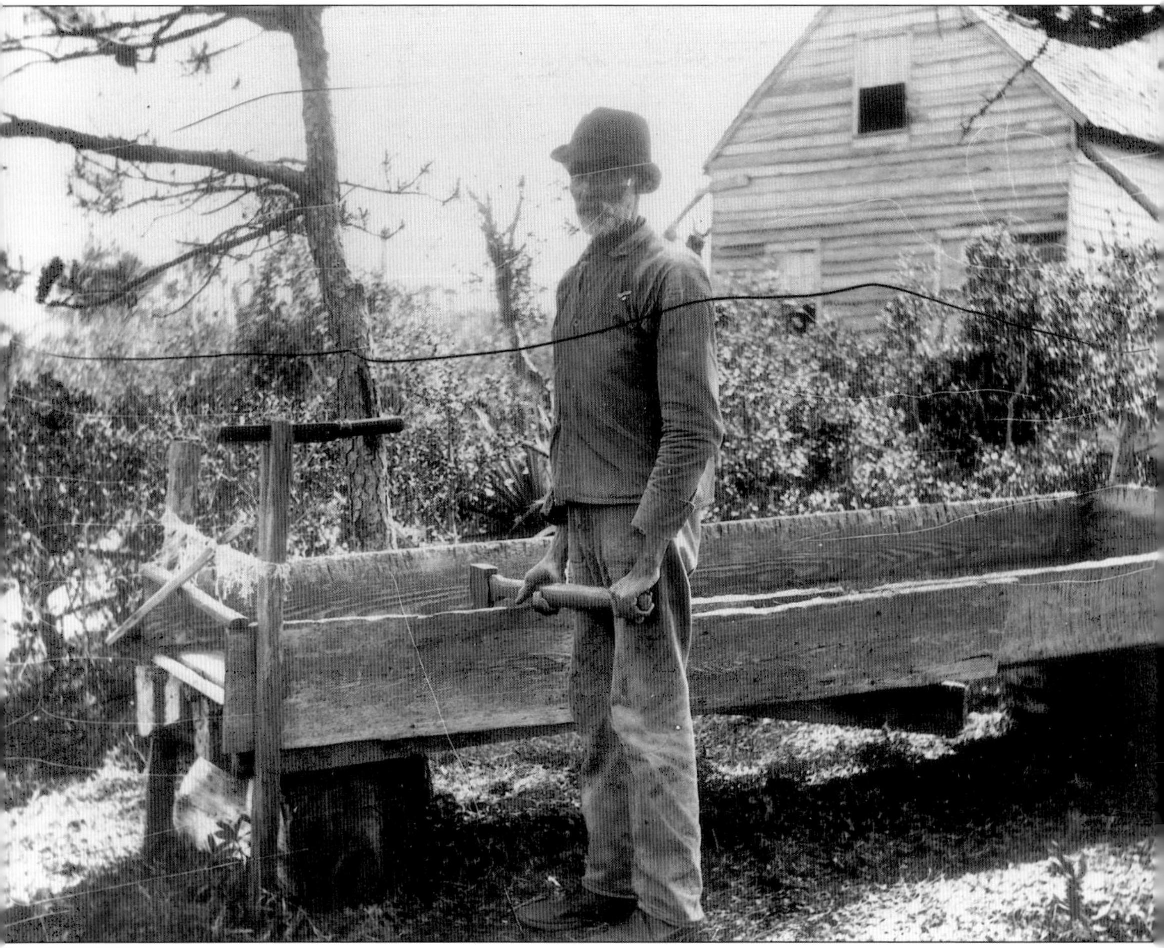

Yaupon tea was a beverage once widely used among the inhabitants of the Outer Banks. During the process of making the tea, twigs from the yaupon with leaves attached were put into a trough and chopped down to approximately an inch long. H.H. Brimley photographed the trough shown above in 1903. (Courtesy North Carolina Division of Archives and History.)

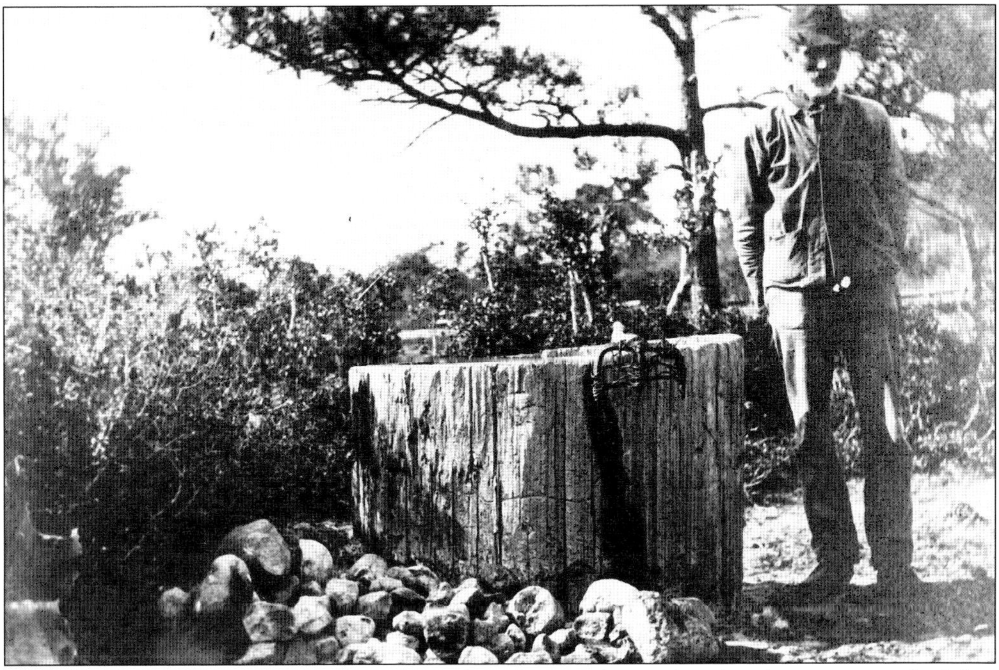

In the next phase of the process, a hollowed out cypress log, or hogshead, approximately 5 feet deep and half buried, is filled with alternating layers of hot stones and chopped yaupon from the trough. Thirty-six hours later the leaves are removed and placed on a platform to continue drying. This photograph was taken by H.H. Brimley at "Trent Woods, Dare County, 1904." (Courtesy North Carolina Division of Archives and History.)

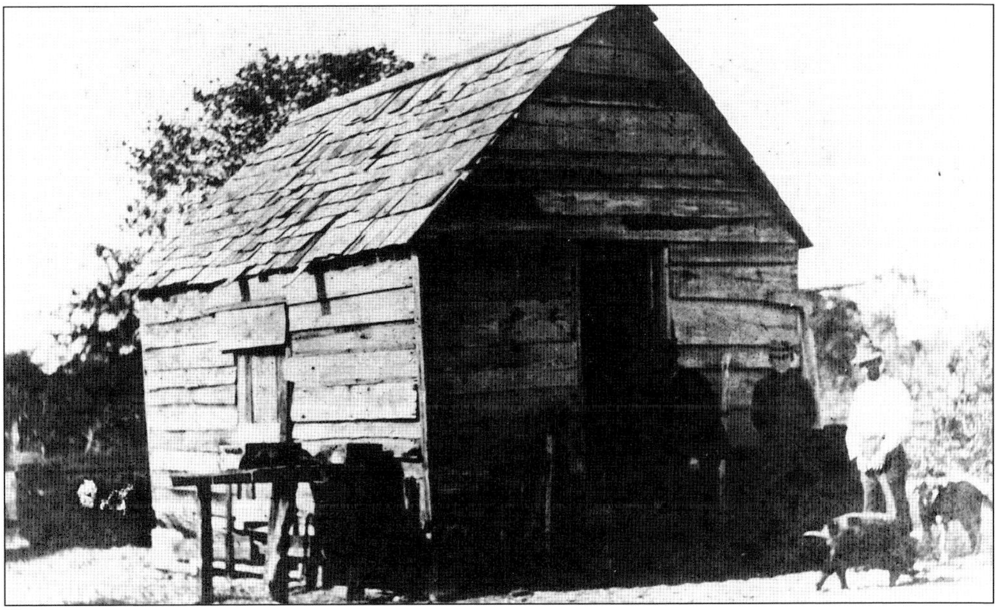

Once dried, the yaupon was stored in buildings such as this one photographed by Brimley in 1905. For a complete discussion of the topic of yaupon tea, consult Brimley's article, "Yaupon Factory" in the December 17, 1955 issue of *The State Magazine*. (Courtesy North Carolina Division of Archives and History.)

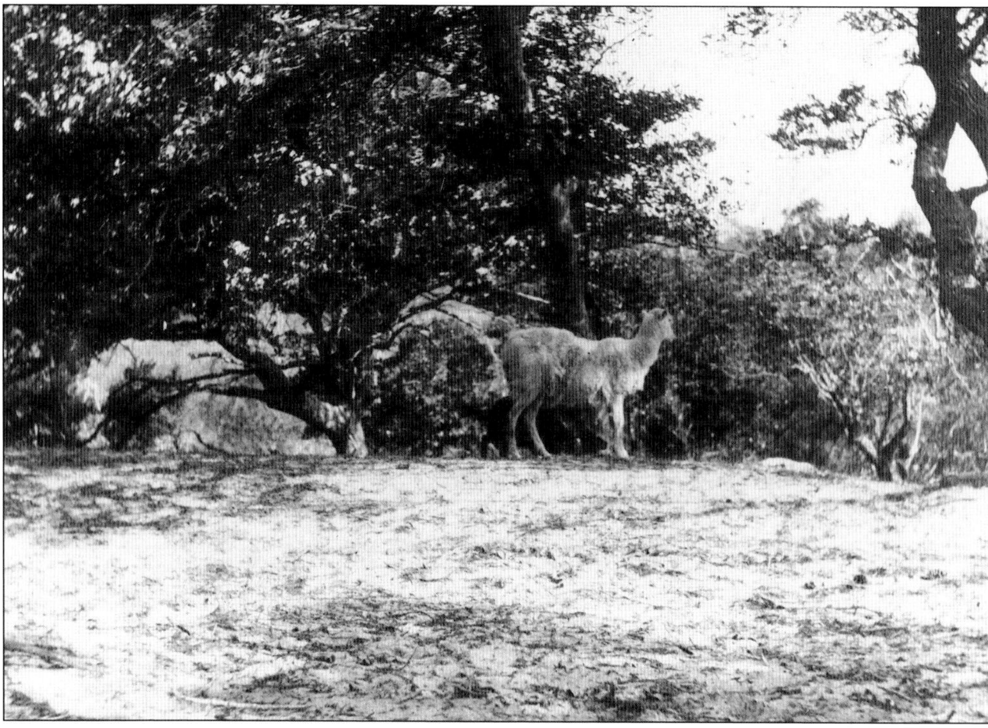

Wild sheep such as these photographed in 1902 were a common site on Hatteras Island. (Courtesy North Carolina Division of Archives and History.)

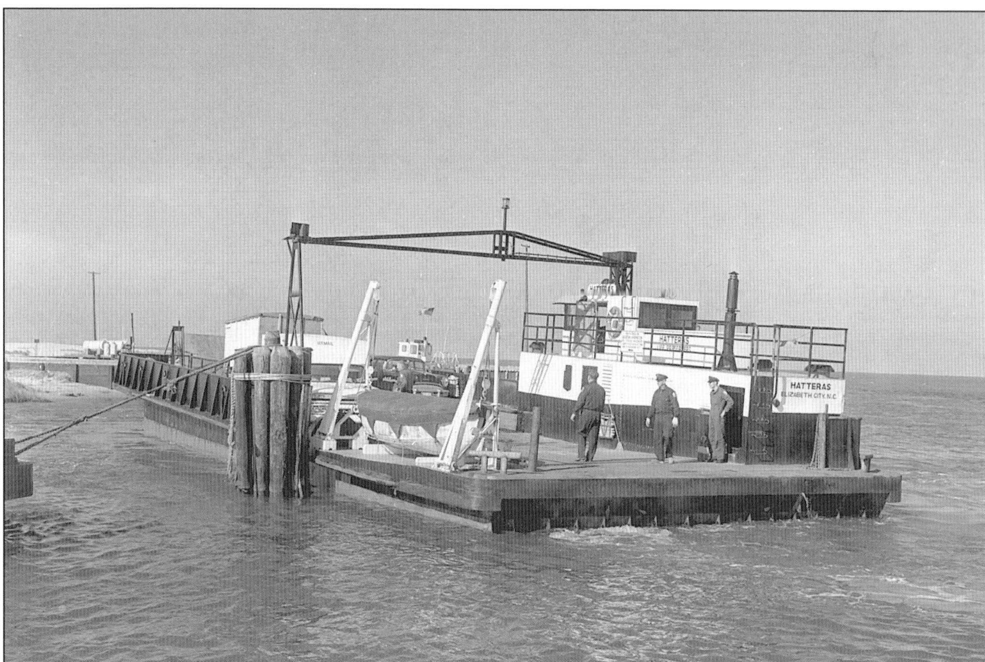

The *Hatteras* carried vehicles across the waters of Hatteras Inlet. (Courtesy North Carolina Department of Transportation.)

Pat Ethridge, keeper of the Creeds Hill Lifesaving Station, won a Gold Lifesaving Medal of Honor when he assisted surfmen from the Cape Hatteras station in rescuing crewmen from the *Ephraim Williams* on December 18, 1884. Keeper Benjamin Dailey and surfmen Charles Fulcher, Thomas Gray, Jabez Jennett, Isaac Jennett, and John Midgett of Cape Hatteras Station also received Gold Lifesaving Medals of Honor on that occasion. (Courtesy North Carolina Division of Archives and History.)

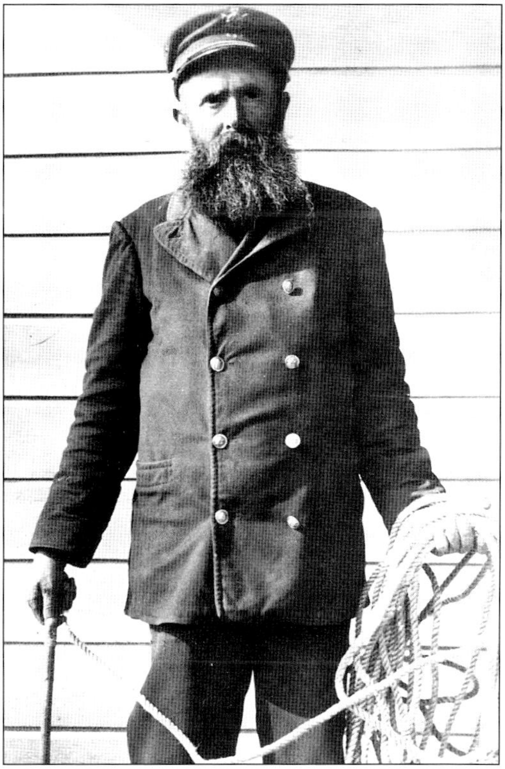

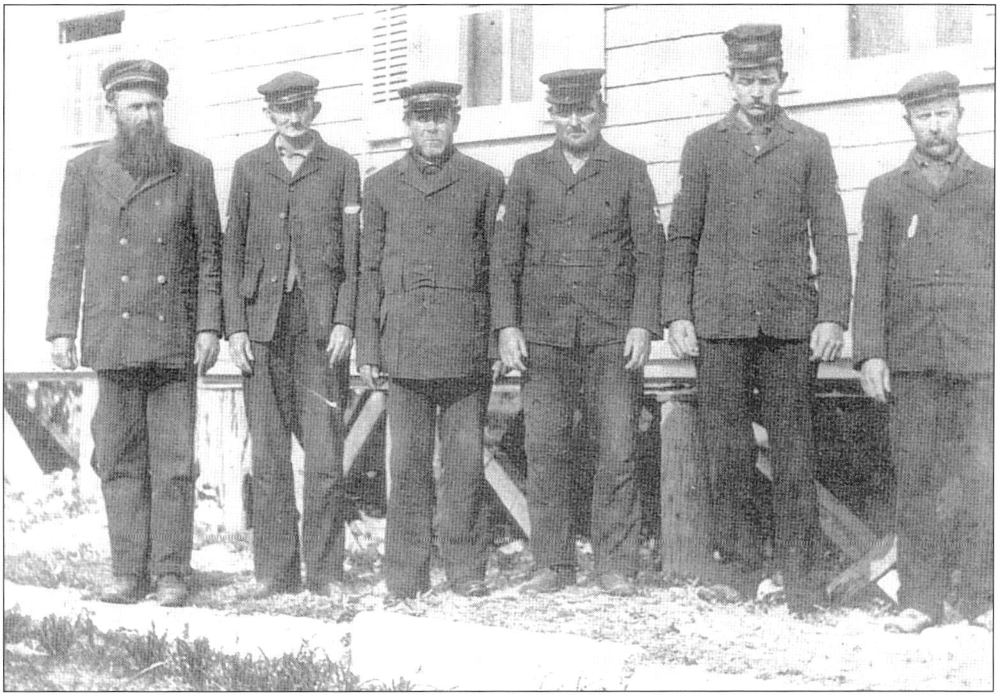

Pat Ethridge and the men from the Cape Hatteras Life Saving Station can be seen in this 1903 photograph. (Courtesy North Carolina Division of Archives and History.)

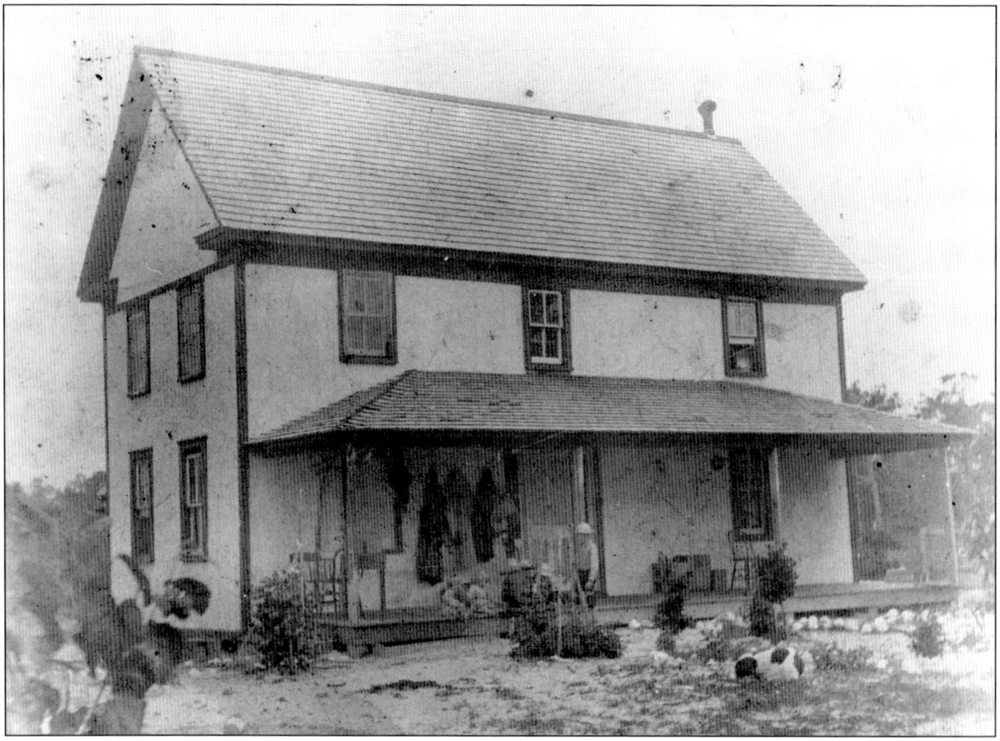

H.H. Brimley captured this scene at the home of Dr. J.J. Davis at Cape Hatteras in 1901. (Courtesy North Carolina Division of Archives and History.)

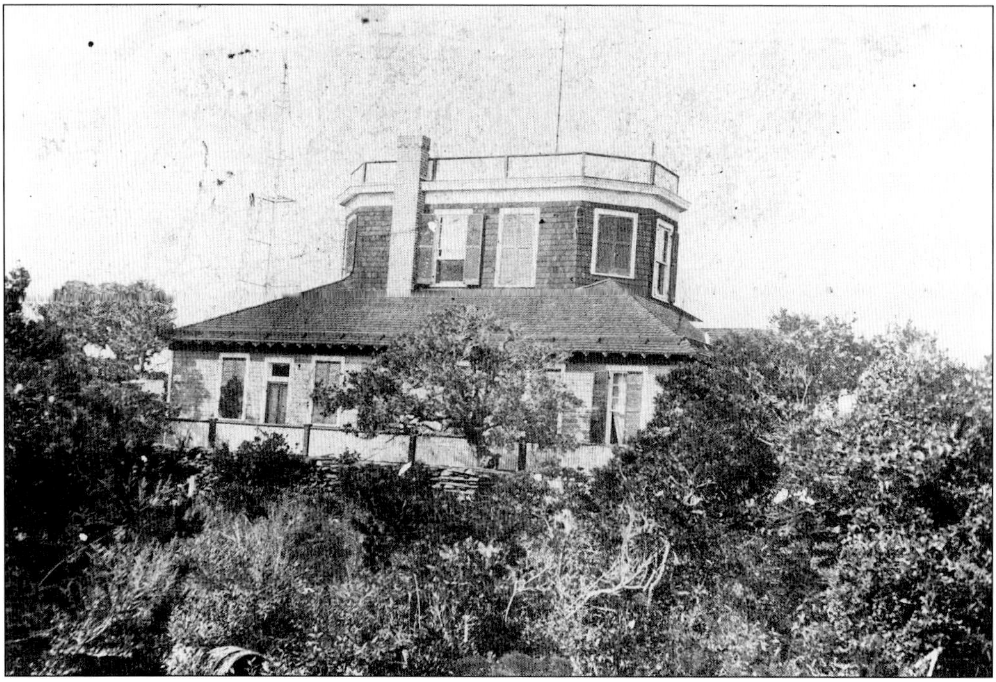

This image of the U.S. Weather Service Station at Hatteras was taken in 1904. (Courtesy North Carolina Division of Archives and History.)

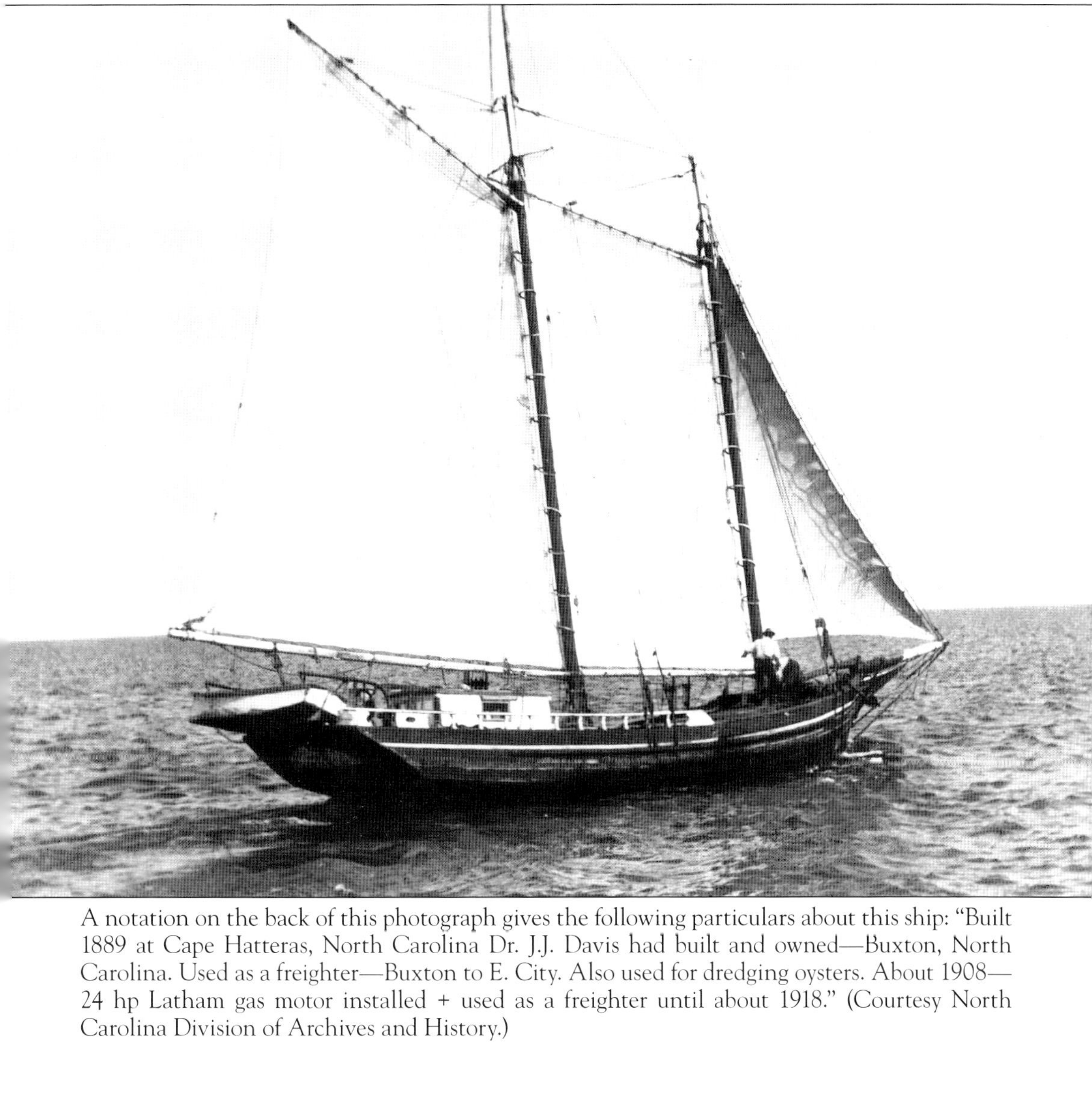

A notation on the back of this photograph gives the following particulars about this ship: "Built 1889 at Cape Hatteras, North Carolina Dr. J.J. Davis had built and owned—Buxton, North Carolina. Used as a freighter—Buxton to E. City. Also used for dredging oysters. About 1908—24 hp Latham gas motor installed + used as a freighter until about 1918." (Courtesy North Carolina Division of Archives and History.)

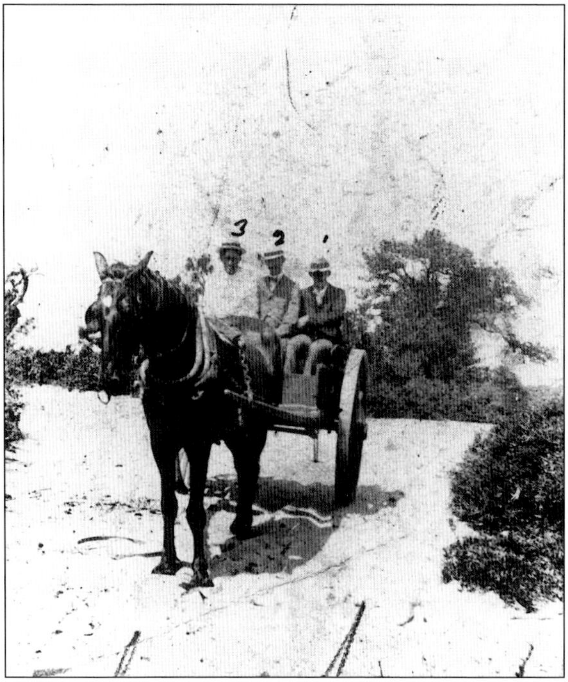

J.J. Davis, Hugh Davis, and Ben Ethridge ride a typical Outer Banks cart near Cape Hatteras in 1907. (Courtesy North Carolina Division of Archives and History.)

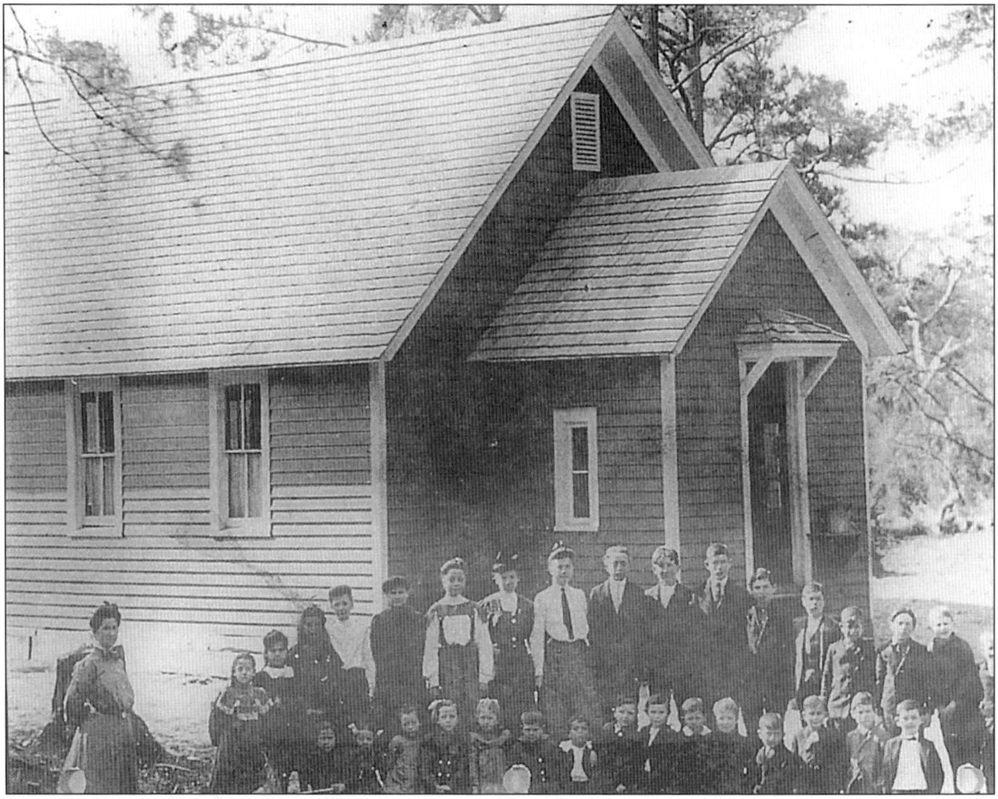

The children of the Cape Hatteras school posed for this H.H. Brimley picture, *c.* 1900. (Courtesy North Carolina Division of Archives and History.)

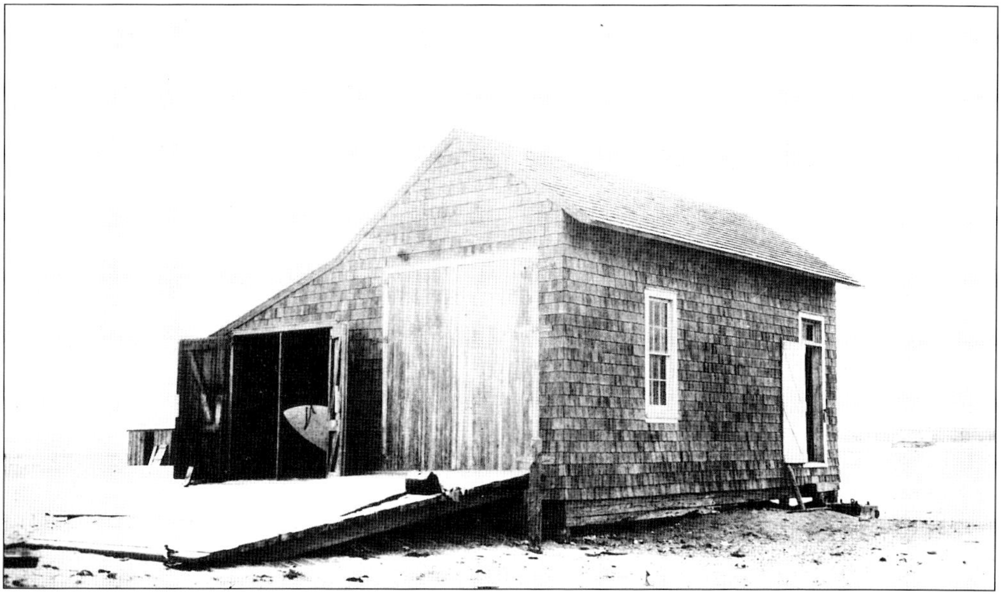

The Creeds Hill Beach Boathouse appeared in this state in the summer of 1917. (U.S. Coast Guard.)

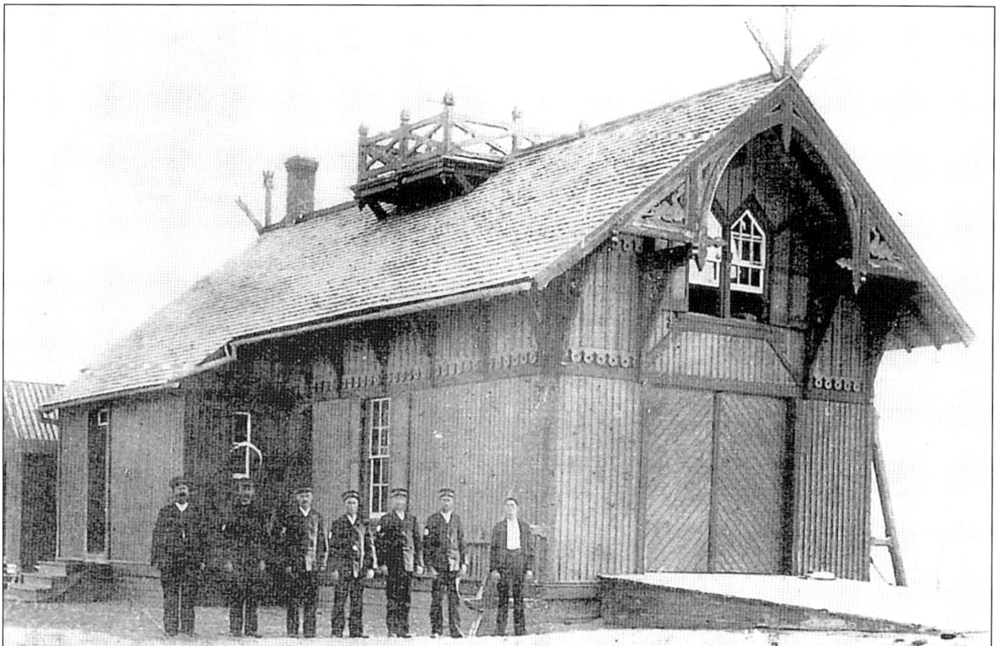

The Creeds Hill Lifesaving Station was located near Cape Hatteras. (U.S. Coast Guard.)

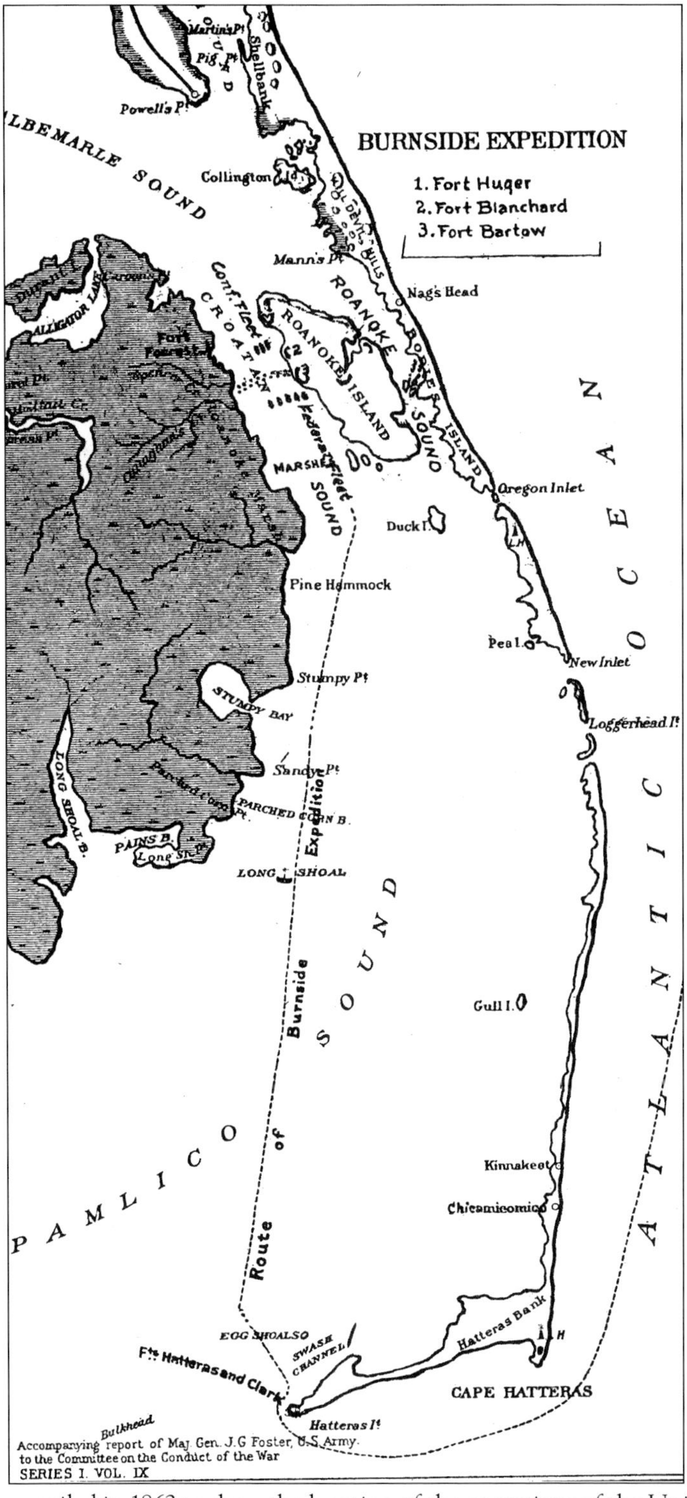

This map was compiled in 1862 to show the location of the operations of the Union forces along the Outer Banks.

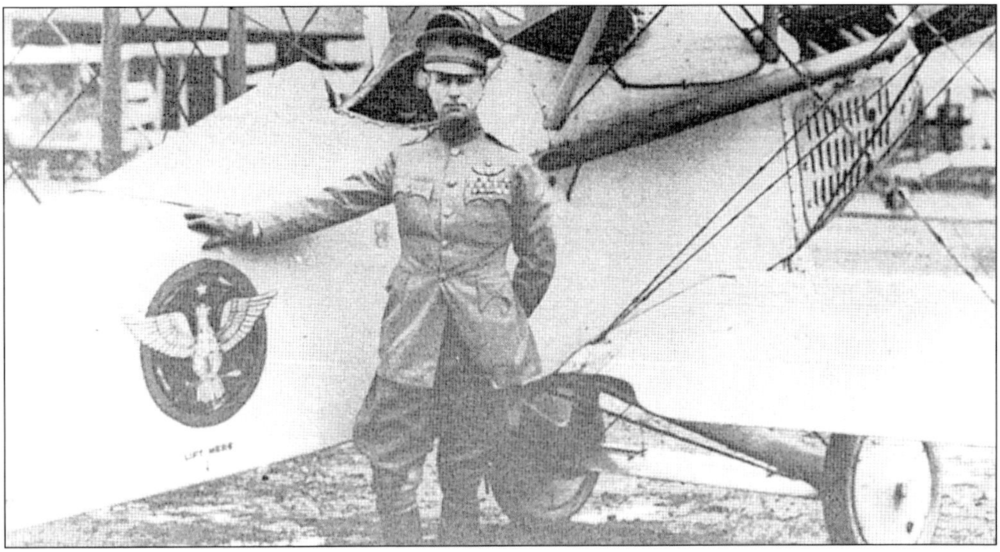

General Billy Mitchell pioneered the use of aircraft against naval targets. He carried out some of his most important demonstrations off Cape Hatteras. The airfield at Buxton is named in his honor.

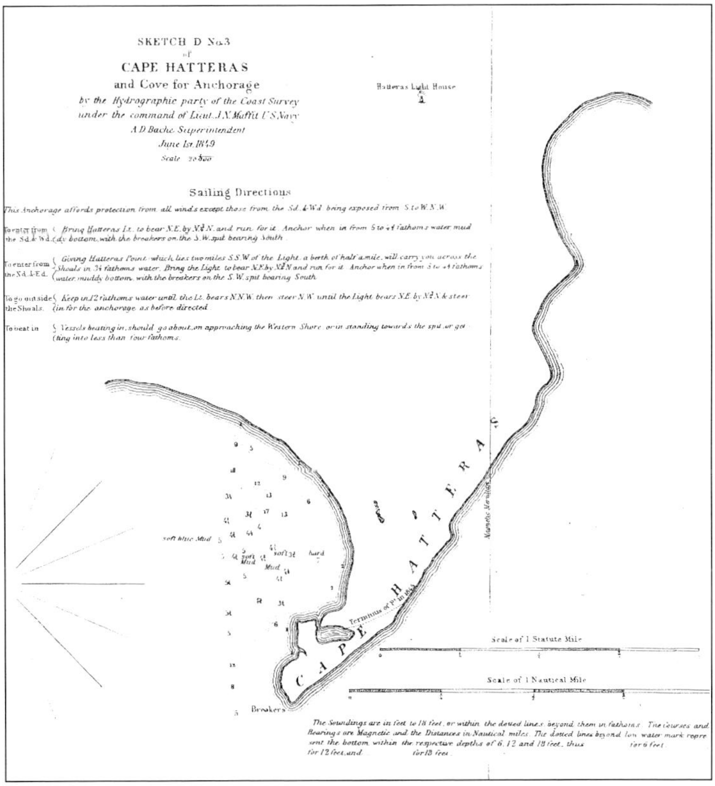

Lieutenant J.N. Maffit of the U.S. Navy compiled this chart of Cape Hatteras in 1849. Later, this young man would go on to become one of the most famous naval commanders for the Confederacy.

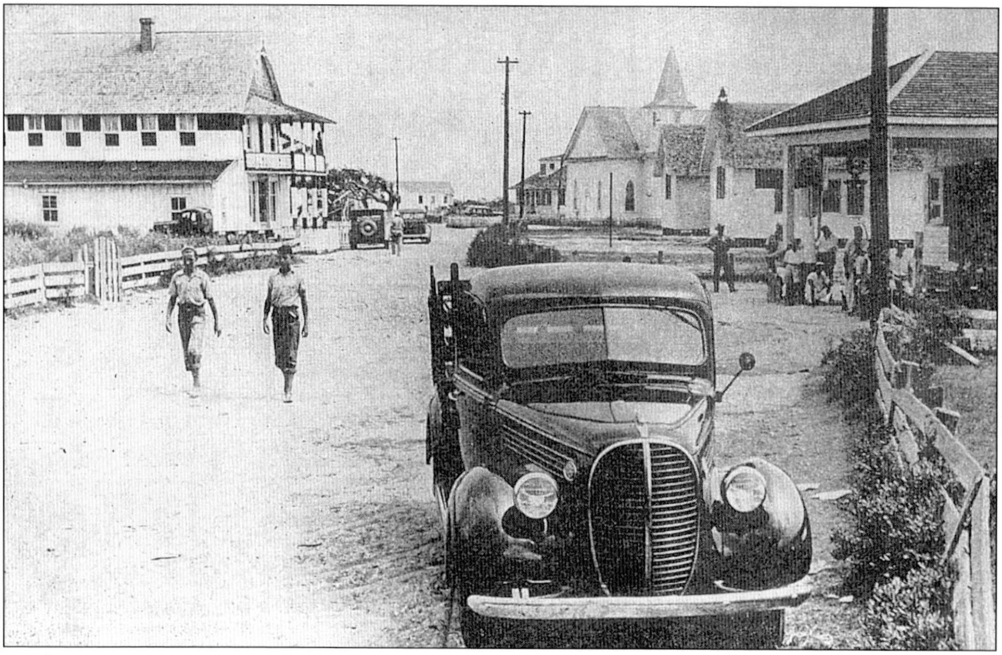
Carl Goerch captured this view of the Hatteras Village in 1945.

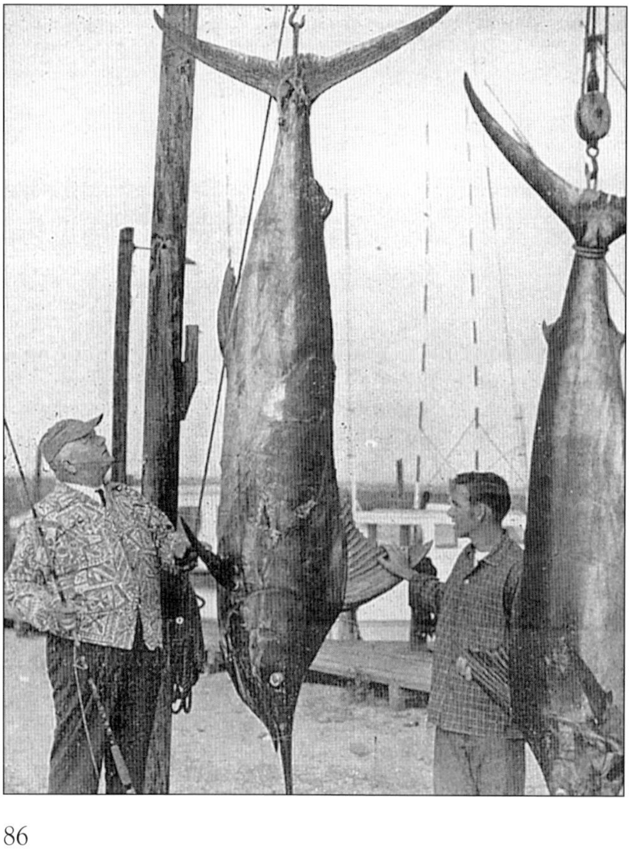
Blue marlin were taken by anglers on a fishing trip out of Hatteras.

Three

OCRACOKE AND PORTSMOUTH

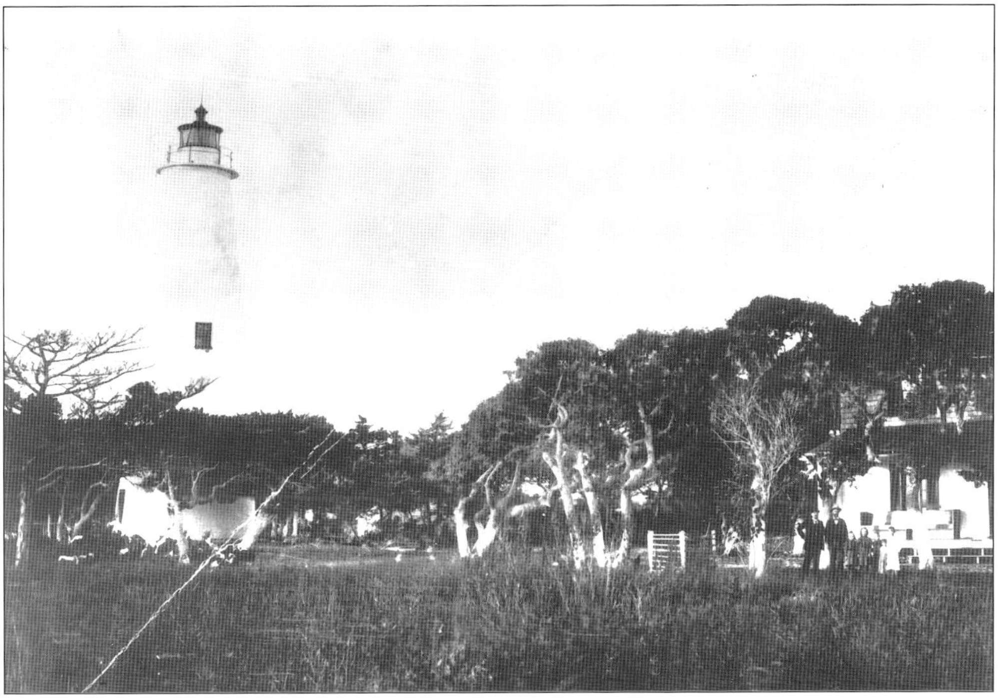

The Ocracoke Lighthouse, photographed here *c.* 1890, was built in 1823 on Ocracoke Island. This lighthouse was constructed to replace another lighthouse at Ocracoke Inlet, the wooden Shell Castle Lighthouse, which was struck by lightning and burned in 1818. (Courtesy North Carolina Division of Archives and History.)

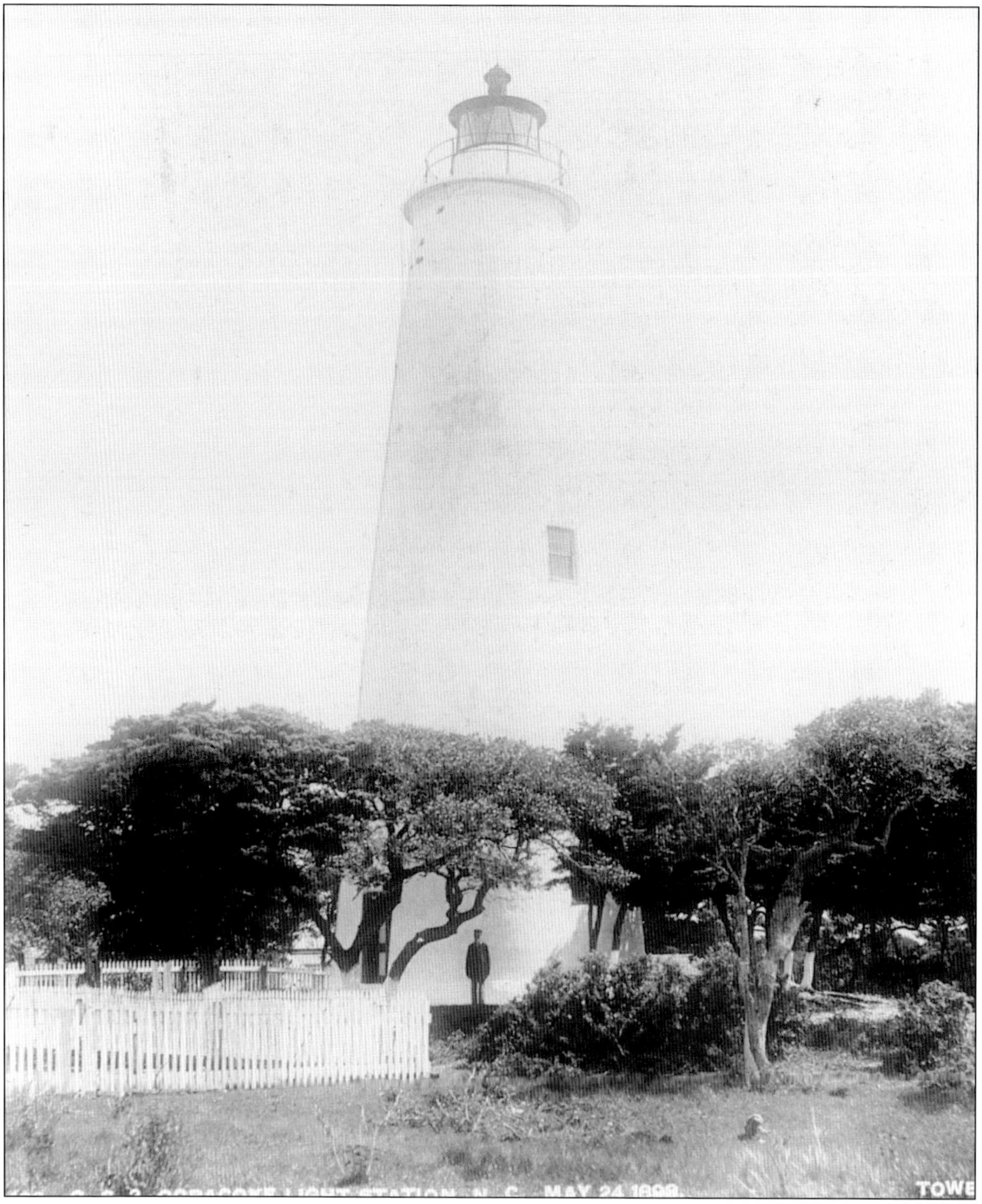

Ocracoke Lighthouse has been in service since 1823. This gives it the distinction of being the oldest active lighthouse in North Carolina. (U.S. Coast Guard.)

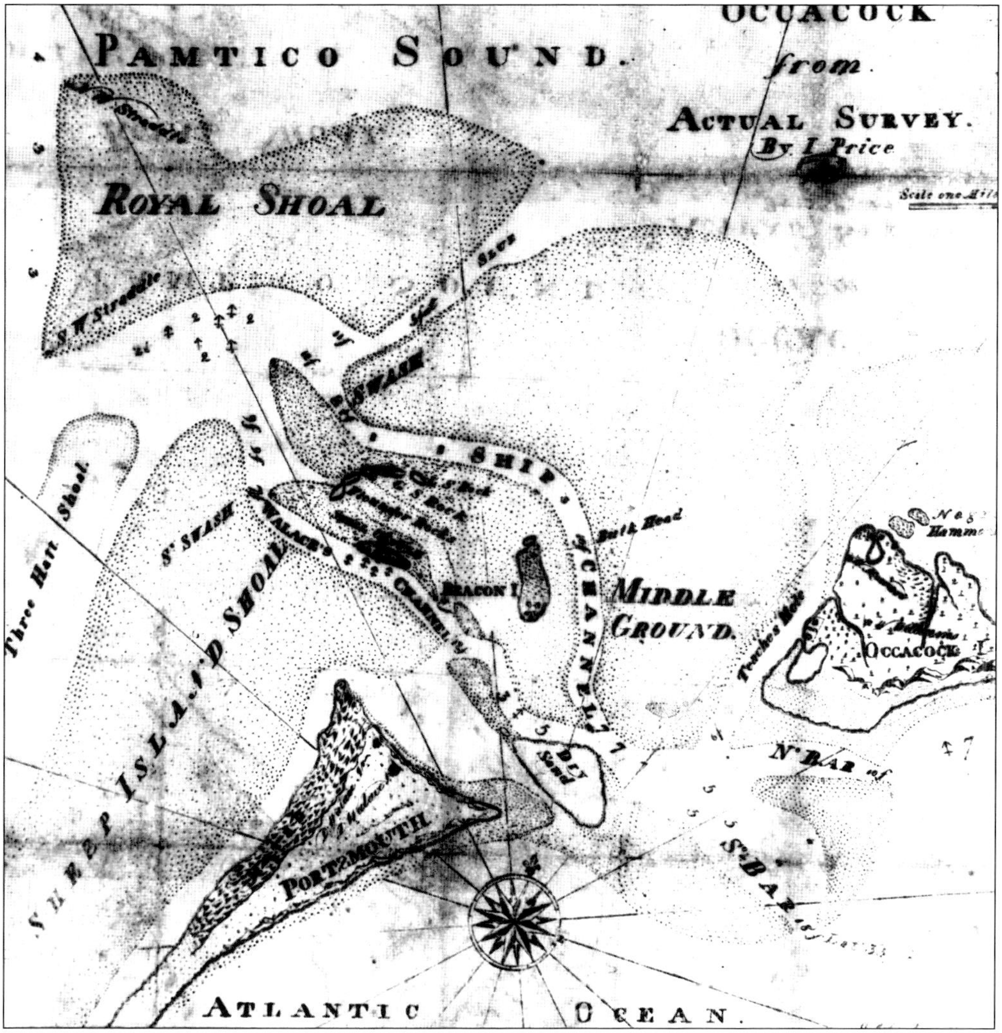

Jonathon Price's *Map of Occacock* was created *c.* 1791. In an accompanying brochure, Price listed the following particulars about Ocracoke.

> Occacock was heretofore, and still retains the name of, an island. It is now a peninsula: a heap of sand having gradually filled up the space which divided it from the bank. It continues to have its former appearance from the sea: the green trees, that cover it, strikingly distinguishing it from the sandy bank to which it has been joined. Its length is three miles, and its breadth two and one half. Small live oak and cedar grow abundantly over it, and it contains several swamps and rich marshes, which might be cultivated to great advantage; but its inhabitants, depending upon another element for their support, suffer the earth to remain in its natural state. They are all pilots; and their number of head of families is about thirty.
>
> This healthy spot is in autumn the resort of many of the inhabitants of the main. One of its original proprietors, who has attained his ninetieth year, still resides on it, and does not appear to feel any of the infirmities of age."

(Courtesy North Carolina Division of Archives and History.)

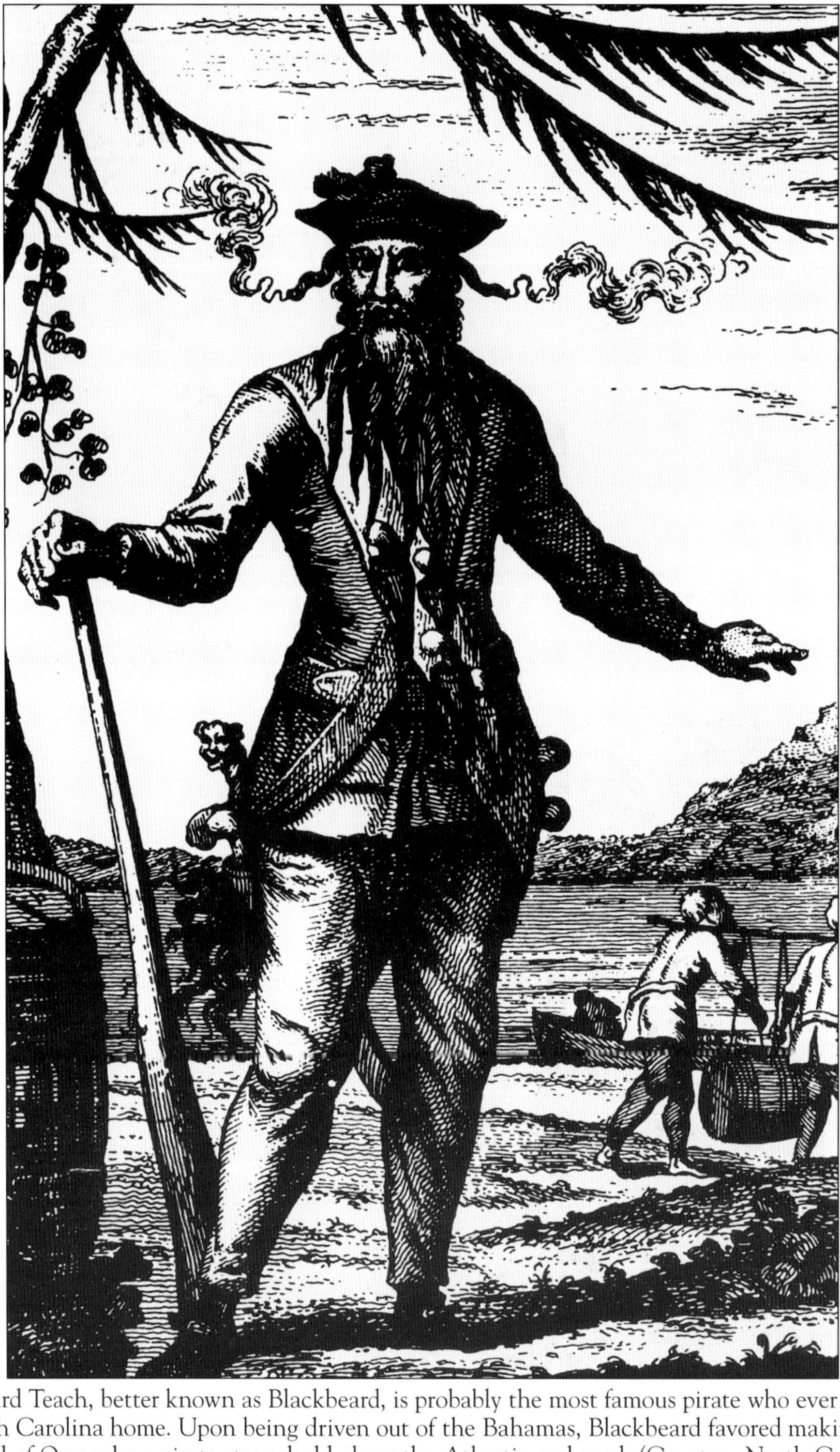

Edward Teach, better known as Blackbeard, is probably the most famous pirate who ever called North Carolina home. Upon being driven out of the Bahamas, Blackbeard favored making the island of Ocracoke a pirate stronghold along the Atlantic seaboard. (Courtesy North Carolina Division of Archives and History.)

This portion of *A Preliminary Survey of Ocracoke Inlet, North Carolina*, compiled under the direction of Commander William T. Muse in 1857, shows the location of Teach's Hole and the village of Ocracoke.

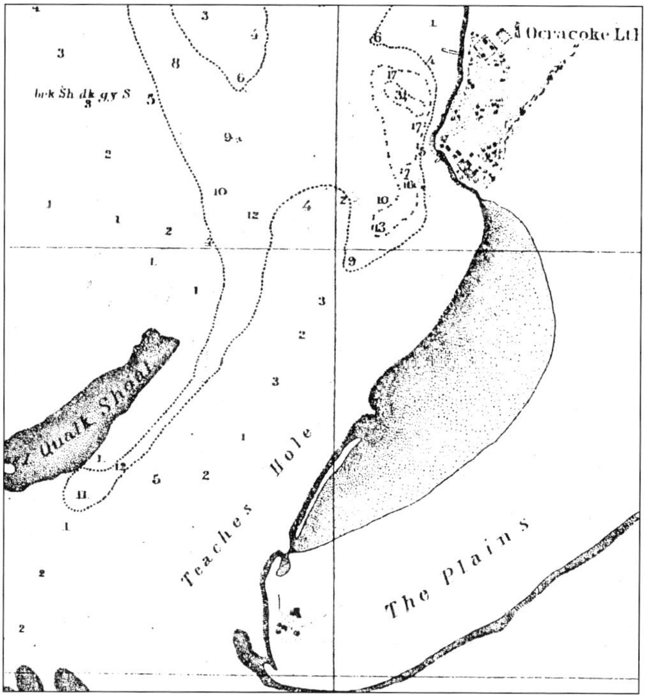

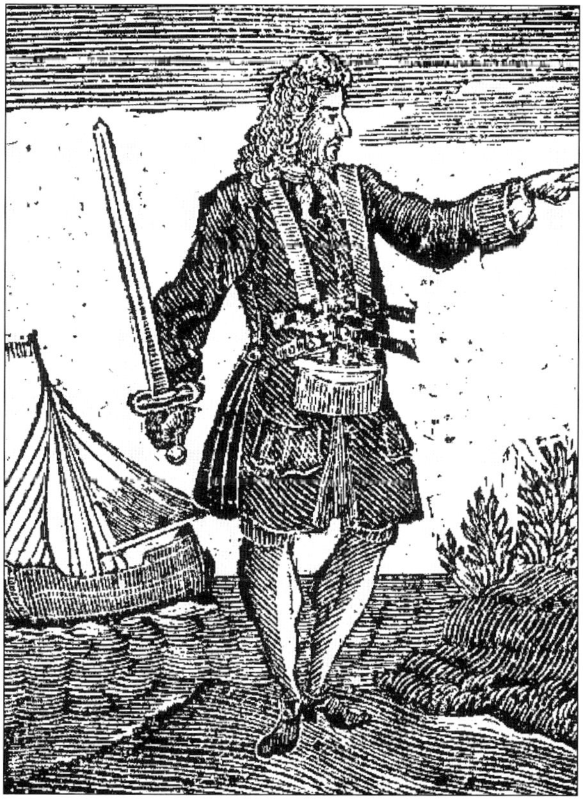

The pirate Charles Vane visited his old friend Blackbeard's base at Ocracoke Island.

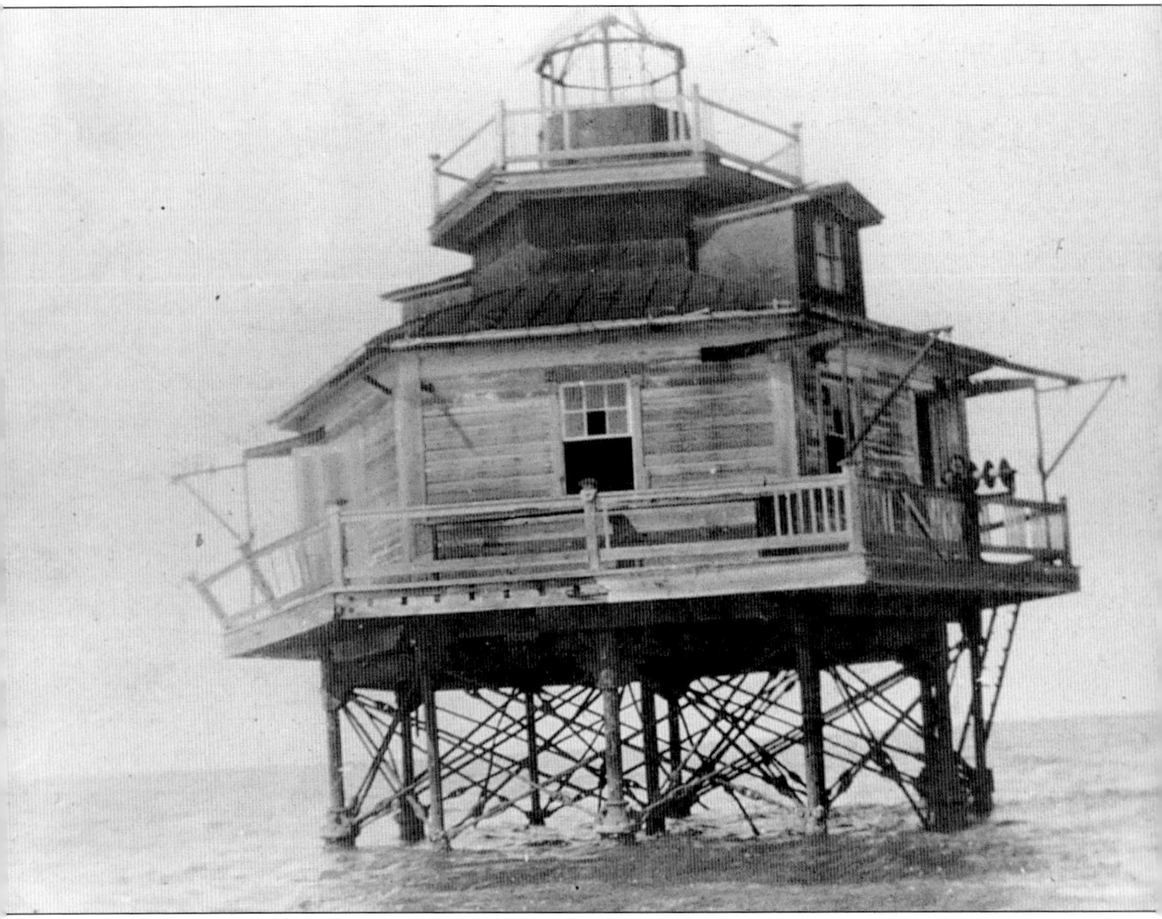

This lighthouse guided ships through Ocracoke Inlet and across the Pamlico Sound. The structure was abandoned following a harsh storm in August 1903. (Courtesy National Park Service, Cape Lookout National Seashore.)

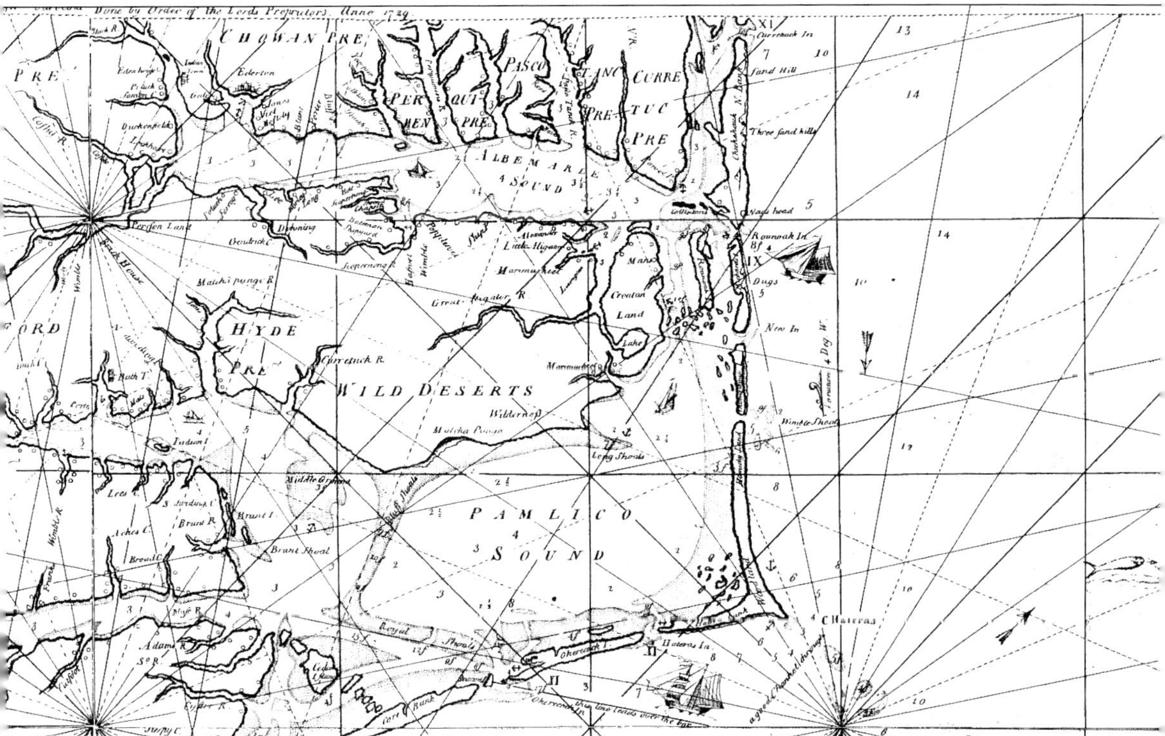

This portion of Captain James Wimble's chart of the North Carolina Coast was prepared in 1738. Note the village and anchorage depicted at "Okerecock." (Courtesy North Carolina Division of Archives and History.)

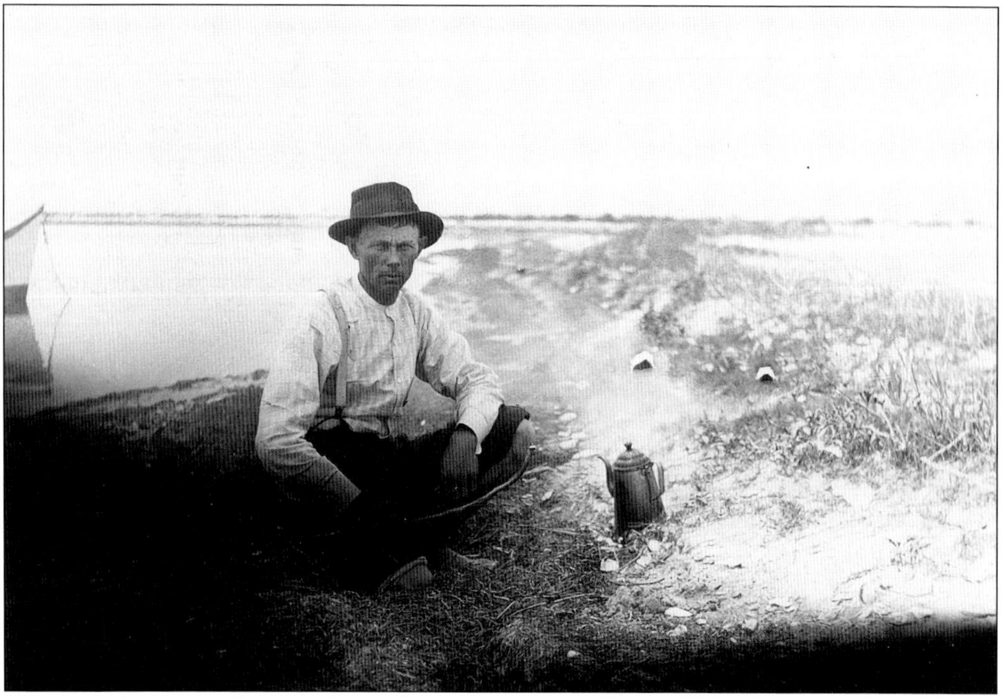

H.H. Brimley camped at Ocracoke Island, *c.* 1912. (Courtesy North Carolina Division of Archives and History.)

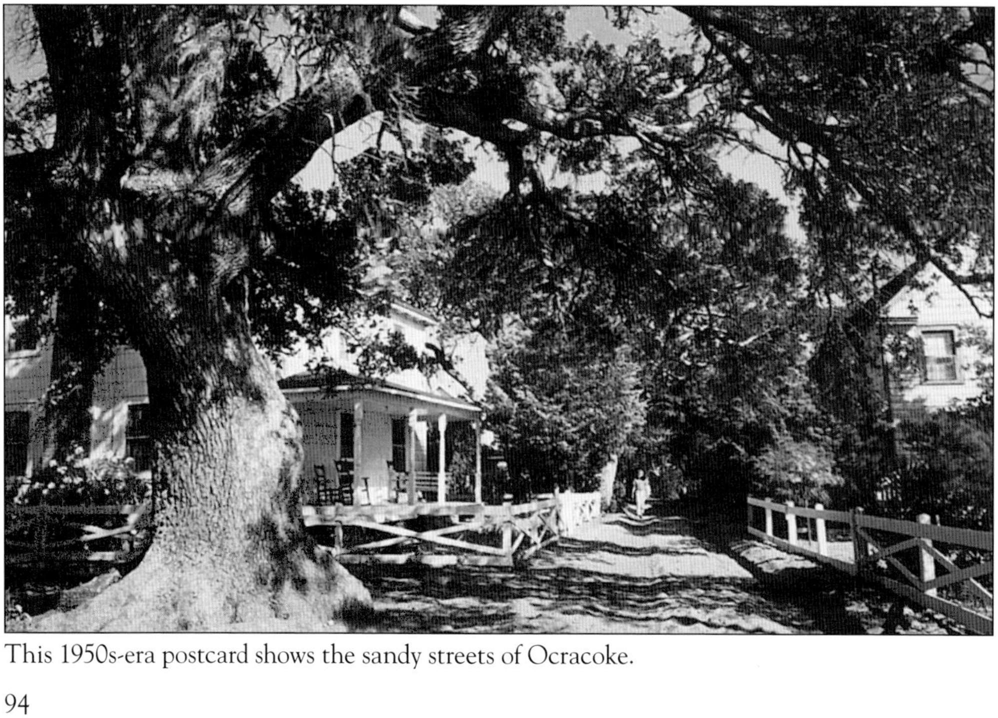

This 1950s-era postcard shows the sandy streets of Ocracoke.

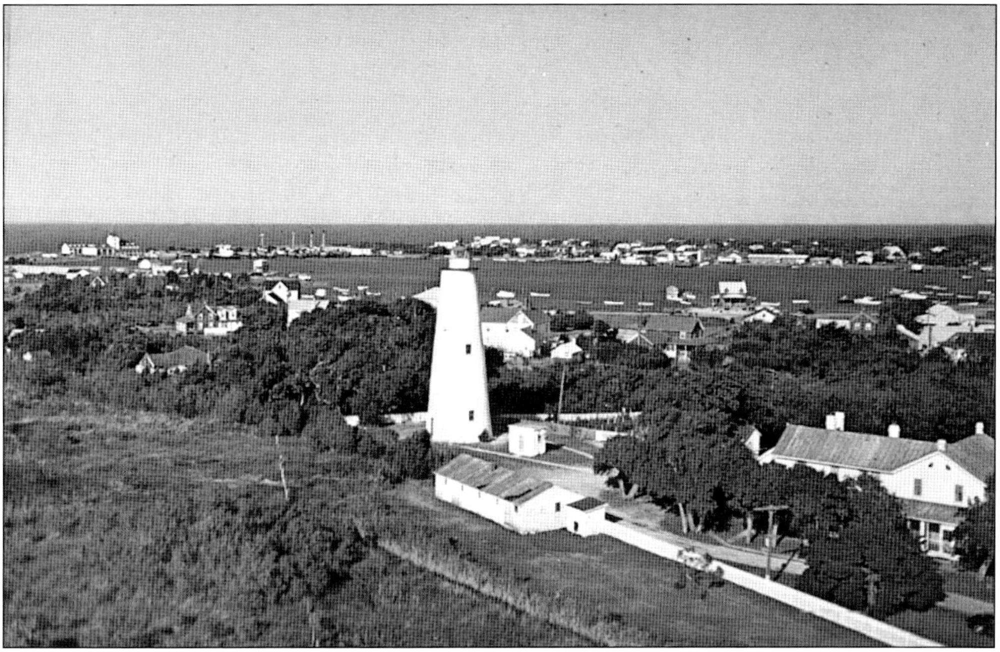

This birds-eye view of Ocracoke was taken *c.* 1960.

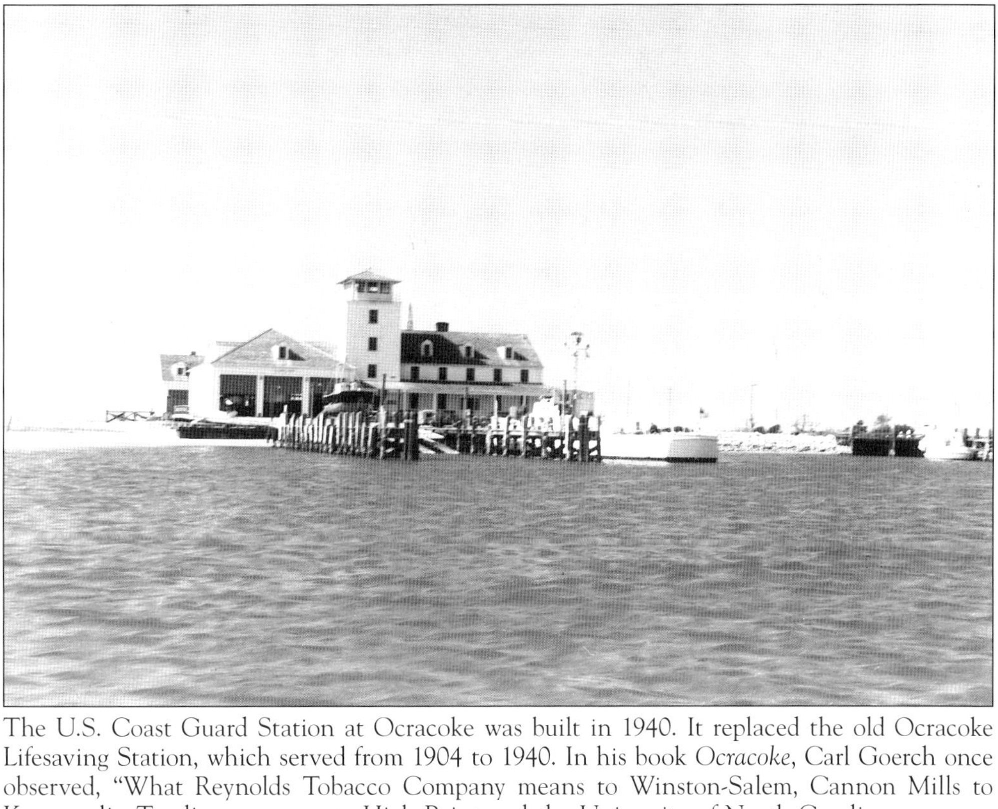

The U.S. Coast Guard Station at Ocracoke was built in 1940. It replaced the old Ocracoke Lifesaving Station, which served from 1904 to 1940. In his book *Ocracoke*, Carl Goerch once observed, "What Reynolds Tobacco Company means to Winston-Salem, Cannon Mills to Kannapolis, Tomlinson means to High Point and the University of North Carolina means to Chapel Hill—the Coast Guard means to Ocracoke." (U.S. Coast Guard.)

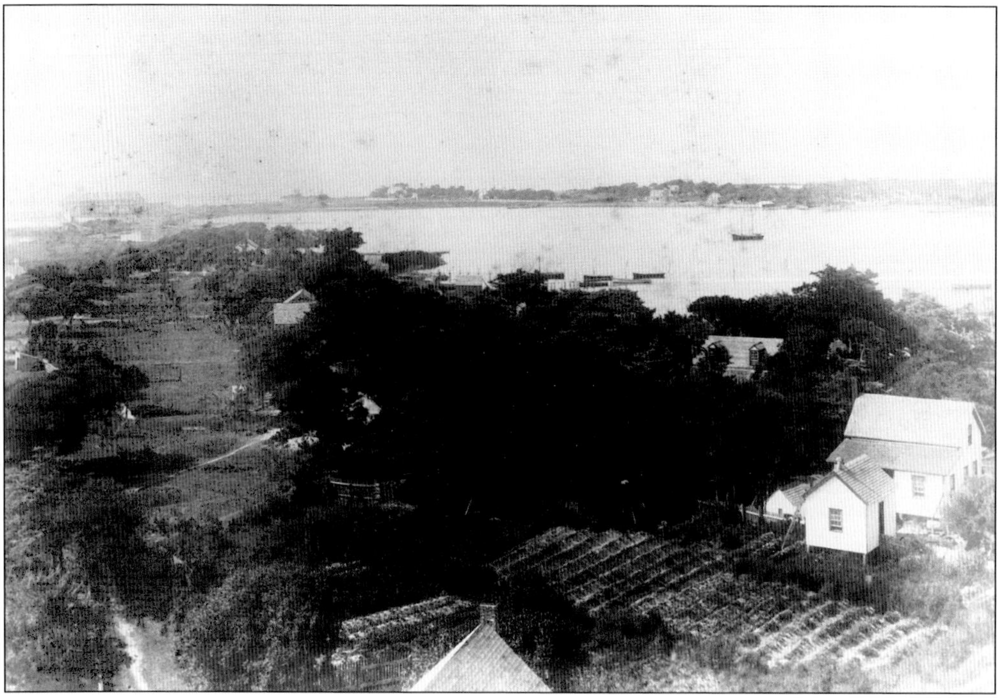

This photograph of Ocracoke was taken from the lighthouse in 1890. (Courtesy North Carolina Division of Archives and History.)

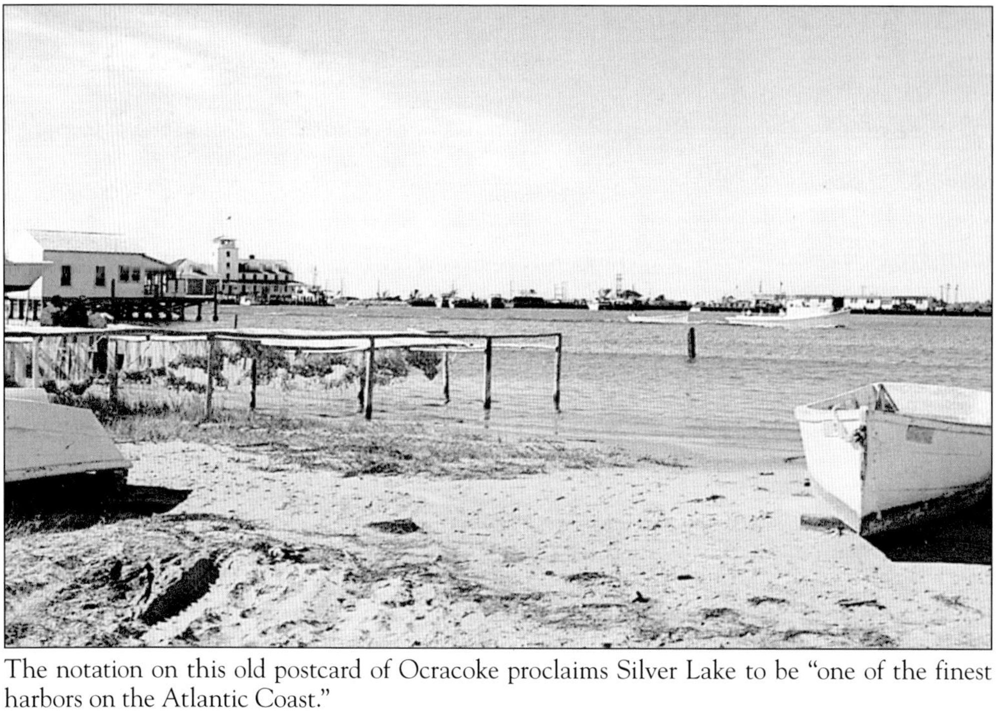

The notation on this old postcard of Ocracoke proclaims Silver Lake to be "one of the finest harbors on the Atlantic Coast."

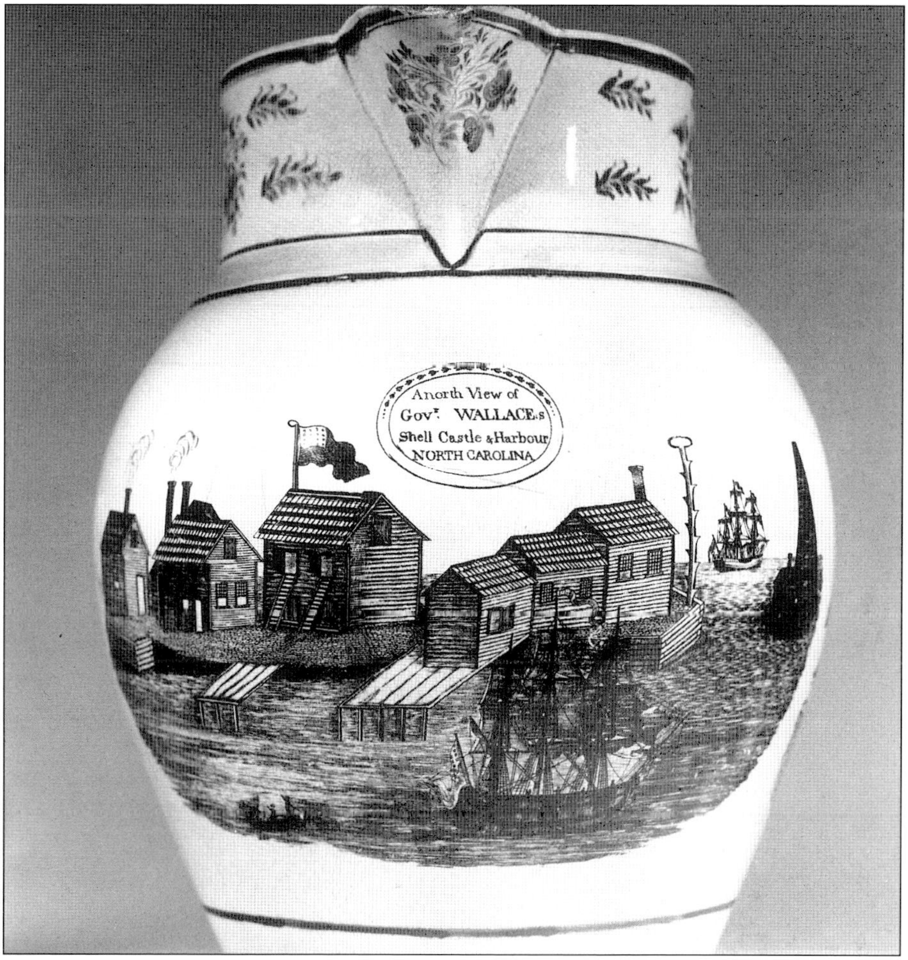

The painting on this pitcher illustrates the once thriving community of Shell Castle, located inside Ocracoke Inlet on Shell Castle Island. In 1791, Jonathon Price wrote the following description of this important commercial shipping center:

> SHELL CASTLE, built on a rock of oyster shells half a mile in length and about sixty feet in width, dry at low water. On the north side of it is nothing but a large bed of shells, from two, to two and one half feet of water. The tide ebbs and flows from twelve to eighteen inches. Wallace's channel runs on the south side, within forty feet of the rock; its depth there is three fathoms and one half.
>
> The castle was built by John Gray Blount, Esq; of Washington, and Mr. John Wallace, in 1790. The last gentleman resides on it: besides his dwelling-house and its out-houses, which are commodious, here are ware-houses for a large quantity of produce and merchandize, a lumber yard and a wharf, along side of which a number of vessels are constantly riding. These late improvements contribute much to the usefulness of the establishment, and give it the appearance of a trading factory. A notary public's office is kept here."

The grand plans envisioned for Shell Castle were dashed when the channel running by the facility shoaled up in the early 1800s. (Courtesy North Carolina Division of Archives and History.)

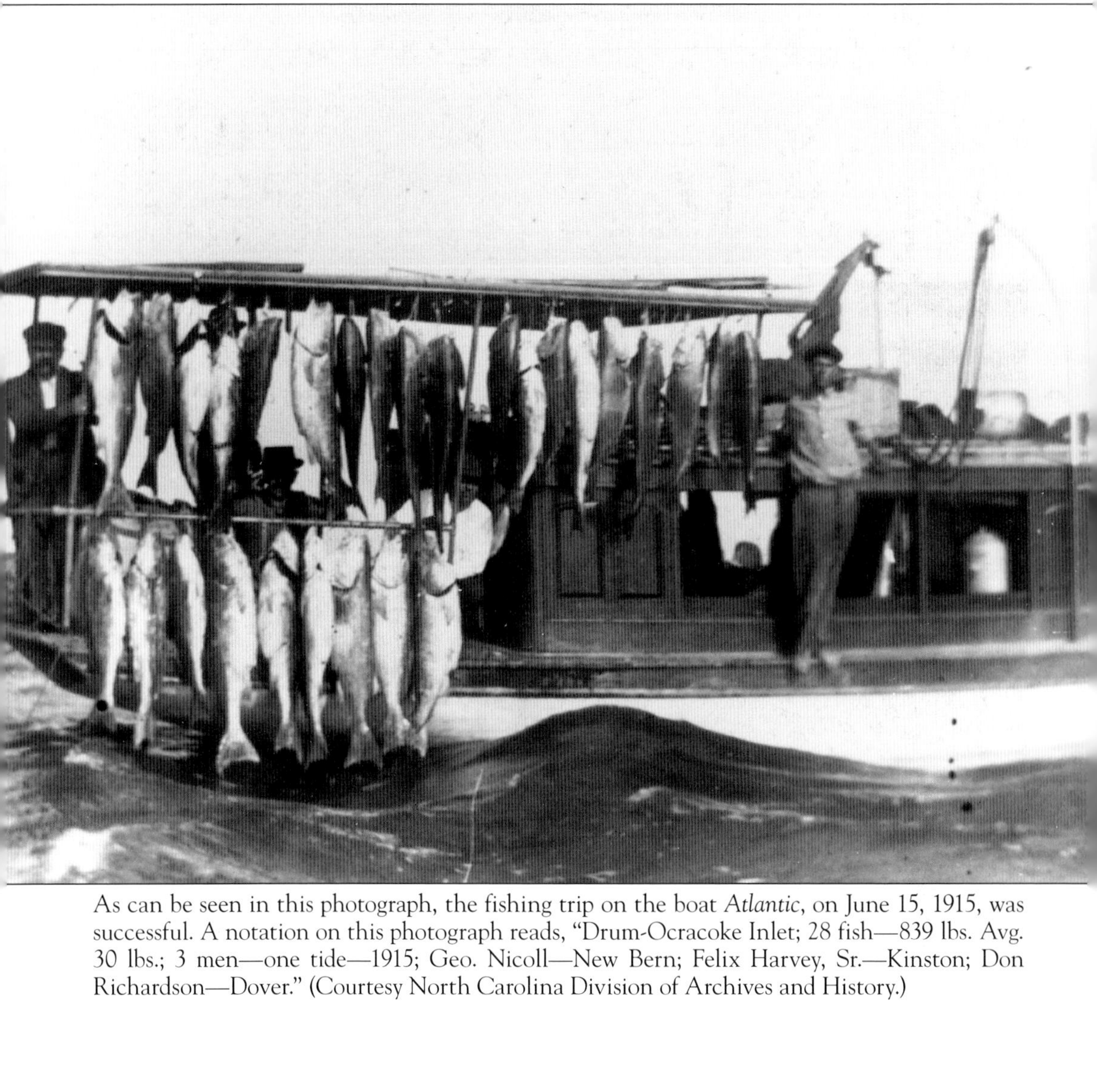

As can be seen in this photograph, the fishing trip on the boat *Atlantic*, on June 15, 1915, was successful. A notation on this photograph reads, "Drum-Ocracoke Inlet; 28 fish—839 lbs. Avg. 30 lbs.; 3 men—one tide—1915; Geo. Nicoll—New Bern; Felix Harvey, Sr.—Kinston; Don Richardson—Dover." (Courtesy North Carolina Division of Archives and History.)

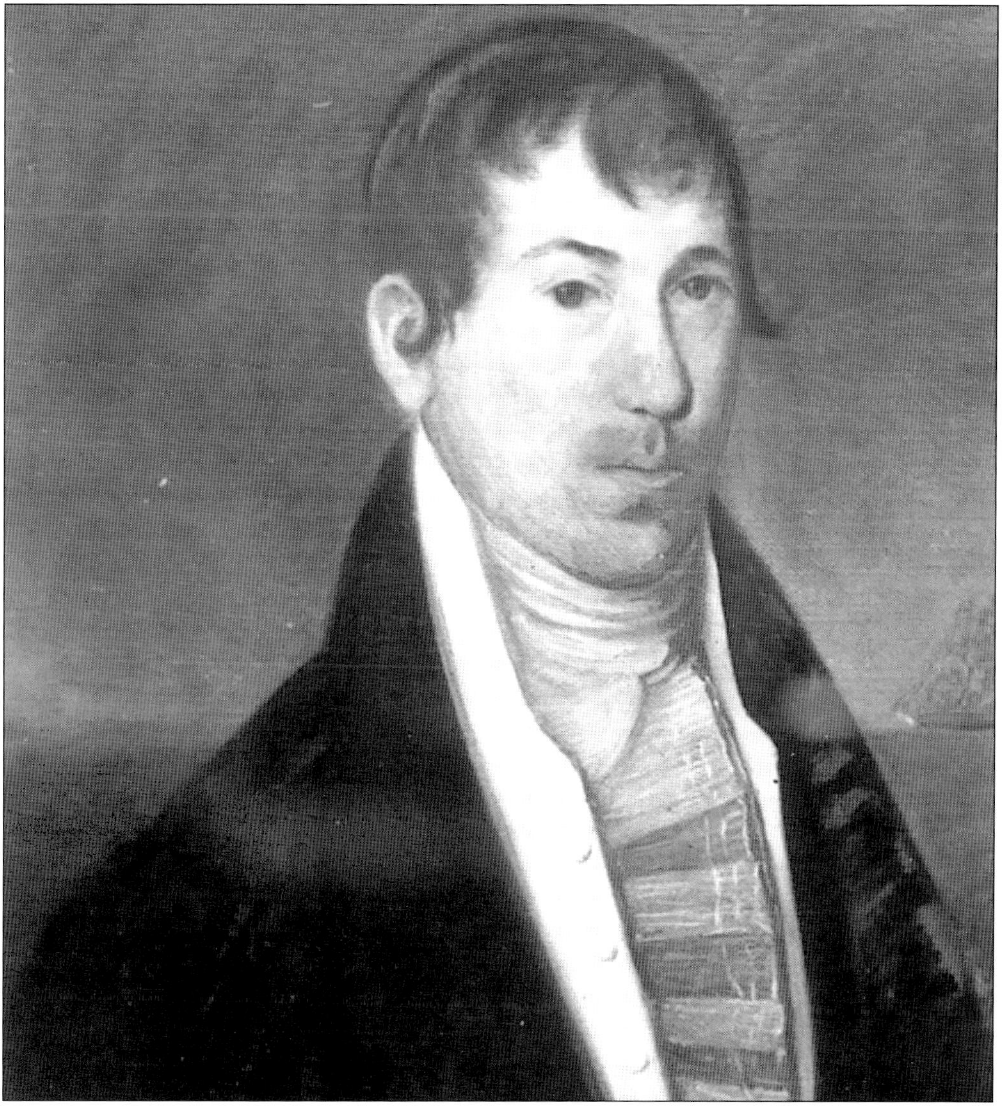

One of the most memorable residents of Portsmouth was Captain Otway Burns. Born and raised in Swansboro, Burns became an accomplished mariner. During the War of 1812, Burns gained notoriety as the captain of the privateer *Snap Dragon*, which captured several prizes while under his command. He was also a renowned shipbuilder.

Following the war, Burns represented Carteret County in both the North Carolina House of Commons and the state senate. His political career came to an end in 1835 when he broke ranks with the legislators from eastern North Carolina and voted for a Constitutional Convention.

In 1835, Burns was appointed to be the keeper of the Brant Island Shoals Light by President Andrew Jackson and, therefore, moved to Portsmouth. There he lived out his days, often parading through town with his captain's uniform, telling yarns of his high sea adventures. As one biographer noted, "He was fond of his brilliant naval uniform and cocked hat, he liked good whiskey, and he liked a good fight, whether on the waterfront or in the legislature."

Captain Otway Burns died at Portsmouth on October 25, 1850, and is buried in Beaufort. (Courtesy North Carolina Division of Archives and History.)

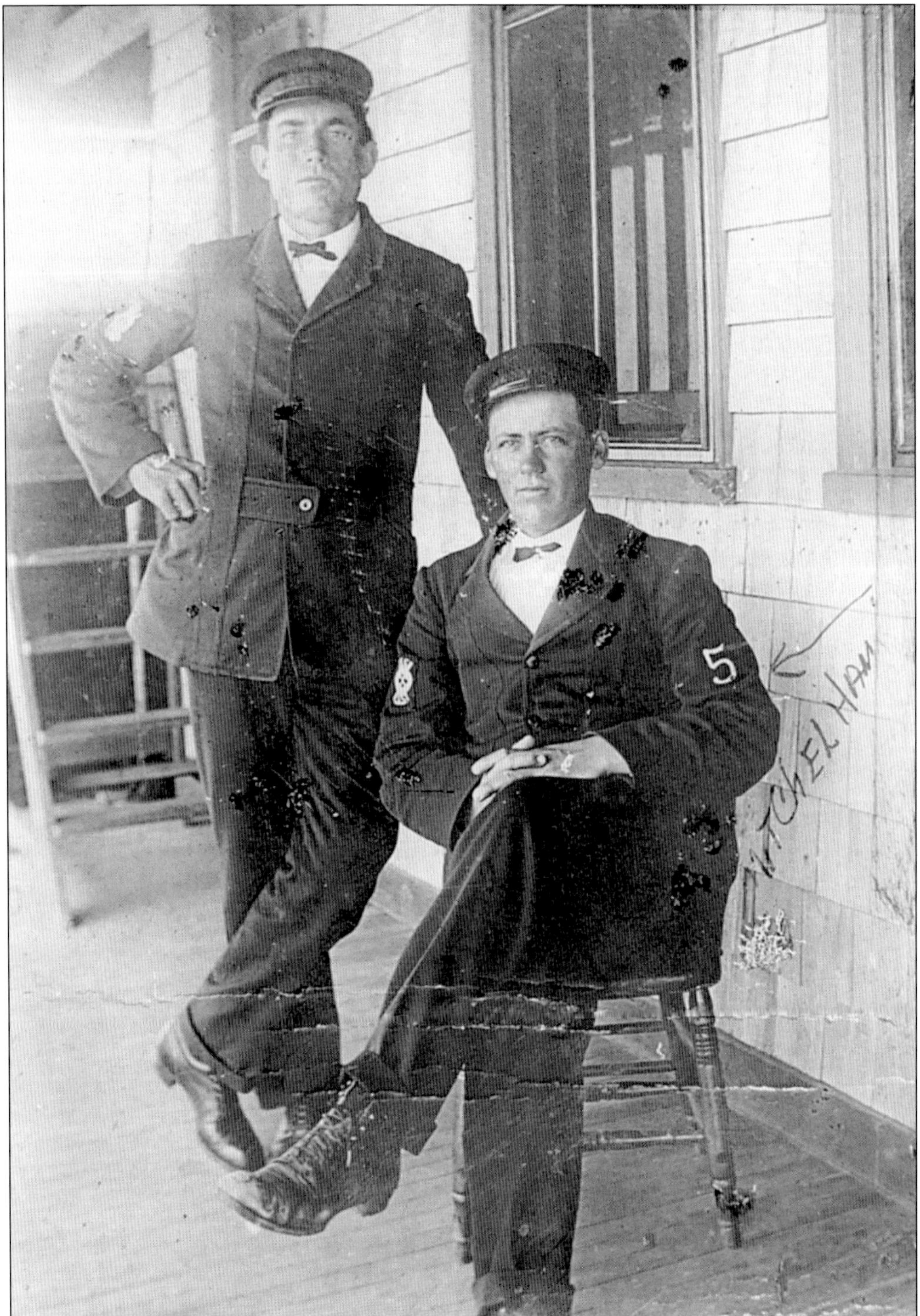

Monroe Gilgo and Mitchell Hamilton, surfman number 5, are on the porch of the Portsmouth Life Saving Station, *c.* 1910. (Courtesy National Park Service, Cape Lookout National Seashore.)

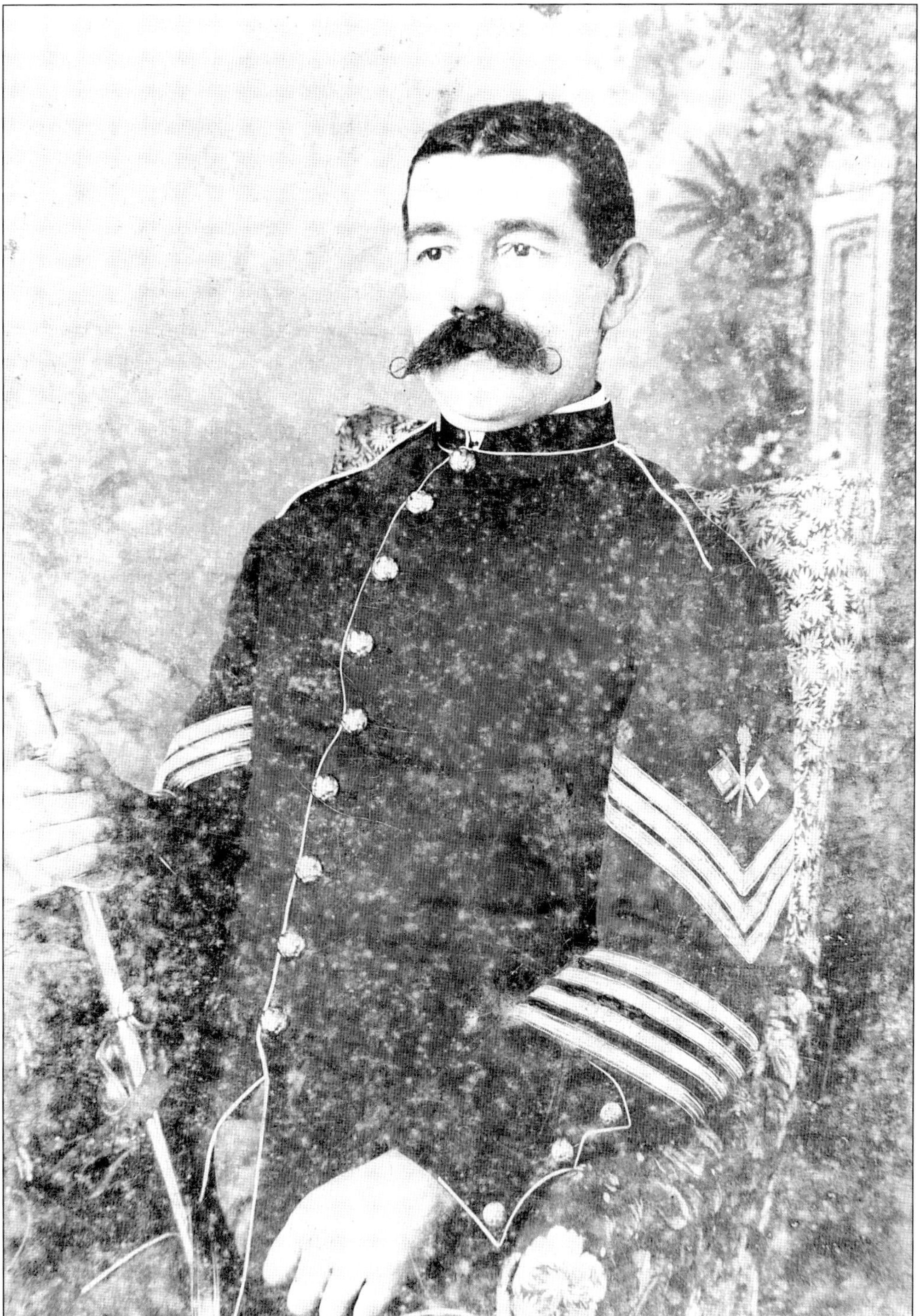

A native of Dublin, Ireland, William Daly served in the U.S. Army Signal Corps office at Portsmouth in the 1880s. Upon his death in 1893, Daly was buried in the Community Cemetery. (Courtesy National Park Service, Cape Lookout National Seashore.)

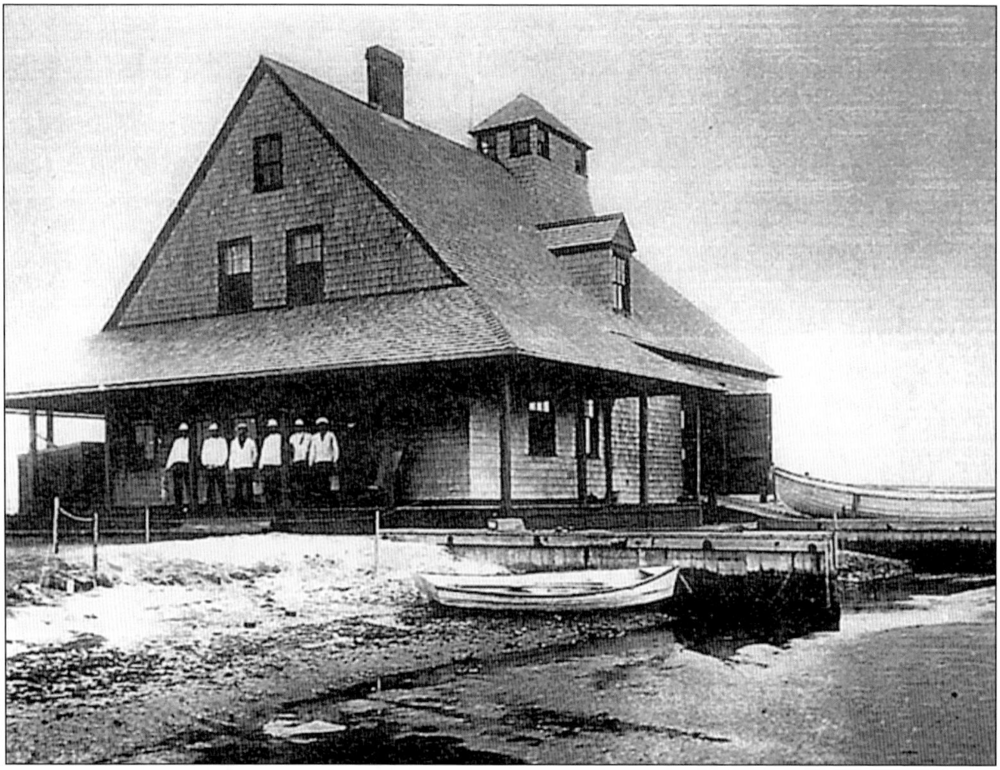

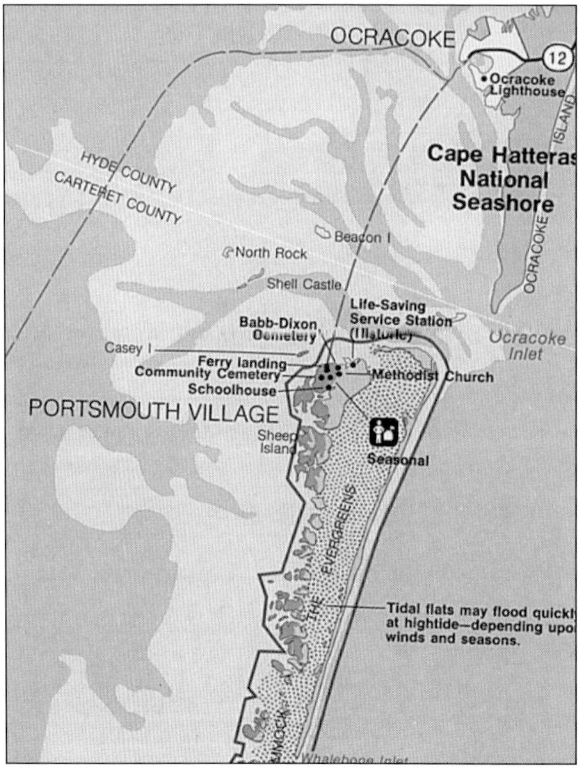

This image of Portsmouth Island Lifesaving Station was taken in 1915. (Courtesy North Carolina Division of Archives and History.)

This National Park Service map shows the Portsmouth Village site in the Cape Lookout National Seashore.

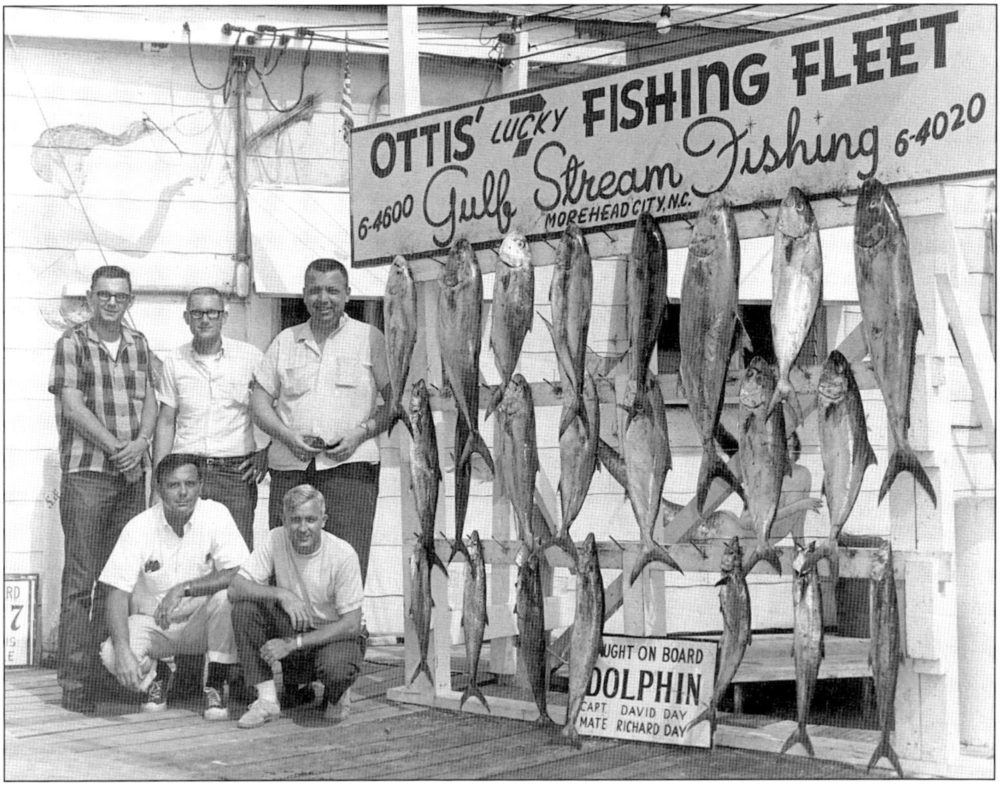

A lucky group of anglers are back from a successful day's fishing in the waters of the Gulf Stream.

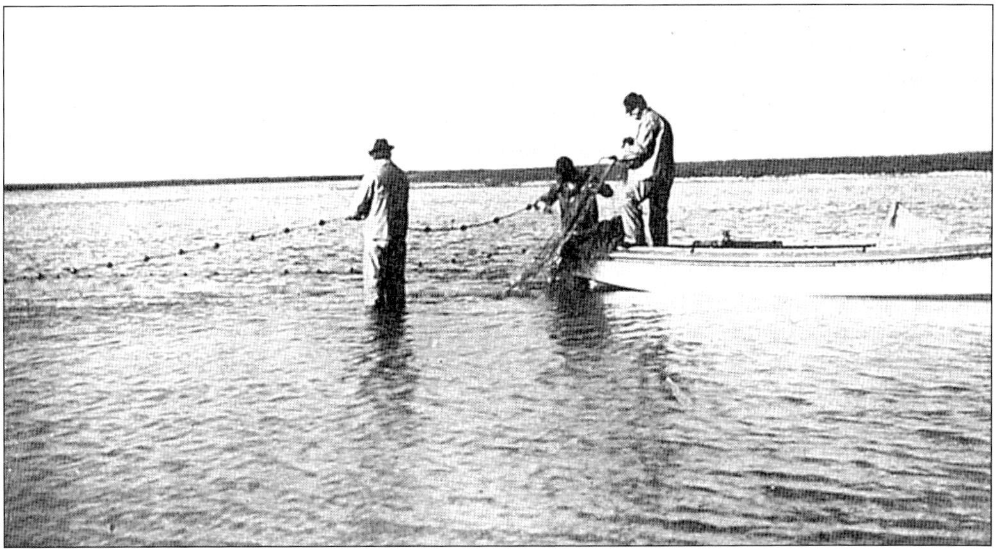

Mullet fishermen probe their luck in Core Sound, 1907. (North Carolina Geological and Economic Survey.)

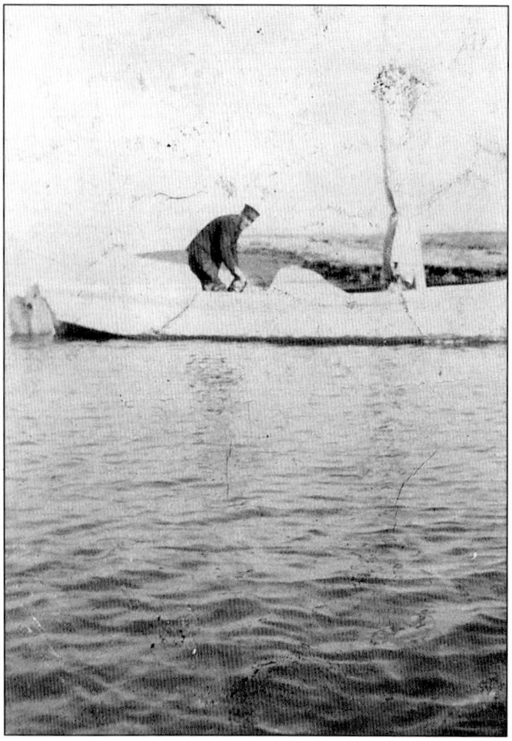

Monroe Gilgo bails the water out of his skiff near Portsmouth, *c.* 1916. (Courtesy National Park Service, Cape Lookout National Seashore.)

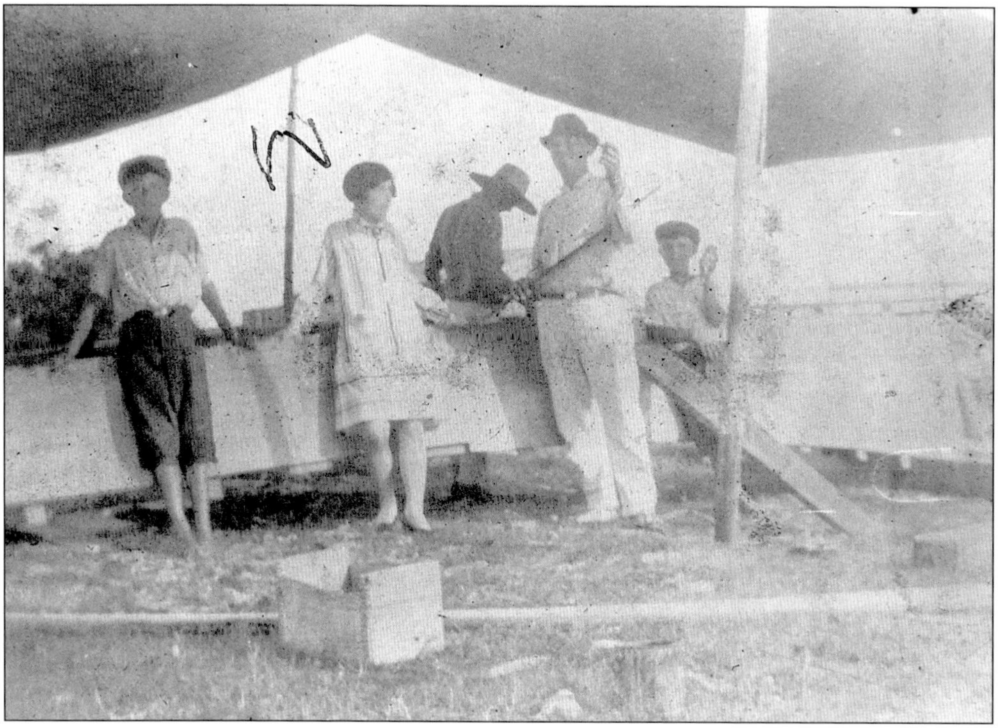

Cecil Gilgo, Ethel Gilgo, Harry Dixon, Wash Roberts, and Lionel Gilgo build a boat at Portsmouth, *c.* 1925. (Courtesy National Park Service, Cape Lookout National Seashore.)

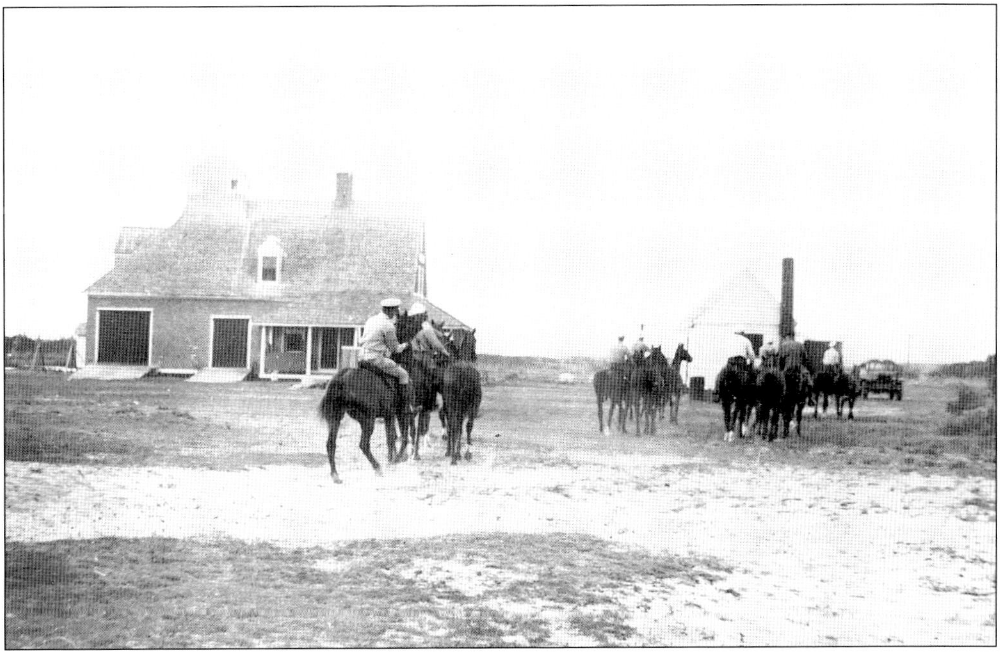

A patrol is mounted on horseback at the Portsmouth Coast Guard Station in 1942, shortly after it was reactivated for WW II. (Courtesy National Park Service, Cape Lookout National Seashore.)

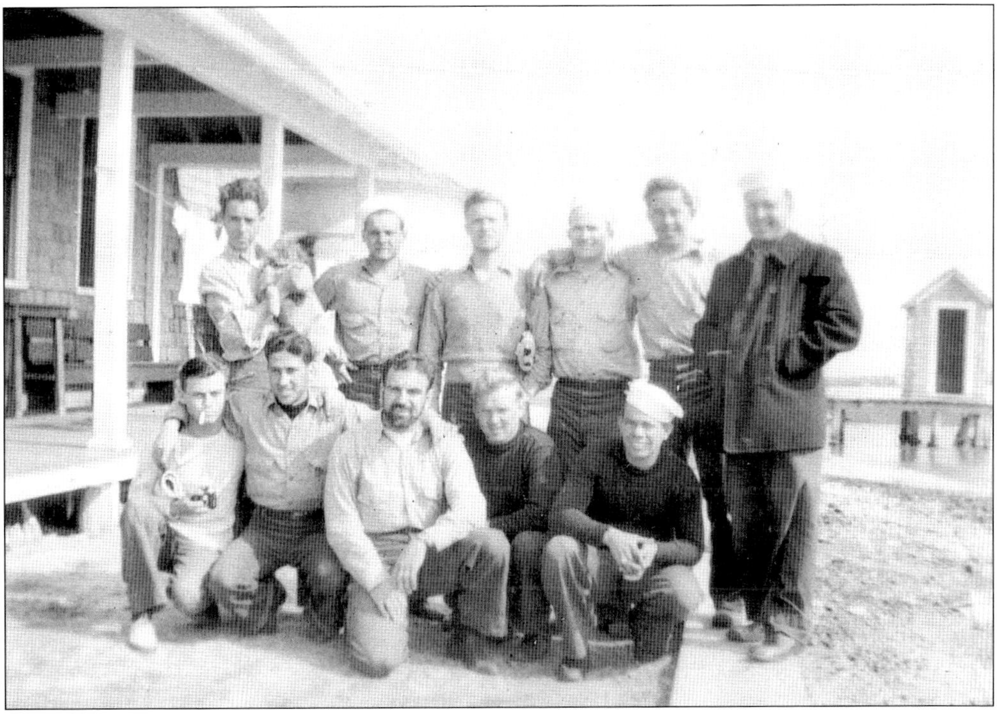

A group of Coast Guardsmen are in front of the Portsmouth Coast Guard Station in 1942. A notation on the back of the photograph draws attention to, "Toilet over creek in rear." (Courtesy National Park Service, Cape Lookout National Seashore.)

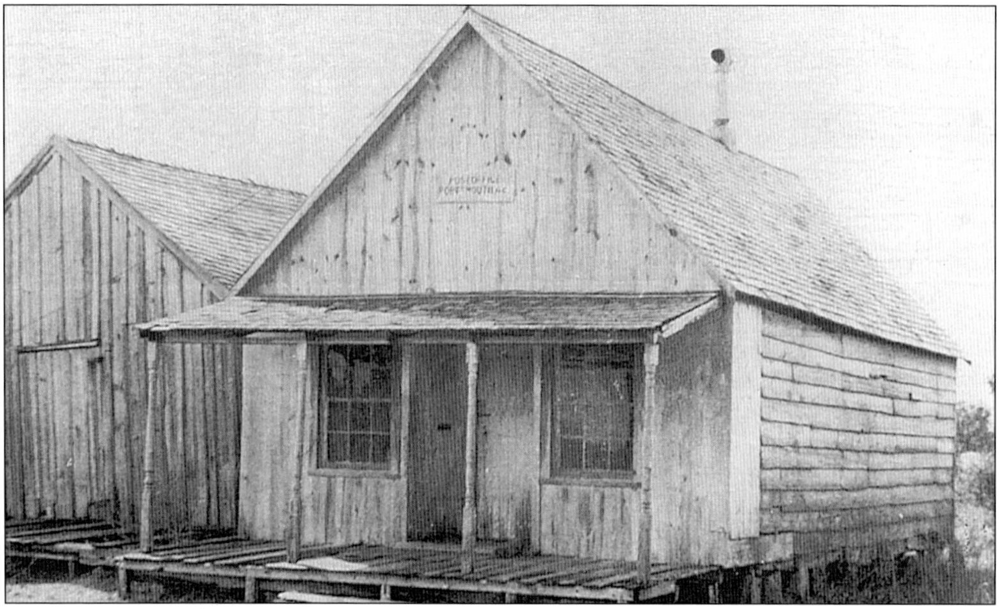

This is the old post office building in Portsmouth. (Courtesy North Carolina Division of Archives and History.)

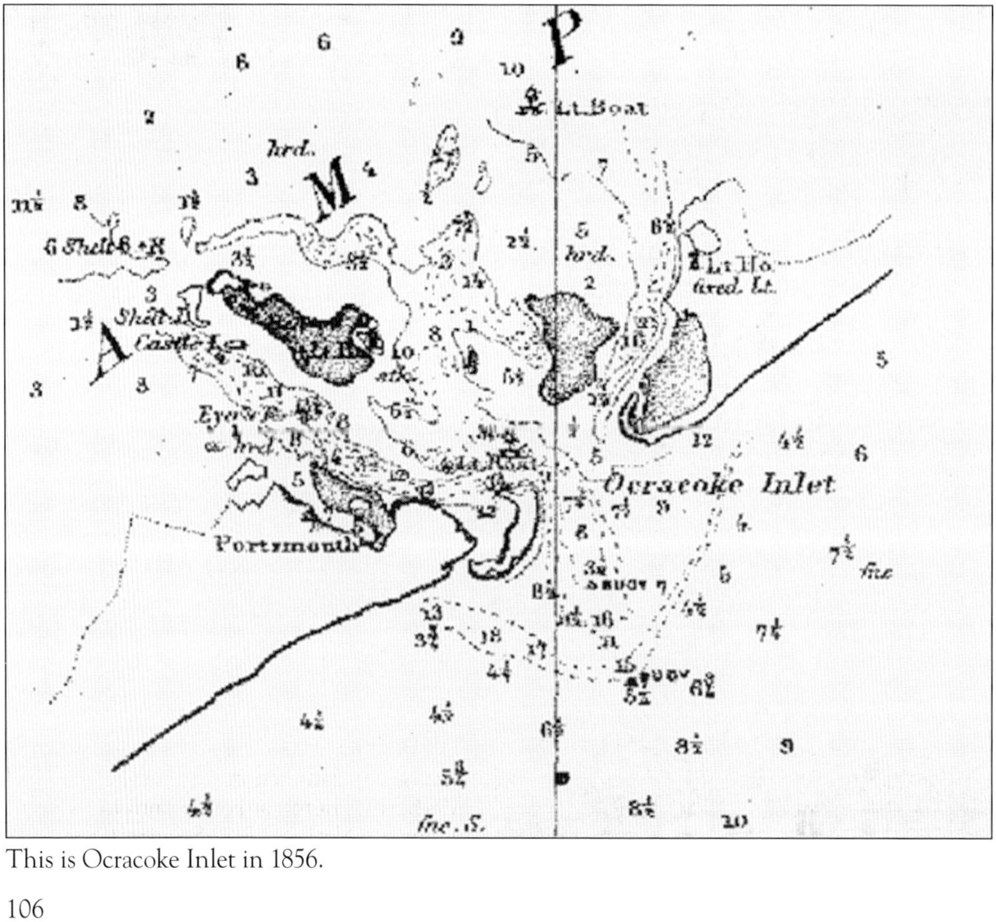

This is Ocracoke Inlet in 1856.

The old Methodist church building at Portsmouth was destroyed by fire in 1913. (Courtesy National Park Service, Cape Lookout National Seashore.)

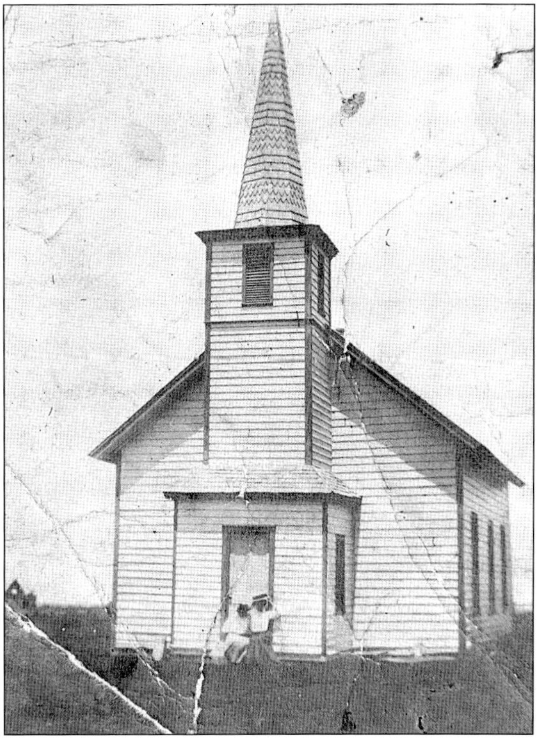

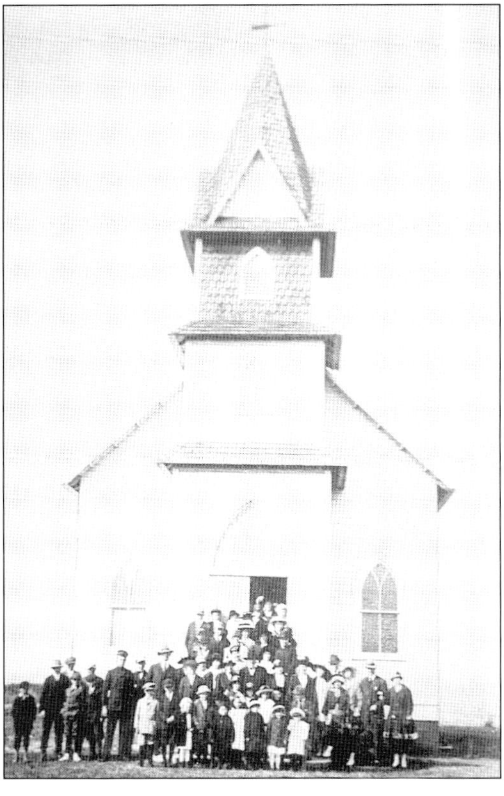

This group gathered in front of the Methodist church at Portsmouth in 1918. (Courtesy National Park Service, Cape Lookout National Seashore.)

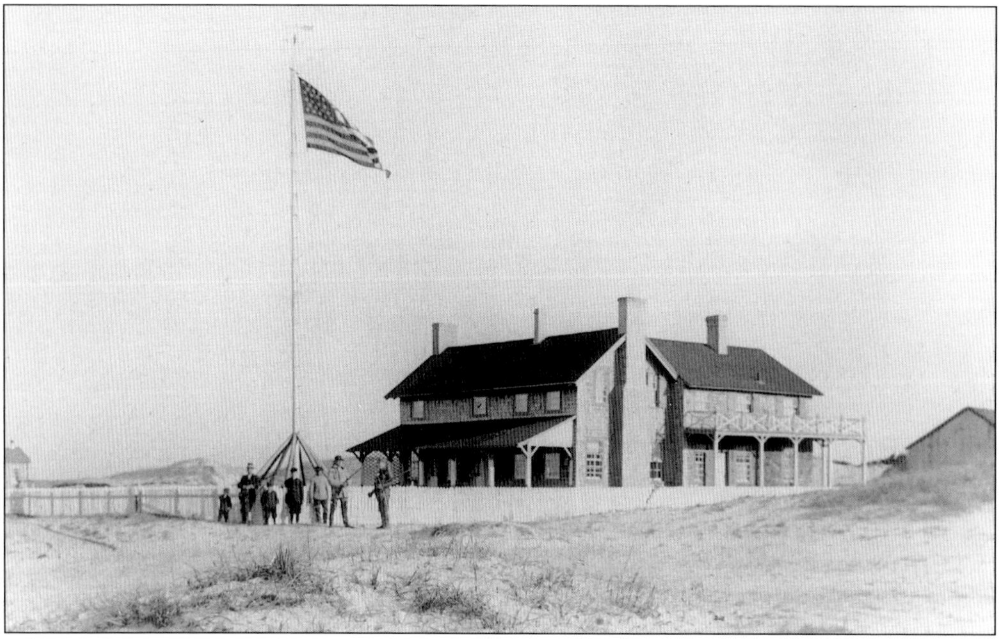

"Shooting trip at Mr. Jordan Mott's house" was the caption on this photograph of a group of hunters gathered in front of the Pilantary Club, which was taken in December of 1915. The man on the left, between the two boys, is thought to be Franklin Roosevelt. (Courtesy F.D. Roosevelt Library.)

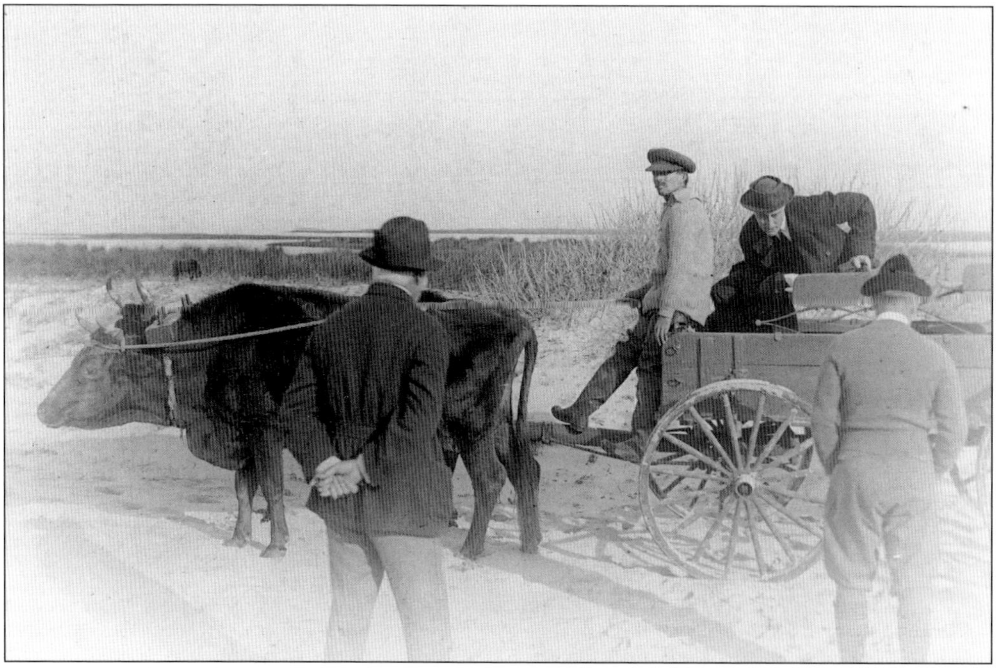

This ox-cart, driven by Alvin Mason, carried Assistant Secretary of the Navy Franklin Roosevelt and wildlife artist Arthur Duane around the Core Banks during their stay at the Pilantary Club. Jordan Mott, owner of the club, is standing on the right. (Courtesy F.D. Roosevelt Library.)

Four

Cape Lookout

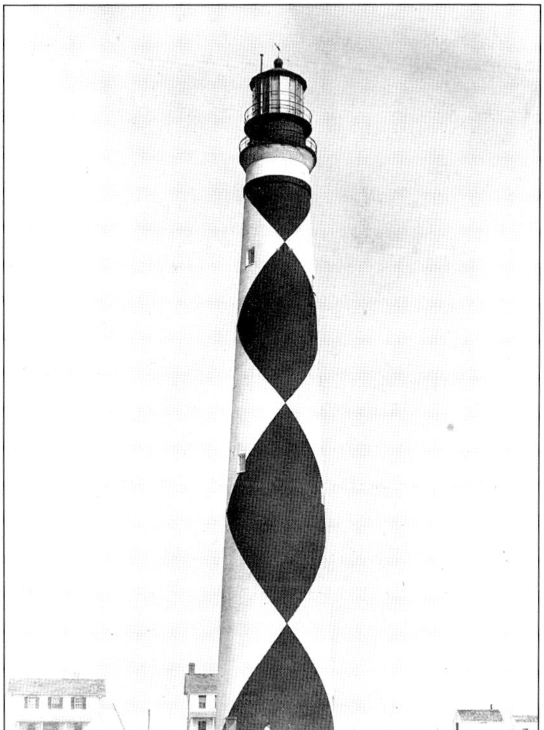

Lighthouse keeper Charles Clifton stands in front of the Cape Lookout Lighthouse, *c.* 1910. (Courtesy National Park Service, Cape Lookout National Seashore.)

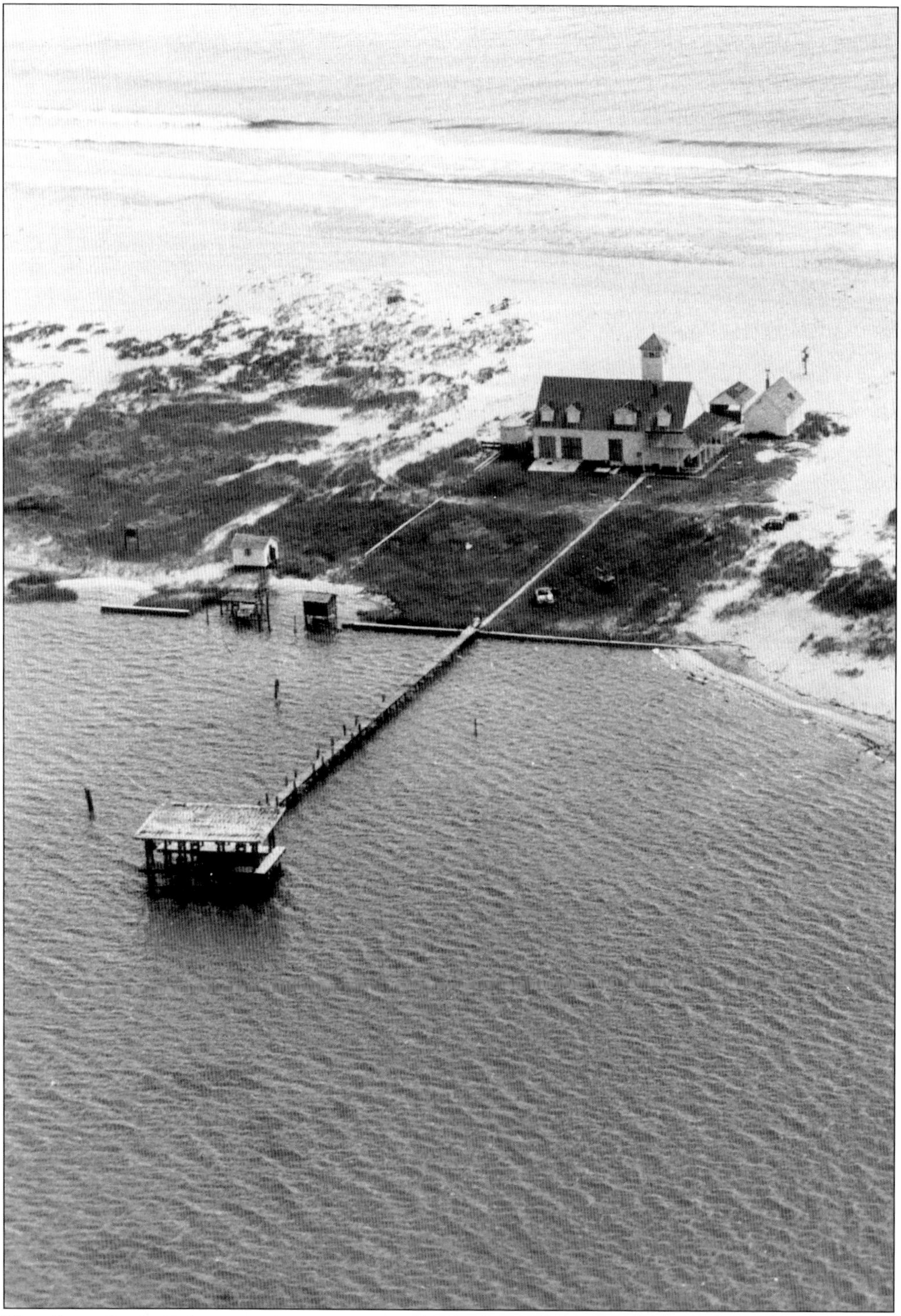

The Core Banks Lifesaving Station was established in 1896 with Alexander Moore as the first keeper. This station stood roughly half way between Ocracoke Inlet and Cape Lookout before it was destroyed by fire. (Courtesy National Park Service, Cape Lookout National Seashore.)

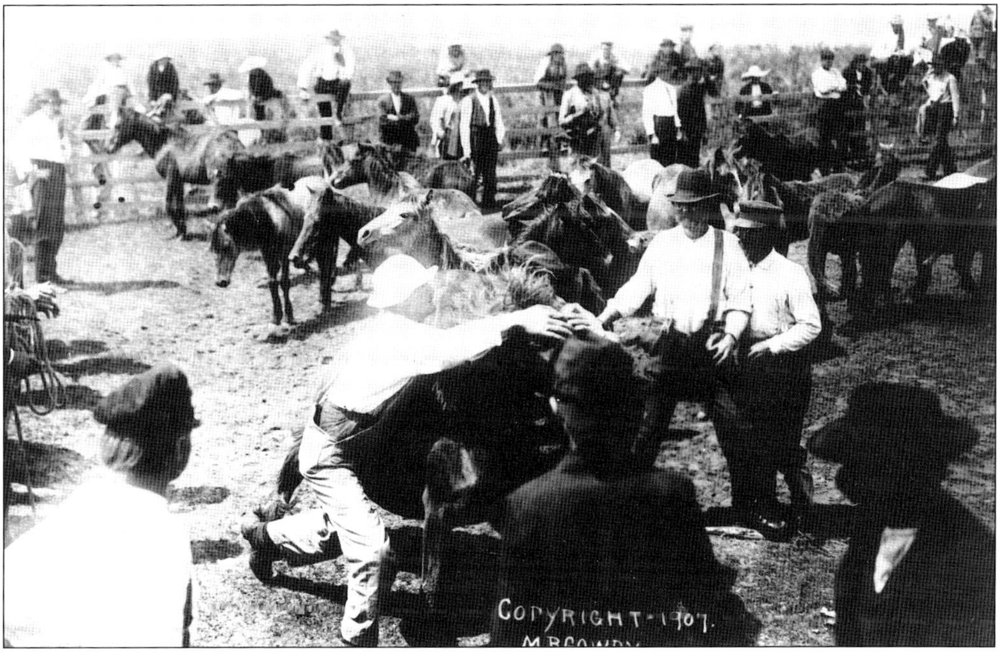

These wild ponies on the Core Banks in 1907 are being rounded up. (Courtesy North Carolina Division of Archives and History.)

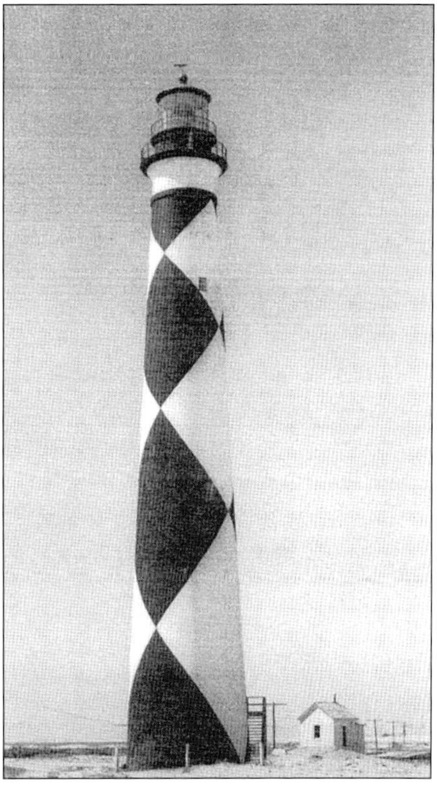

When it was first constructed, the Cape Lookout Lighthouse, seen in this *c.* 1920 photograph, was unpainted. After 1870 this caused some confusion among mariners who had difficulty distinguishing the lighthouse at Cape Lookout from the newly constructed one at Cape Hatteras in the daytime. To alleviate this problem, the Cape Lookout lighthouse was assigned its black-and-white diamond pattern, while the Cape Hatteras Lighthouse was given its black-and-white spiral design.

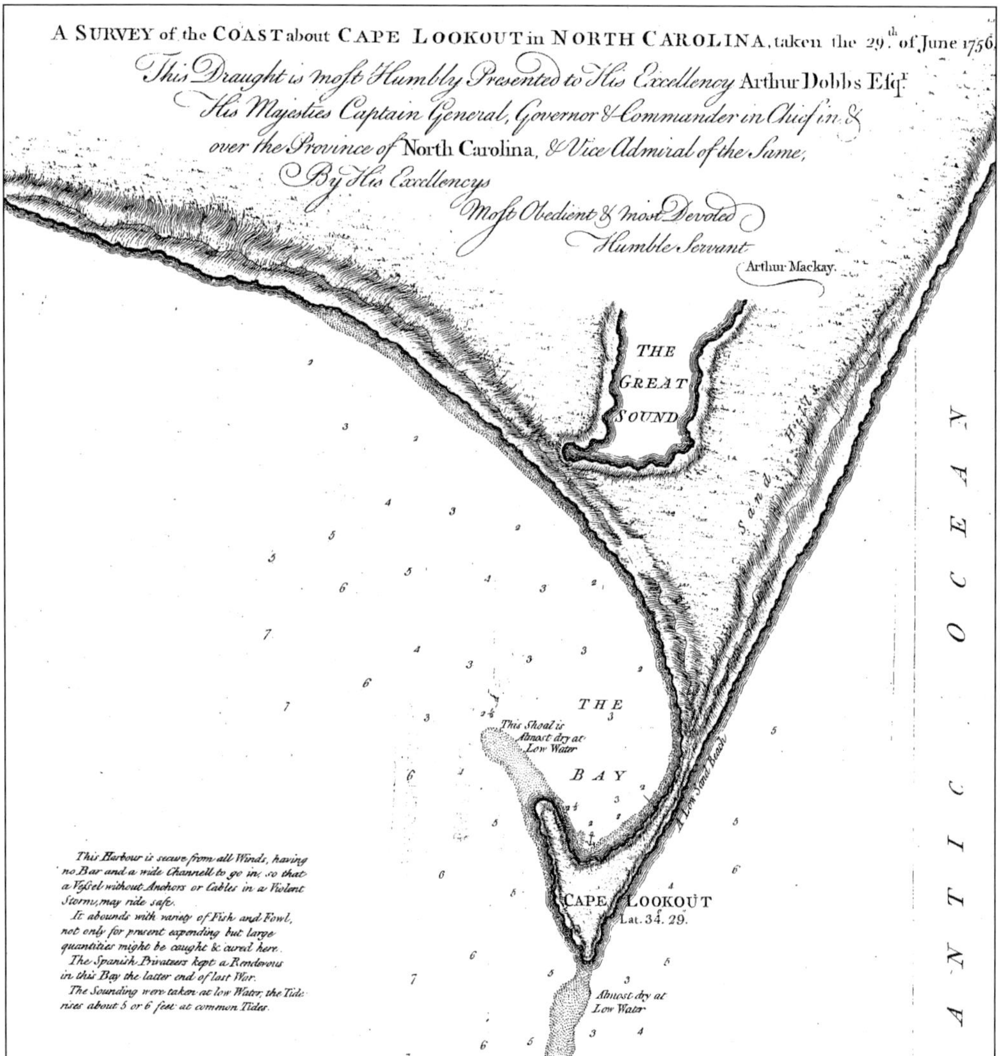

Surveyor Arthur McKay prepared this chart of the Cape Lookout region in 1756. (Courtesy North Carolina Division of Archives and History.)

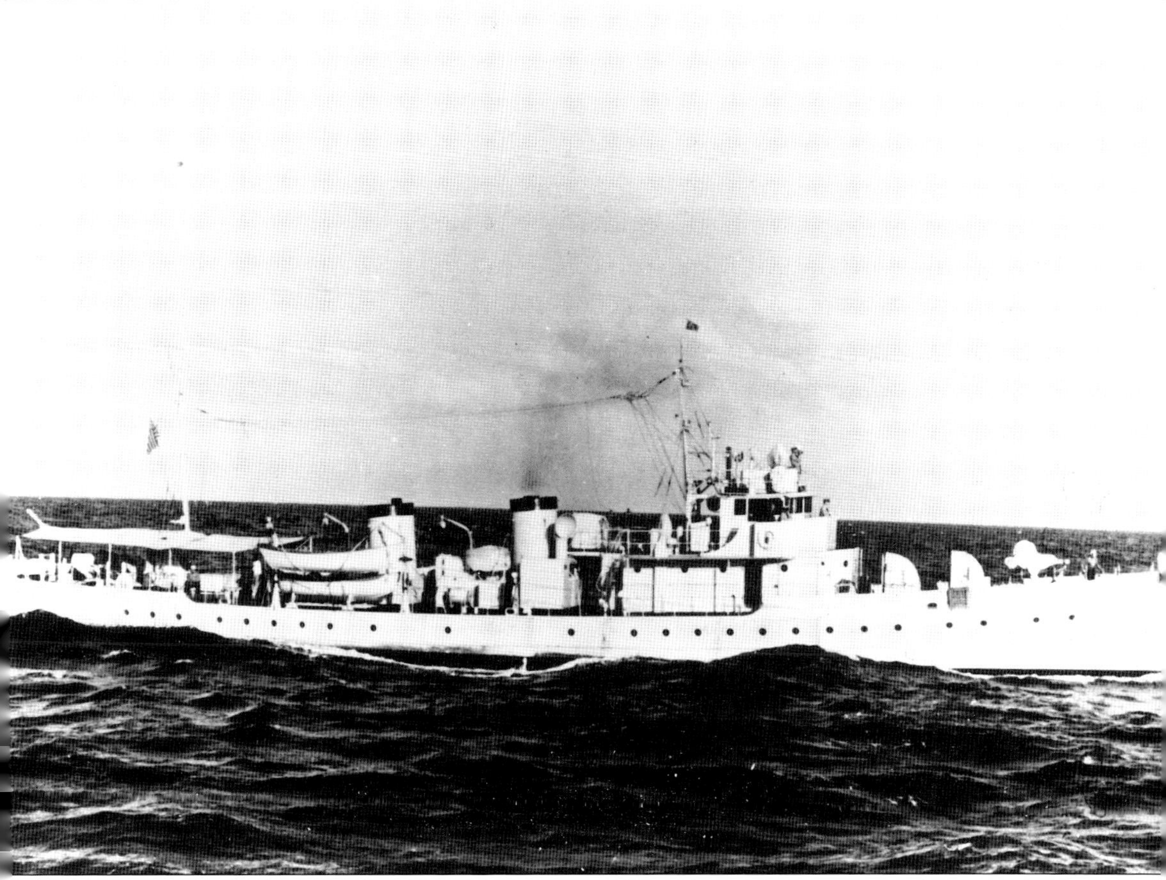

The CGC *Icarus* became the first U.S. Coast Guard vessel to sink a German U-boat in WW II when she sank the *U-352* off Cape Lookout on May 9, 1942. (U.S. Coast Guard.)

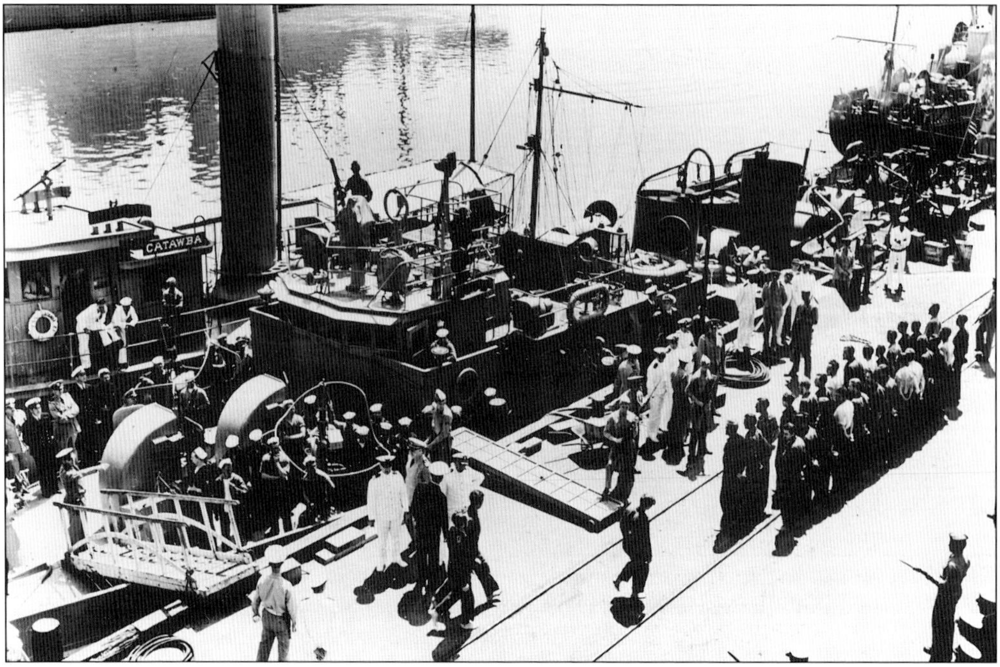

Survivors of the *U-352* are lined up on the dock in Charleston, South Carolina, alongside the *Icarus*. A notation on the photograph states, "The sub's commanding officer, Kapitan Leutnant [Lieutenant Commanding] Hellmut Rathke, stands beside his men in the front row (extreme right) while the barefooted executive officer and a sailor (left center) approach formation." (U.S. Coast Guard.)

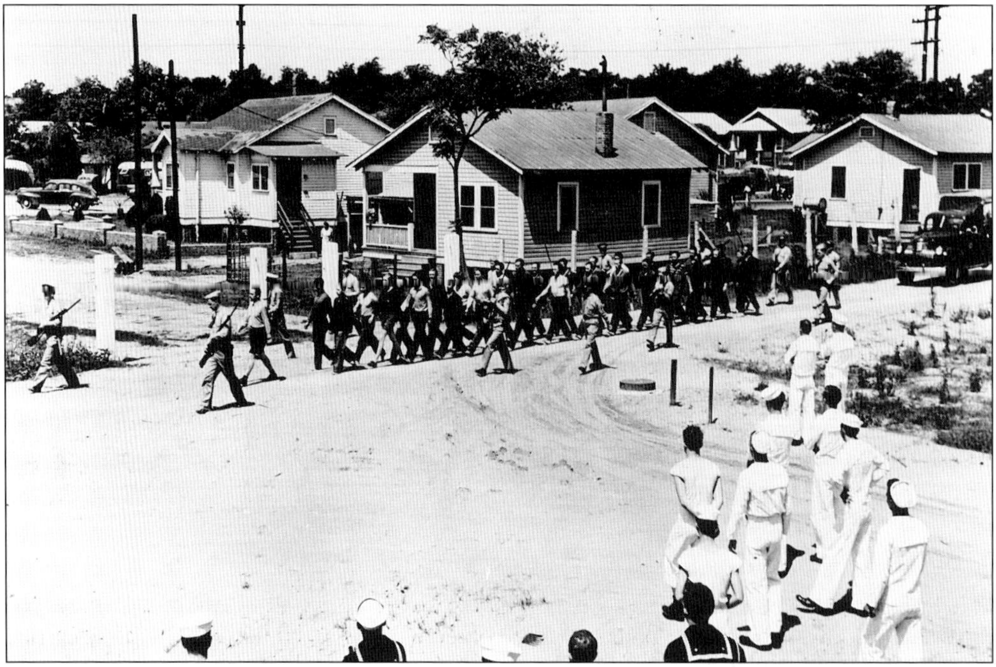

The German prisoners from the *U-352* are being marched off to their quarters. (U.S. Coast Guard.)

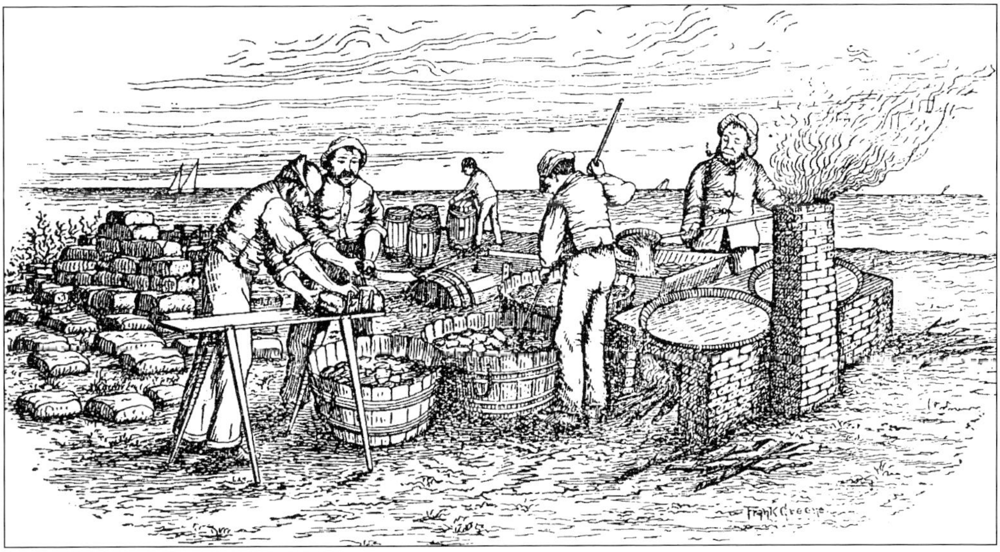

The illustrations on this page and the next were drawn by Frank Greene in 1894. They accompanied an article written by H.H. Brimley, "Whale Fishing in North Carolina," which appeared in the April 1894 *Bulletin of the North Carolina Department of Agriculture*.

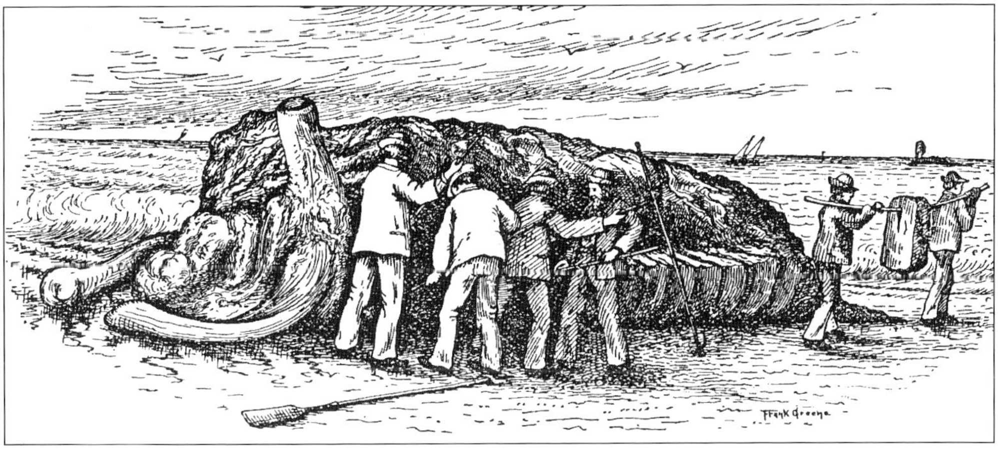

Whaling had a long and colorful history along the Outer Banks, especially the Core Banks, Shackleford Banks, and Bogue Banks. Brimley observed in 1894, "The Whale Fishery carried on around Beaufort Inlet has been in existence for years, and the whalers of that locality are second to none in the knowledge of the business of whaling, and in the coolness and courage in carrying it out."

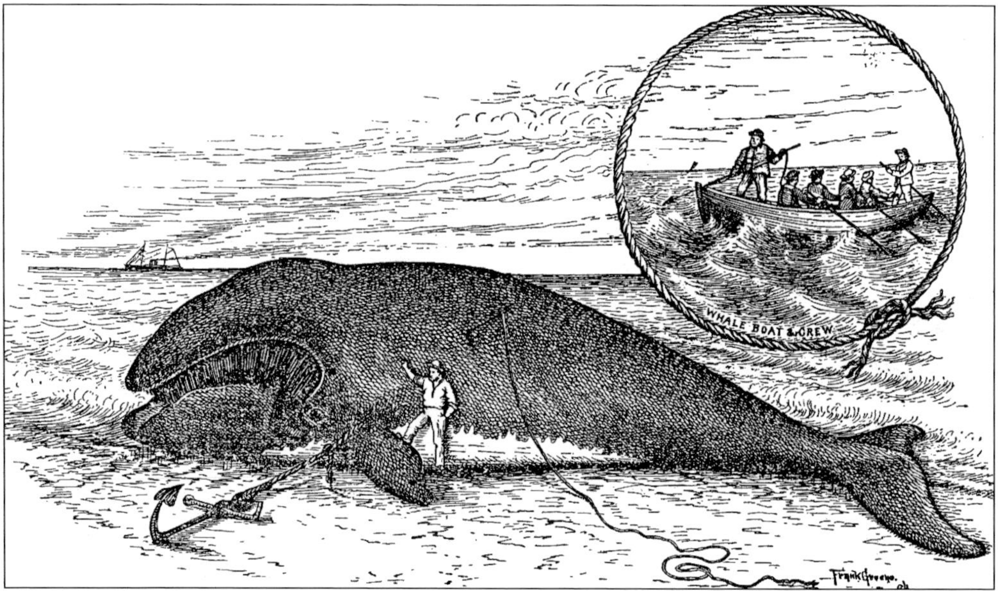

Whaling was carried on along the Outer Banks into the first quarter of the 20th century. In their book, *Whaling on the North Carolina Coast*, Marcus and Sallie Simpson write, "The last shore crew for whaling disbanded when a fire destroyed most of its gear in 1917."

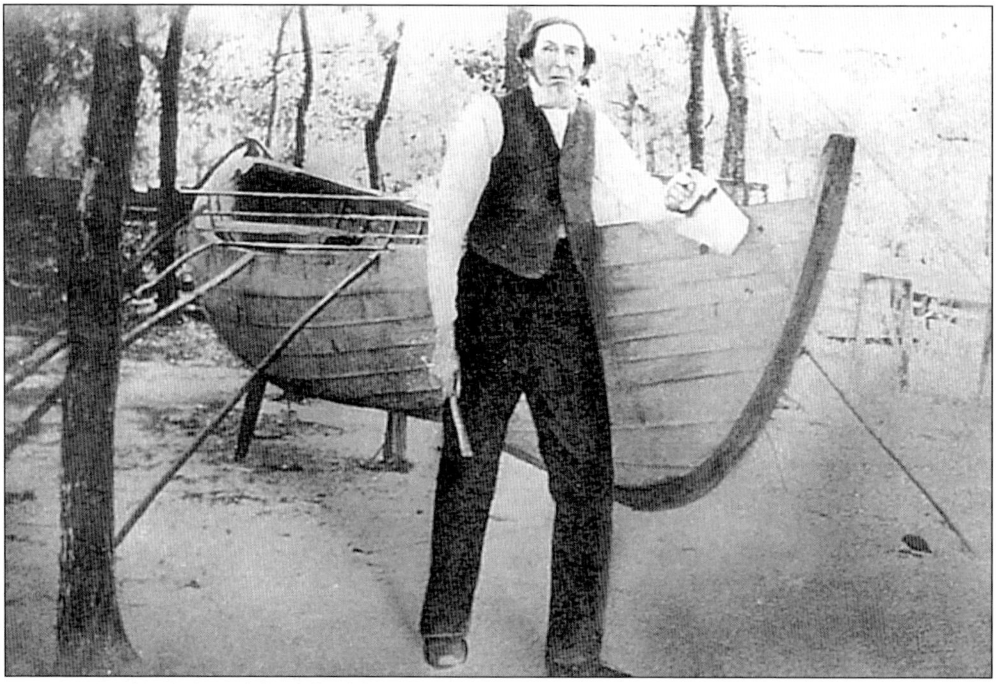

Devine Guthrie, famed boat-builder of Shackleford Banks, is busy at work on a whaleboat. (North Carolina Division of Archives and History.)

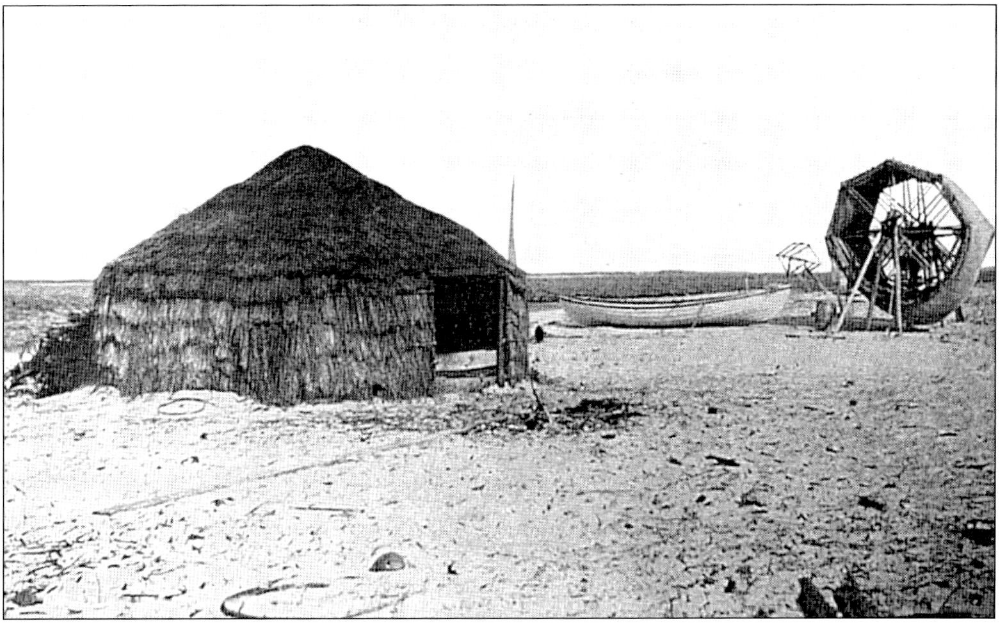

The Mullet fishermen's camp was located on the Shackleford Banks near Cape Lookout in 1907. (North Carolina Geological and Economic Survey.)

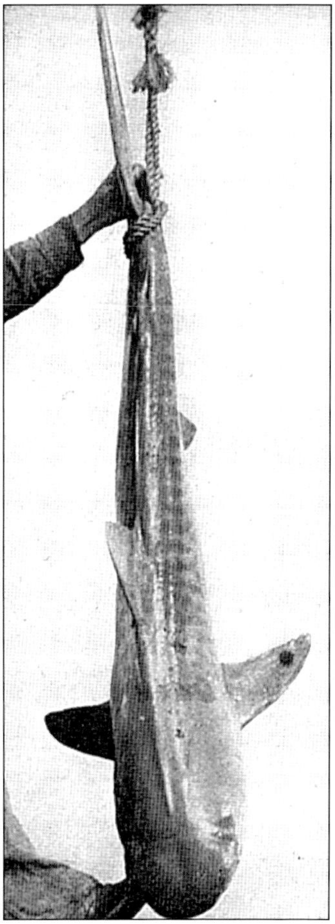

Russell Coles captured this shark by Cape Lookout in 1918.

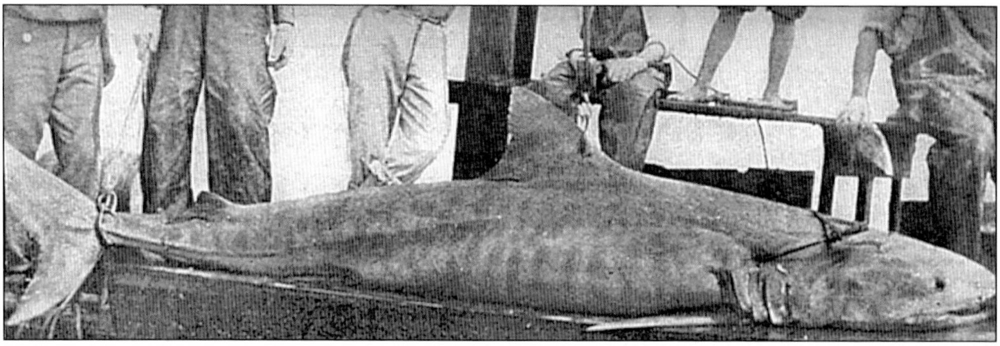

Coles made notes concerning the numerous sharks he encountered through the years, especially when he was working from a shark fishing station at Cape Lookout from May through July 1918. The sharks were processed for, "leather, food. Oil and fertilizer."

Coles had several adventures with the sharks he hunted at Cape Lookout. One such adventure with a Great White Shark is recounted here to give some idea of the dangers involved:

> After trying for an hour to approach within harpooning distance of a large man-eater which was swimming in shallow water near the scene of my former encounter, I got over-board in a depth of five feet of water and had the boat retire to a distance of a hundred yards with the coil of rope, which was attached to the harpoon which I had with me. I also took with me half a bushel of crushed and broken fish to attract the shark, which was then swimming on or near the surface, half a mile to the leeward of me. Soon the shark could be seen zig-zagging its course toward me, by crossing and re-crossing the line of scent from the broken fish, just as the bird-dog follows up the scent of quail. With harpoon poised, I crouched low, trusting that its approach would be continued in this manner, until, by a long cast, I could fasten my harpoon in its side. The scent of the broken fish, however, was so strong that they were definitely located, and the shark charged from a hundred feet away with a speed which has to be seen to be appreciated.
>
> I met the onrushing shark by hurling my harpoon clear to the socket into it, near the angle of the jaw, and, as the iron entered its flesh, the shark leaped forward, catching me in the angle formed by its head and the harpoon handle, which caught me just under the right arm, bruising me badly, while my face and neck were somewhat lacerated by coming in contact with the rough hide of the side of its head. As my right arm was free, it was a great chance for using the heavy knife, with which I was armed, had my tackle been strong; but the force of the blow snapped the poorly made harpoon at the socket and the shark escaped, although it carried its death wound. I never again employed the same black-smith to forge my harpoons, but that poorly-made iron surely brought to a sudden ending a most exciting situation."

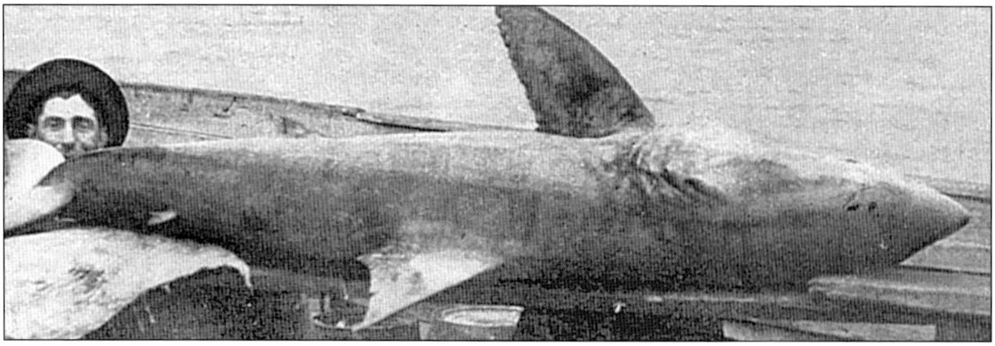

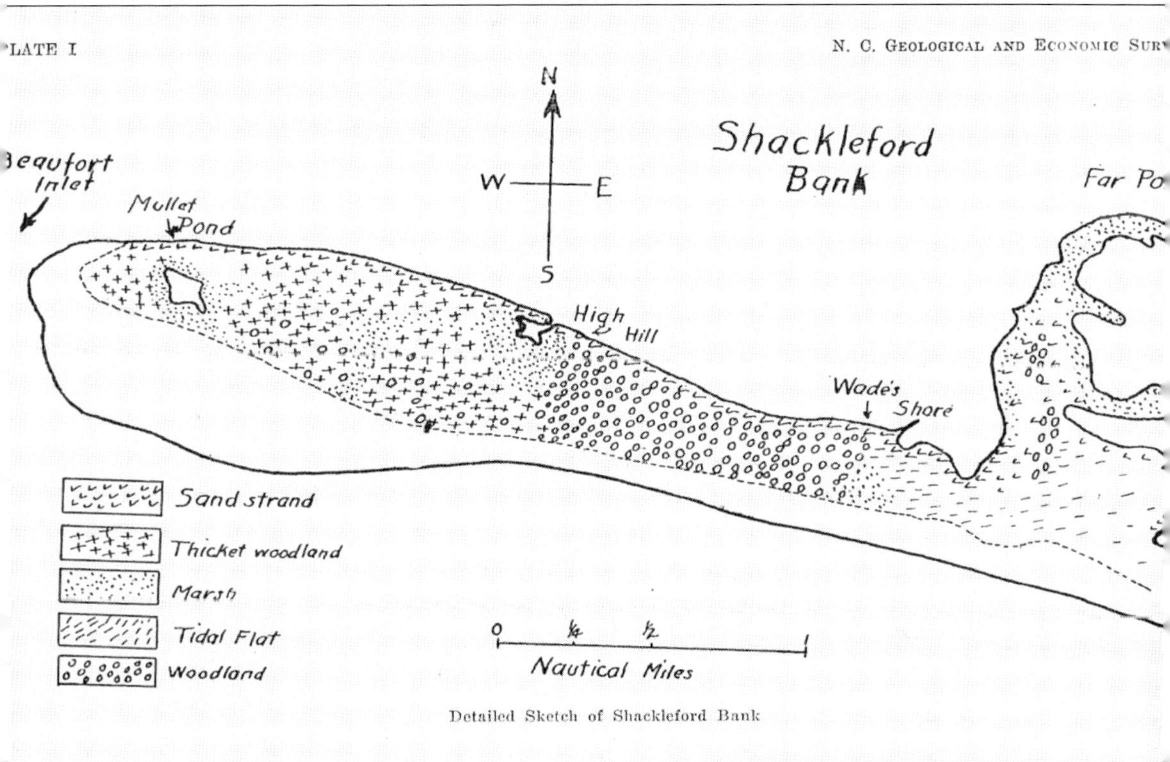

This map of the Shackleford Banks was prepared by I.F. Lewis in 1017.

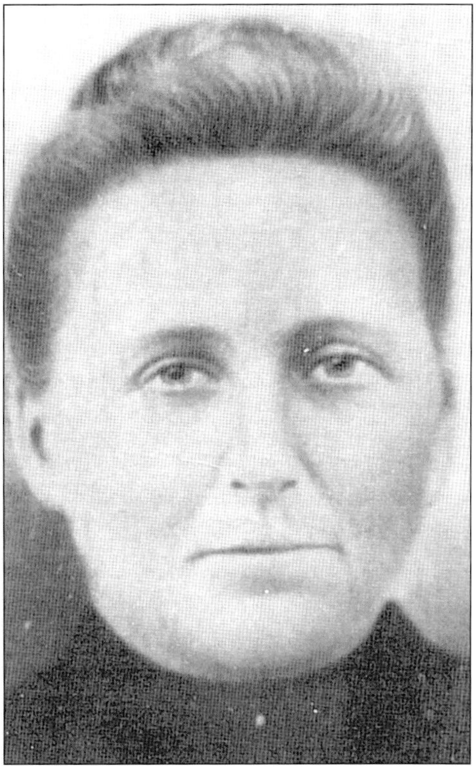

Charlotte Ann Mason served as the assistant keeper of the Cape Lookout Lighthouse during the 1870s. (Courtesy National Park Service, Cape Lookout National Seashore.)

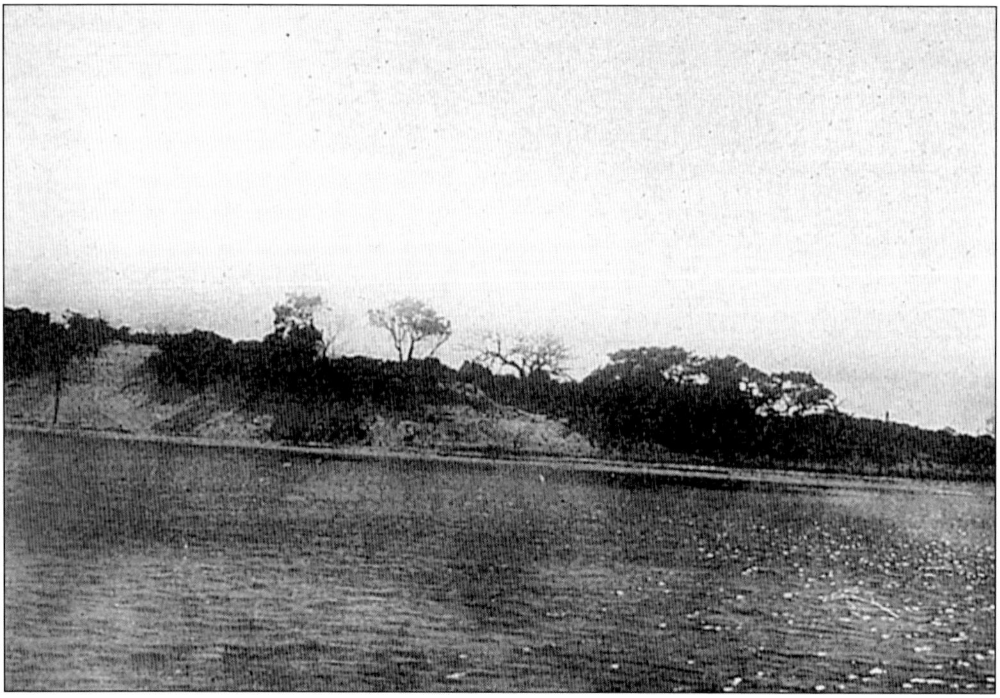

High Hill, pictured here, is a prominent landmark on the Shackleford Banks. (North Carolina Geologic and Economic Survey.)

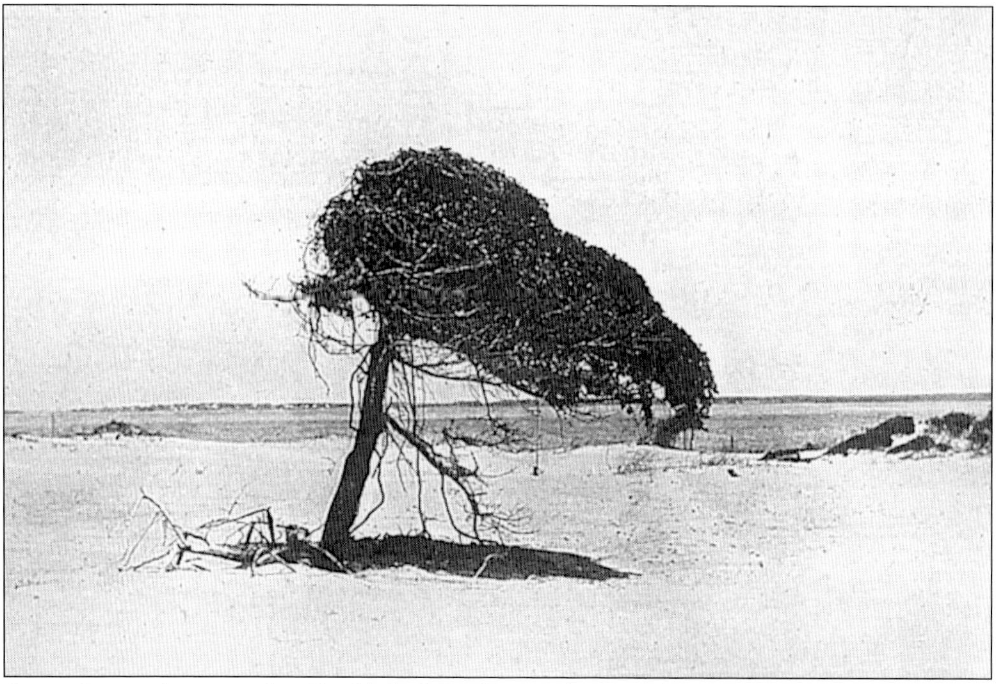

A windswept dune on the Shackleford Banks can be seen here, *c.* 1917. (North Carolina Geologic and Economic Survey.)

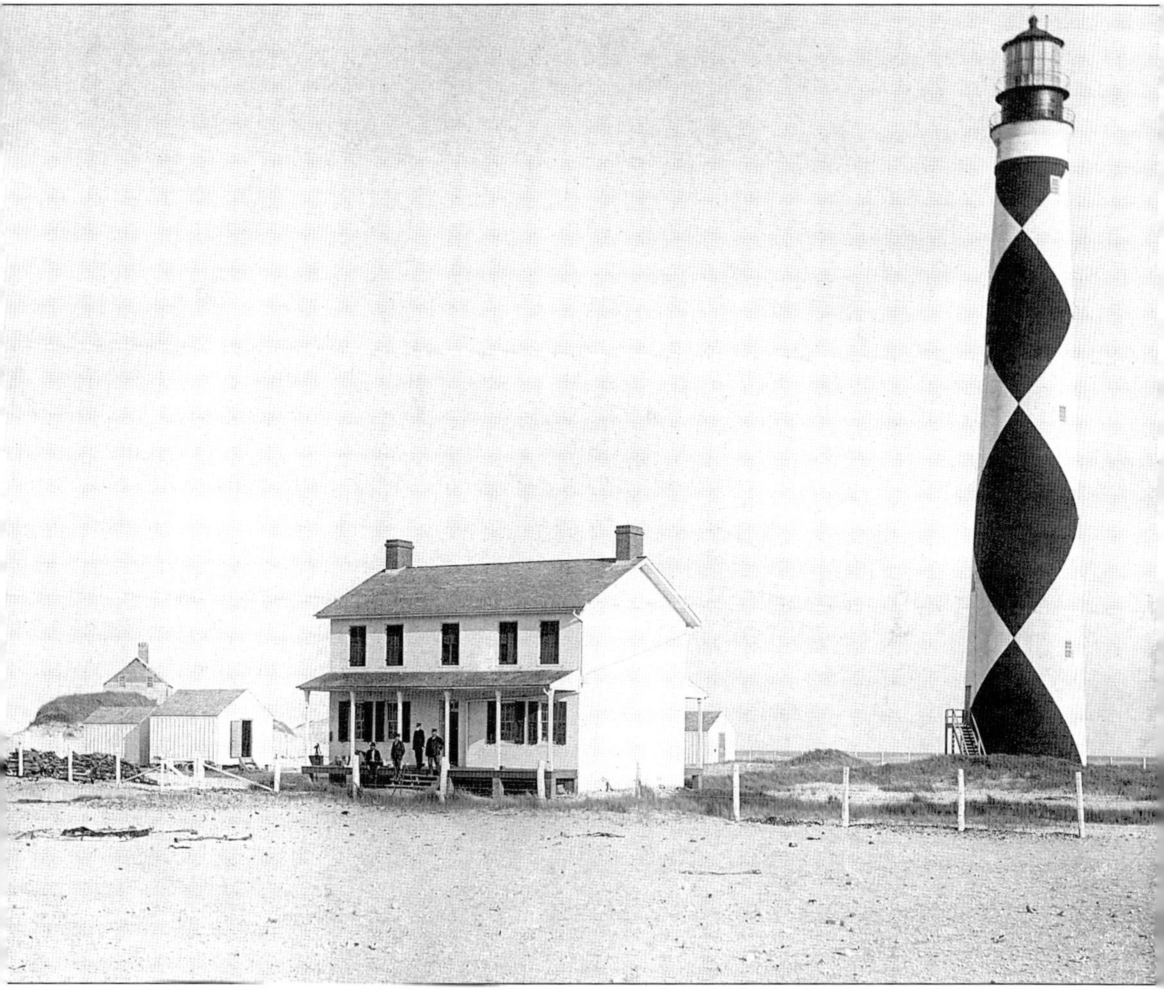

Pictured here is the Cape Lookout Lighthouse, *c.* 1880. (Courtesy National Archives.)

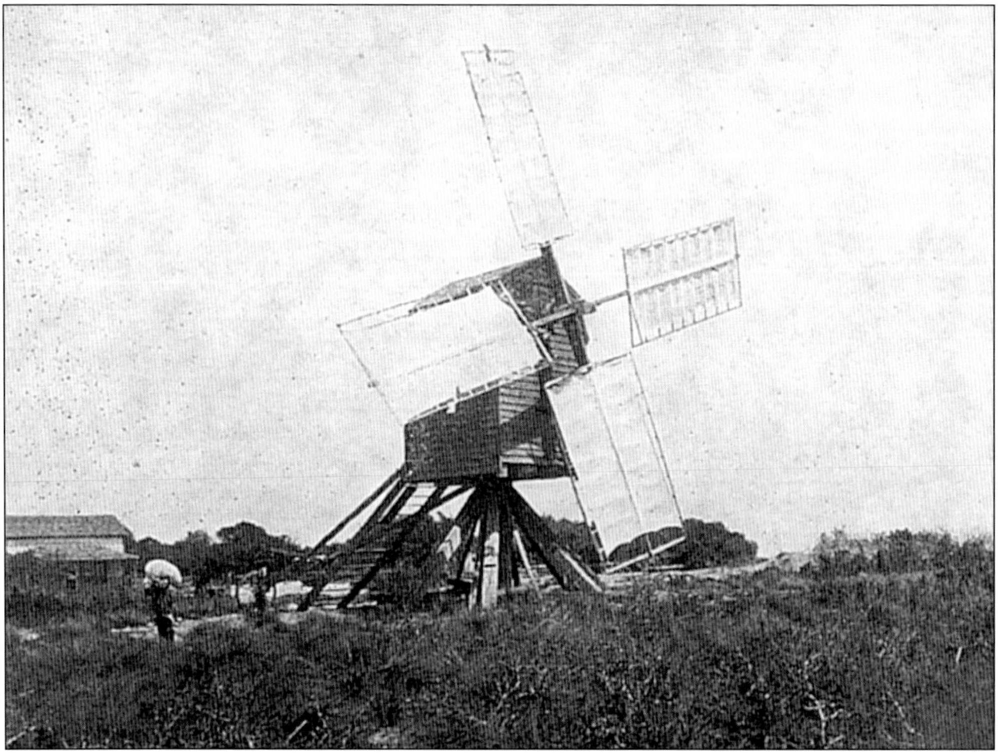

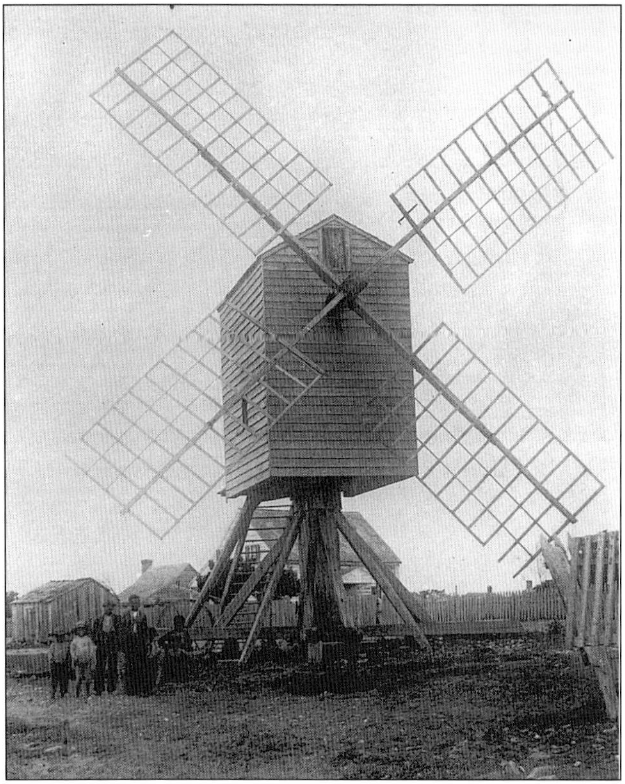

This windmill on Harker's Island stood near the present site of the Cape Lookout National Seashore Visitor's Center.

A windmill stood on the mainland, opposite Shackleford banks near Beaufort. (North Carolina Division of Archives and History.)

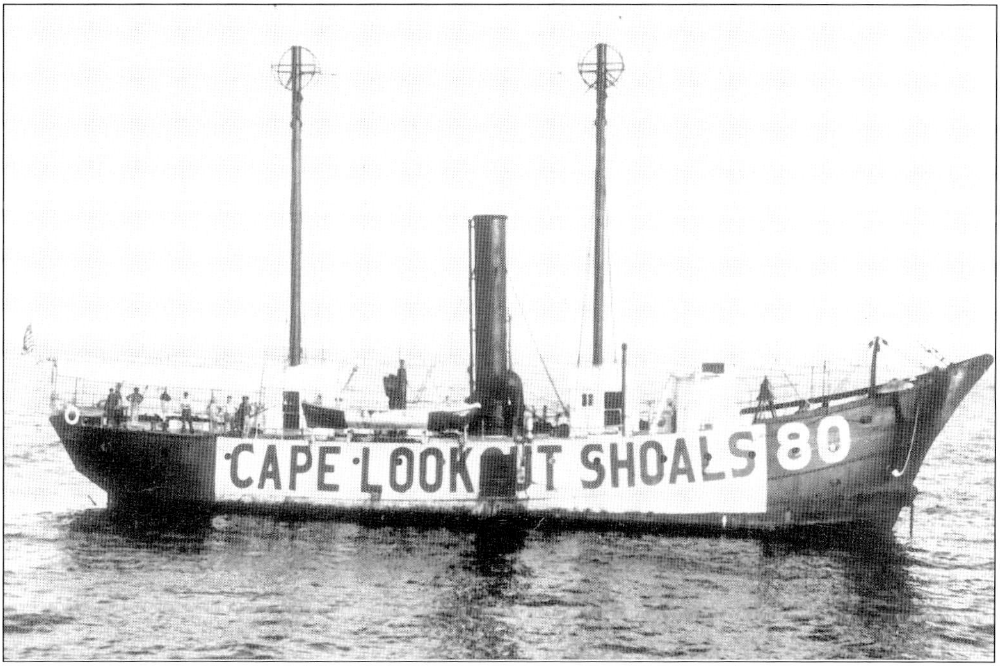

Lightship #80 first took up station in the shoals off Cape Lookout in 1904. She had an eventful career that spanned nearly 30 years at Cape Lookout. One of the most tragic events occurred on July 25, 1913, when the steamer *City of Atlanta* ran over the lightship's whaleboat, killing three crewmen. (Courtesy National Park Service, Cape Lookout National Seashore.)

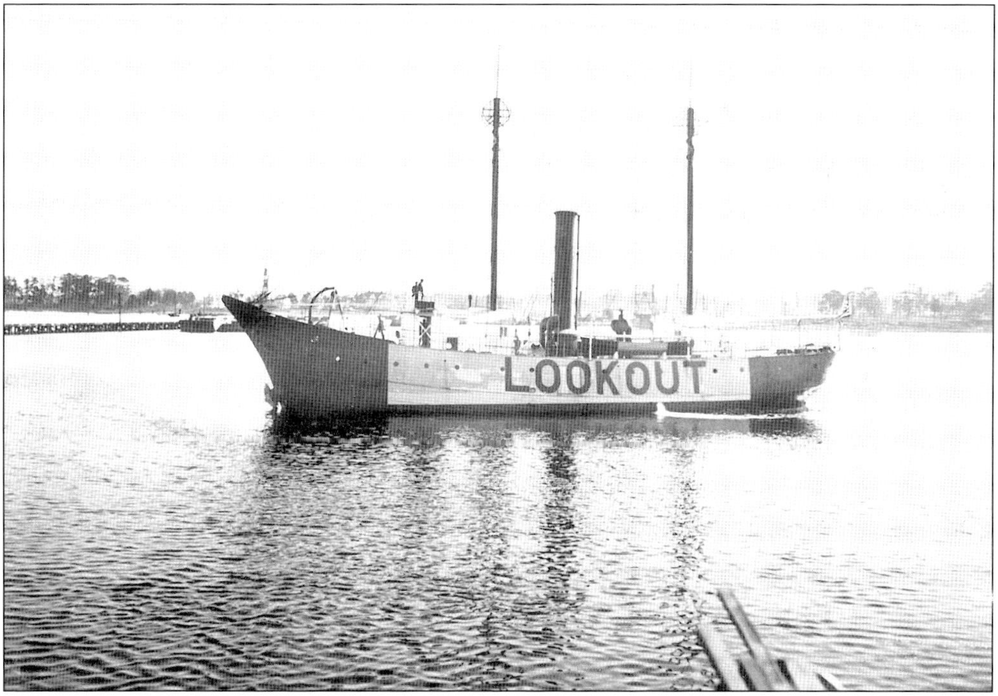

The *Cape Lookout Lightship* can be seen in port. The lightship was replaced by unmanned buoys in 1933. (Courtesy National Park Service, Cape Lookout National Seashore.)

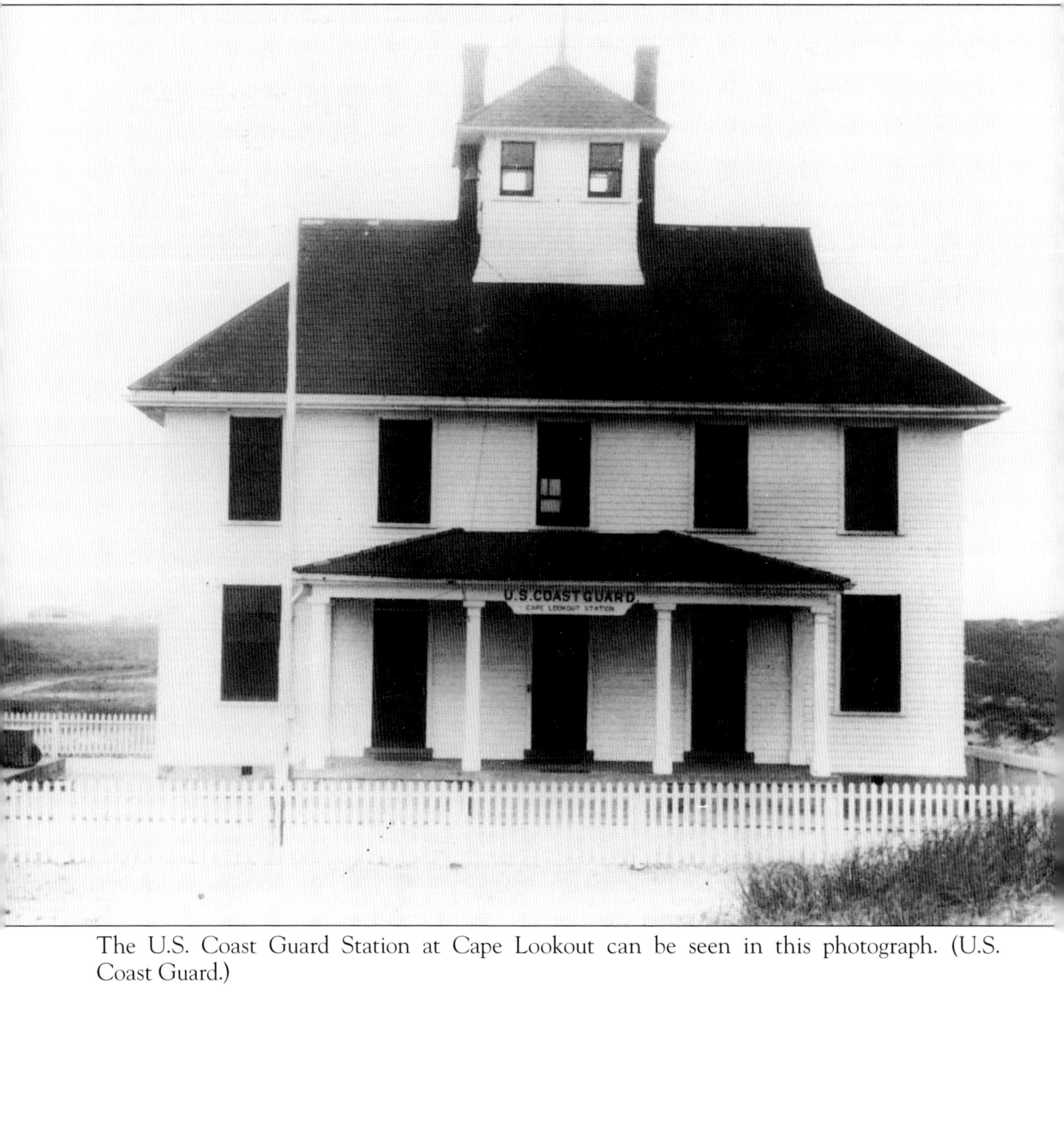

The U.S. Coast Guard Station at Cape Lookout can be seen in this photograph. (U.S. Coast Guard.)

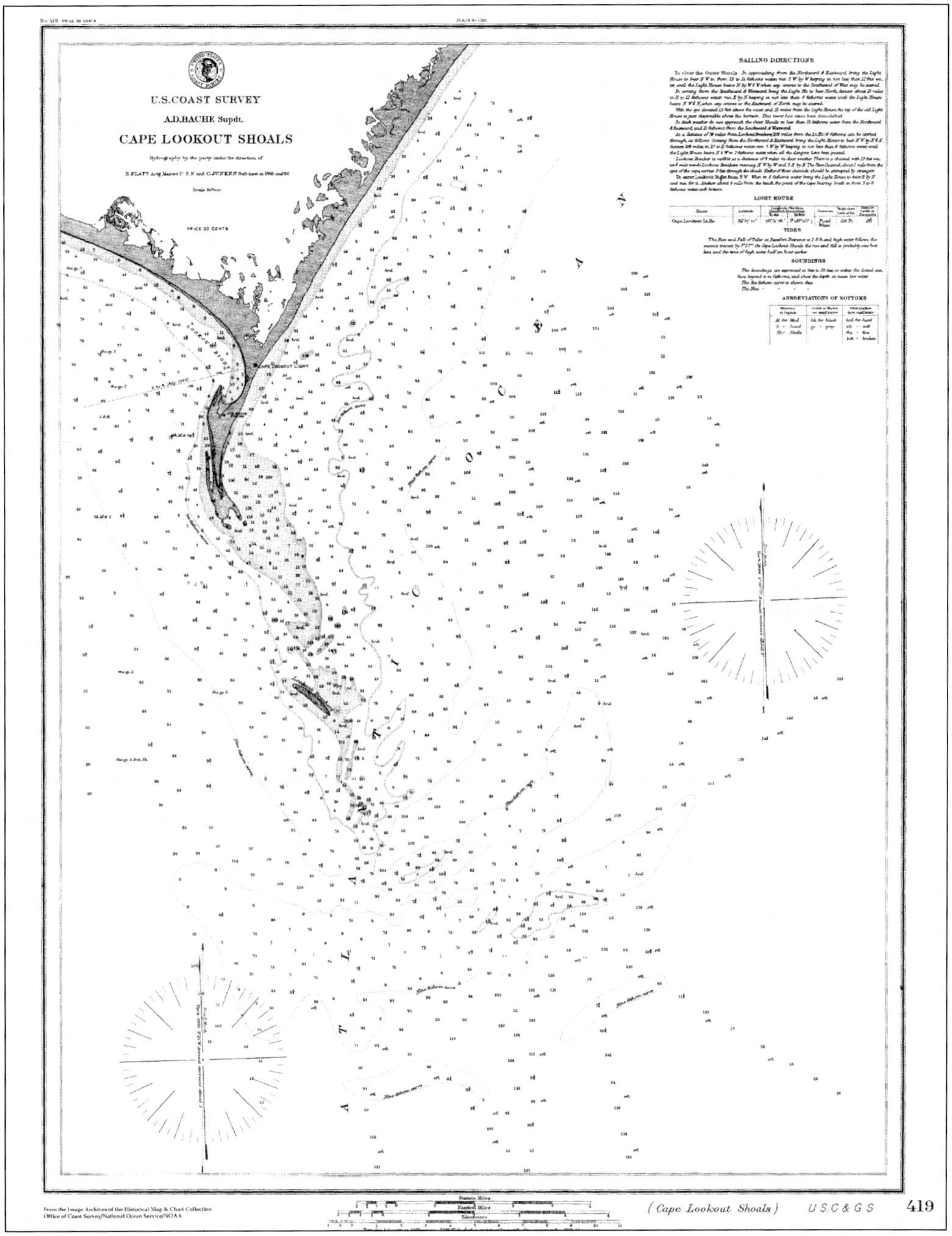

Seen here is a maritime map of the Cape Lookout Shoals.

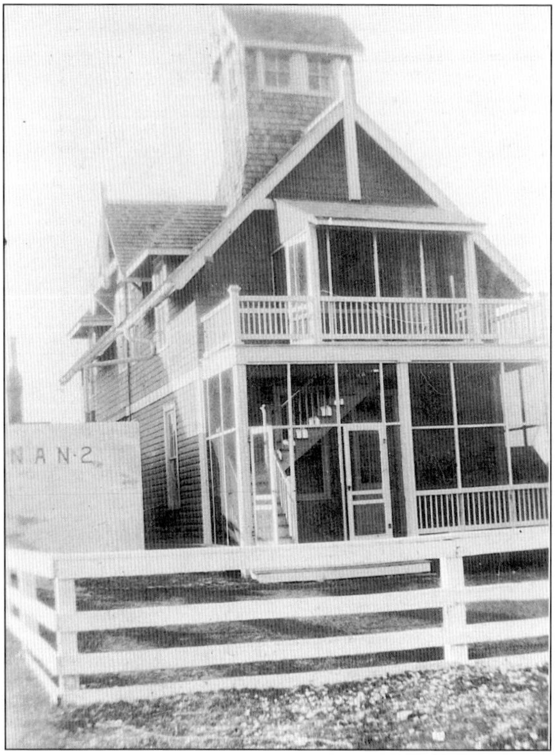

The Life Saving Station at Cape Lookout was converted into a radio station by the U.S. Navy and operated until 1940. Radio operator John Miller took this photograph in the last year of the station's existence. (Courtesy National Park Service, Cape Lookout National Seashore.)

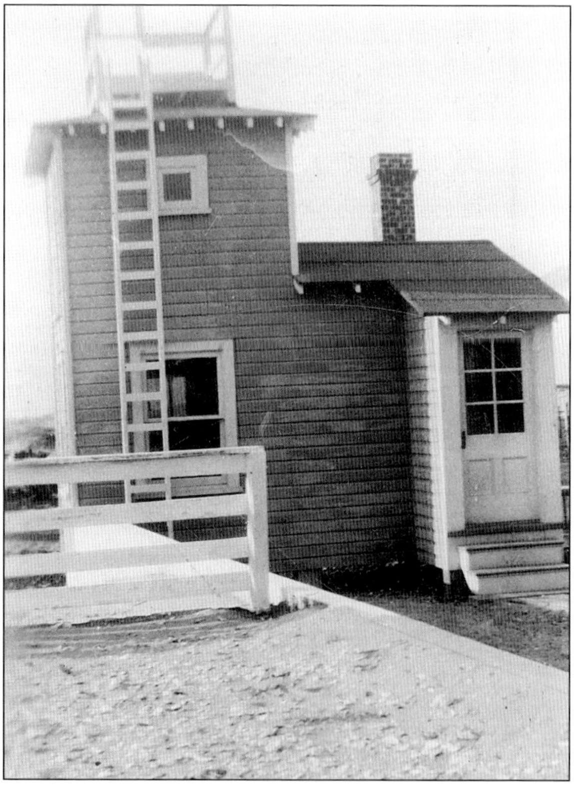

The U.S. Navy utilized this building as a radio shack at Cape Lookout. (Courtesy National Park Service, Cape Lookout National Seashore.)

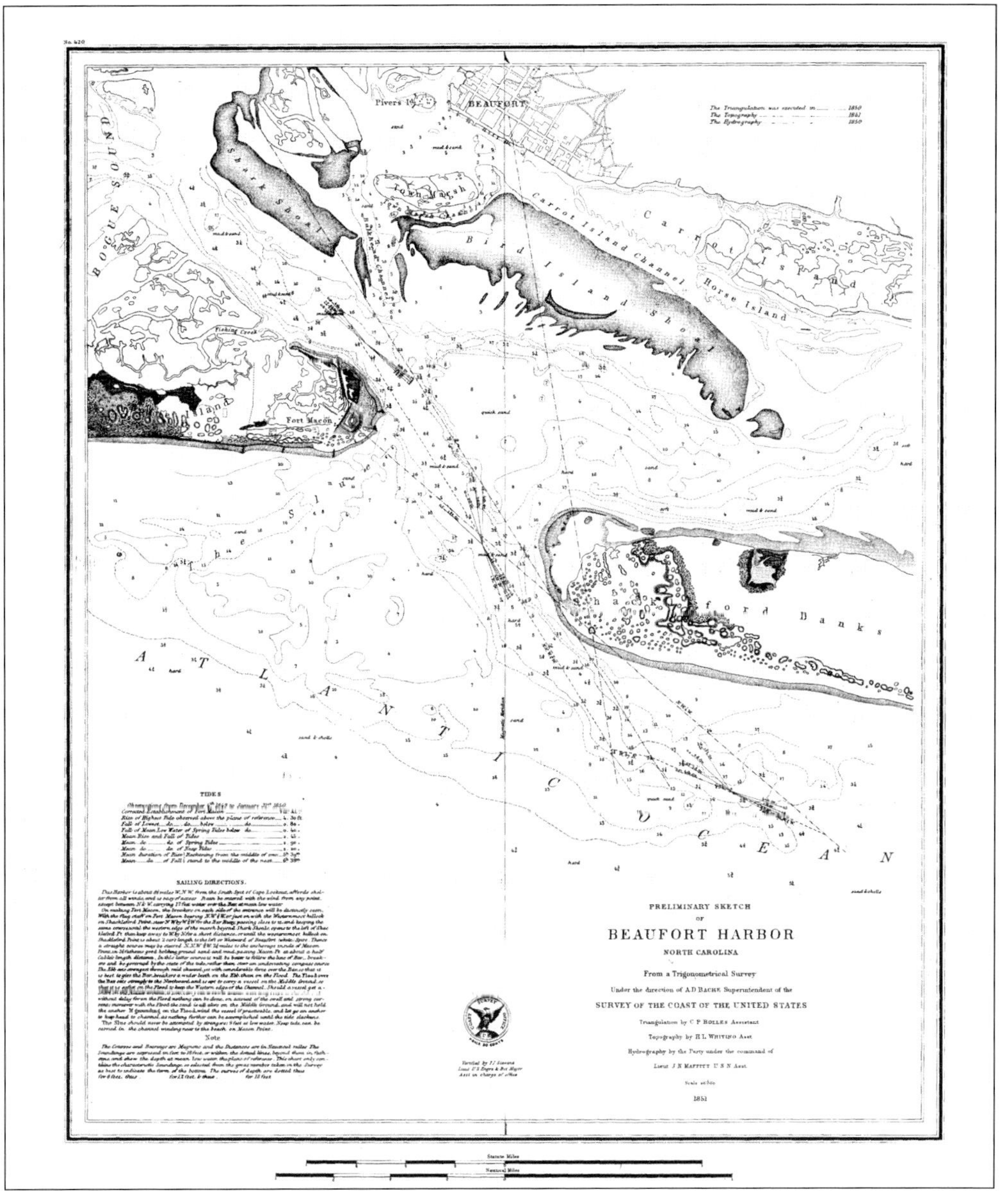

This chart of the Beaufort Harbor dates back to 1851.

ACKNOWLEDGMENTS

A work of this nature and scope is not possible without the kindly assistance of numerous individuals. Steve Massengill of the North Carolina Division of Archives and History and Steve Price of the U.S. Coast Guard were extremely helpful. Karen Duggan of Cape Lookout National Seashore provided access to the wonderful collection of material housed at the park headquarters. Staff members of the North Carolina Maritime Museum, the Office of the Coast Survey, and the Museum of the Albemarle helped make this book possible. Thank you.

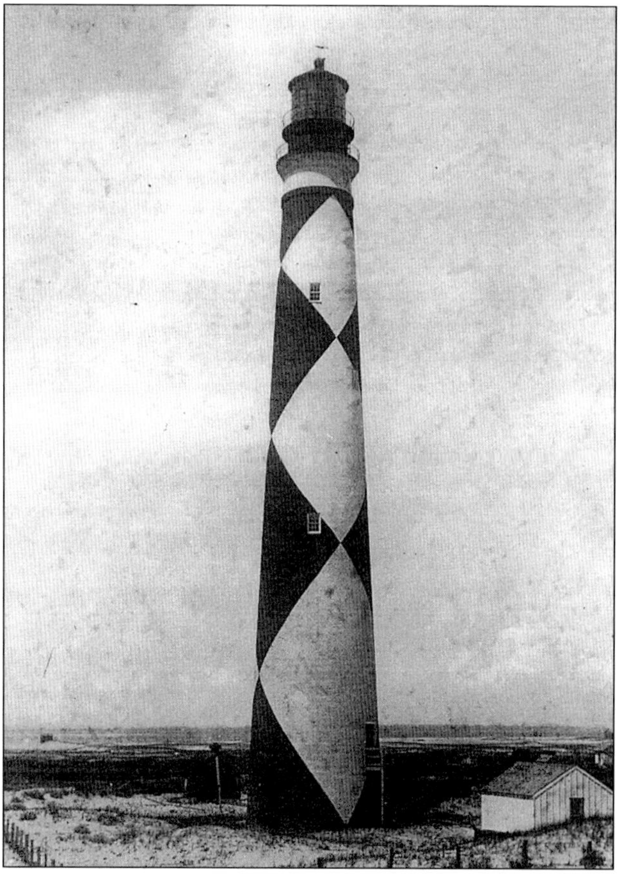

This photograph captures the Cape Lookout Lighthouse *c.* 1880.